Praise for *Strategic Transfor*

M000249659

"*Strategic Transformation of Higher Education* lays out the fundamental issues challenging all of higher education in the contemporary world, where the basic goals and methods of education are more challenged than just about any period in our history. Even the challenges to America's pioneering institutions—to create citizen leaders for a democracy unlike any ever seen in the world—did not match the challenges to today's institutions who also face additionally a weltering array of modalities for delivering education, as well as a conflicting sets of goals for its purpose. This book is a fine overview of the elements and challenges to 'change' leadership in higher education, and is especially valuable in its global comparisons of the goals and funding of systems in many different countries. Also, its discussion of eight exemplars of change in the area of online and competency-based education is valuable for pointing out ways that quality, skills, improved access, and affordability might be shared, rather than conflicting, values."

—**Esther Barazzone**, president, Chatham University

"This is a most interesting and challenging volume. I have long known that it is 'easier to move a graveyard than to change a college curriculum,' but Stewart E. Sutin and W. James Jacob offer readers a powerful rationale and strategy for change as well as the global imperative to do so—and sooner rather than later. This book is truly a 'must read' for all policy makers, college and university trustees, administrators, and especially the faculty of higher education. Sadly, most faculty members have little understanding of the revenue sources that are critical to institutional survival, much less any interest in finding solutions to the impending shortfall of revenue with the continuing increases in operations. This book offers practical suggestions and strategies for moving forward with much-needed reforms in providing more students with successful learning experiences and an education that provides them with the skills they need for living and succeeding in an increasingly complex and competitive global environment. We will be using this work in our graduate classes."

—**John E. Roueche**, president, Roueche Graduate Center,
National American University; Sid W. Richardson Regents chair emeritus,
The University of Texas at Austin

"Here is a book that demands our attention. Sutin and Jacob present a compelling case for the need for transformation of higher education if institutions are to survive. The authors point out the challenges of operating in an environment that includes decreased funding, cost increases, greater expectations from employers, global competition, a projected skills gap, and accreditation concerns. Globalization and advances in technology are affecting our society in ways that higher education can no longer ignore. The book's brief case studies show how leaders who make plans and decisions without considering the consequences of unanticipated economic cycles jeopardize the existence of their institutions. To assist leaders in navigating today's challenging environment, the authors provide examples of institutions that are successful because they have undergone systemic reform. Higher education leaders, educators, and policy makers need to think seriously about the case for strategic transformation that Sutin and Jacob present so well."

—**George R. Boggs**, president and CEO emeritus, American Association of Community Colleges; superintendent/president emeritus, Palomar College

Strategic Transformation of Higher Education

Challenges and Solutions in a Global Economy

Stewart E. Sutin and W. James Jacob

ROWMAN & LITTLEFIELD
Lanham • Boulder • New York • London

Published by Rowman & Littlefield
A wholly owned subsidiary of The Rowman & Littlefield Publishing Group, Inc.
4501 Forbes Boulevard, Suite 200, Lanham, Maryland 20706
www.rowman.com

Unit A, Whitacre Mews, 26-34 Stannary Street, London SE11 4AB

British Library Cataloguing in Publication Information Available

Library of Congress Cataloging-in-Publication Data is Available

ISBN 978-1-4758-2108-6 (cloth: alk. paper)
ISBN 978-1-4758-2109-3 (pbk: alk. paper)
ISBN 978-1-4758-2110-9 (electronic)

∞™ The paper used in this publication meets the minimum requirements of American National Standard for Information Sciences—Permanence of Paper for Printed Library Materials, ANSI/NISO Z39.48-1992.

Printed in the United States of America

To Rowna Levitt Sutin and Natalie Kaye Criddle Jacob, whose consistent support and encouragement were a source of inspiration

Contents

List of Figures

List of Tables

List of Abbreviations and Acronyms

AACC	American Association of Community Colleges
AACSB	Association to Advance Collegiate Schools of Business
AACU	Association of American Colleges and Universities
ABET	Academic Board for Engineering and Technology
ACE	American Council on Education
ACT	American College Testing
AFT	American Federation of Teachers
APA	American Psychological Association
APHERP	Asia Pacific Higher Education Research Partnership
APLU	Association of Public and Land Grant Colleges
AQF	Australian Qualifications Framework
ARWU	Academic Ranking of World Universities
ASEAN	Association of Southeast Asian Nations
ASU	Arizona State University
BA	Bachelor of Arts
BMEC	Ministry of Education, Brazil
BRICS	Brazil, Russia, India, China, and South Africa
CBE	Competency-based education
CCAC	Community College of Allegheny County
CCS	Common Core Standards
CEO	Chief executive officer
CfA	College for America
CFO	Chief financial officer
CHEA	Council for Higher Education Accreditation
CL	Civitas Learning
CMMS	Computerized maintenance management system
CMOE	China Ministry of Education

CMU	Carnegie Mellon University
C-RAC	Council of Regional Accrediting Commissions
CUNY	City University of New York
DAAD	German Academic Exchange Service
EdD	Doctor of Education
EHEA	European Higher Education Area
ELICOS	English Language Intensive Course for Overseas Students
EMBO	European Molecular Biology Organization
ENADE	National Student Performance Exam, Brazil
ENQA	European Association for Quality Assurance
FICCI	Federation of Indian Chambers of Commerce and Industry
FSUD	Flexible State University at Daytona
FTE	Full-time equivalent
FYP	Five-Year Plan
G20	Group of Twenty
GCC	Grove City College
HEI	Higher education institution
IACs	Industry advisory councils
IIE	Institute of Industrial Engineers
ISUP	Independent State University at Peoria
K-12	Kindergarten through Grade 12
MA	Master of Arts
MBA	Master of Business Administration
MHRD	Ministry of Human Resource Development, India
MINT	Math, informatics, natural sciences, or technology/engineering
MIT	Massachusetts Institute of Technology
MOOC	Massive open online course
MSCHE	Middle States Commission on Higher Education
NASBO	National Association of State Budget Officers
NCA–HLC	North Central Association of Colleges and Schools–The Higher Learning Commission
NCATE	National Council for Accreditation of Teacher Education
NCEE	National Center on Education and the Economy
NEASC–CIHE	New England Association of Schools and Colleges–Commission on Institutions of Higher Education
OBI	Ontario Brain Institute
OECD	Organisation for Economic Co-operation and Development
P-12	Pre-school through Grade 12
P-16	Pre-school to four-year higher education degree

PCC	Pasadena City College
PhD	Doctor of Philosophy
Pitt	University of Pittsburgh
PRIA	Public Relations Institute of Australia
PROUNI	*Programa Universidade para Todos* (University for All Program), Brazil
PSU	Pennsylvania State University
PSWC	Penn State World Campus
P-TECH	Pathways in Technology Early College High School
QS	Quacquarelli Symonds
REF	Research Excellence Framework, UK
REUNI	Restructuring and Expanding Plans of Federal Universities, Brazil
RMIT	Royal Melbourne Institute of Technology
ROA	Return on assets
RUSA	*Rashtriya Uchchatar Shiksha Abhiyan* (National Higher Education Mission), India
SACS	Southern Association of Colleges and Schools
SC	Steering committee
SEIU	Service Employees International Union
SINAES	National Assessment of Higher Education System, Brazil
SNHU	Southern New Hampshire University
STEM	Science, Technology, Engineering, and Math
SUPE	State University of Peninsula at Erie
SWOC	Strengths, weaknesses, opportunities, and challenges
SWOT	Strengths, weaknesses, opportunities, and threats
SYSU	Sun Yat-sen University
TEQSA	Tertiary Education Quality and Standards Agency
THE	*Times Higher Education*
UCLA	University of California, Los Angeles
UGC	University Grants Commission
UK	United Kingdom
UN	United Nations
UNESCO	United Nations Educational, Scientific and Cultural Organization
UPMC	University of Pittsburgh Medical Center
US	United States of America
USC	University of Southern California
USDHH	U.S. Department of Health and Human Services
USDOE	U.S. Department of Education
VIT	Valley Institute of Technology

List of Abbreviations and Acronyms

WASC–ACCJC   Western Association of Schools and Colleges–
              Accrediting Commission for Community and Junior
              Colleges
WASC–ACSCU   Western Association of Schools and Colleges–
              Accrediting Commission for Senior Colleges and
              Universities
WGU   Western Governors University

Foreword

For the past decade we have witnessed a variety of studies on how higher education is being transformed in the dynamic context of the global economy. Some of these studies are nation specific, others regional, and still others comparative across regions. The themes they pursue are also varied, ranging from enduring themes such as access and equity, the public-private dilemma, regionalism, mobility and migration, and quality assurance to more recent interests in innovation and entrepreneurship.

But just as the authors of this well-written book on *Strategic Transformation* note, there remains a "gap" in the literature and one that they masterfully fill. There is a gap with respect to the alignment issue, referred to as the skills gap, and the ever-present dilemma of funding higher education, made more prescient in the new ecology of neoliberalism and the decline of notions of higher education for the public good.

The authors have taken on the task of clarifying these complex relationships focused on the skills gap and comparative funding models. As higher education has continued to grow and develop through the massification movement present in most national settings, a central issue has been how to close the skills gap, or, in other words how to seek a greater alignment between the content and structure of learning and the social demand for continuingly changing skills.

This naturally brings forth and highlights the many debates that are taking place on learning outcomes and assessment strategies. Educational planning and planners must struggle with the tension that arises as their societies seek to make higher education "relevant" while at the same time preserving the creative and innovative traditions of higher learning and avoiding the vocationalization of the university. This is no easy task as the authors deftly show, and they show us we are not faced with a zero-sum game when it comes to change.

Part of the issue has to do with the stubbornness of dominant funding models for higher education. As others have noted, universities are slow to change and their business models are first in line in need of reflection and adaptation. Chapter 3 makes the case for change very convincingly and in a rational manner. One of the robust features of this study is a level of practicality when discussing problematic institutional change.

The authors offer not only a global perspective but also a *comparative* global perspective when discussing government policies, practices, and funding models (chapter 4). They do not avoid the many obstacles and challenges to these issues and offer the reader what they refer to as "a practitioner's guide to systemic reform" in the context of a more self-reliant funding environment.

Finally, in sharing with the reader the accumulated years of practical leadership experience that both authors bring to this topic, this book anchors the conceptual material by identifying exemplars of good and new practices and the skills and innovation that "transformative leaders" must have to move their institutions into the globalized future.

This book will serve as an excellent source book and in some ways a guide for those of us who labor in the rocky vineyard of global higher education institutional change and development. Professors Sutin and Jacob have attempted a most difficult job, to bridge the gap between theory and practice in higher education by making available this critical and timely exposition to those who wish to understand the complexity of higher education in the global environment.

John N. Hawkins
University of California, Los Angeles

Preface

The genesis for our book evolved during many years of conversations while serving on the higher education management faculty in the School of Education at the University of Pittsburgh. During our many years of international professional travel and living experiences, we became increasingly aware of the correlation between highly functioning educational systems, socioeconomic gains for those who emerge from those environments, the competitive advantages for their employers, and sustainable economic growth of those countries able to elevate their populations through skill acquisition and behavioral development.

In this context, globalization of commerce, information sharing, technological innovation, increasing use of social media, and changing demographic mix of students pose threats to some, and opportunities for others. The rapidity of market-based changes allows those more agile to find ways to align reflective with creative thinking, while others remain mired amid change-resistant institutional cultures.

We further believe that the legacy revenue-dependent business model for much of higher education is unsustainable in regions characterized by high levels of household debt, stagnant wage gains, and tuition pricing that has grown in multiples of inflation. If there is a singular overarching thesis of our book, we propose that higher education institutional leaders and those responsible for public education policy improve the quality and relevance of education while delivering it in ways that are more efficient, effective, and priced more affordably.

Our shared concerns include preoccupations for students who find themselves underprepared with requisite work and behavioral skills to meet the increasingly complex performance expectations of employers, and underfunded community colleges and universities that are challenged to offer accessible and affordable education to students who are not college or university ready.

The purpose of our book is to suggest ways that institutional leaders, members of boards of trustees, and those responsible for public education policy can revitalize business models while providing higher-quality education at more affordable prices. Our diagnostics suggest that the outlook for improved government appropriations for higher education does not offer cause for optimism. We call for transformative and strategic leaders who inspire confidence among internal and external stakeholders alike. In doing so, our book offers exemplars of change in higher education and lessons we can learn from them.

We offer a guide to systemic reforms, and tools that institutional leaders can call upon. Our book offers a comparative perspective by sharing insights into evolving higher education environments in the United States and select developed economies in Europe and Asia-Pacific. We attempt to avoid the dual temptations of oversimplifying the complexities of taking on institutional transformation while not understating the case for change. Solutions lie somewhere between the extremes of expecting quick fixes on one hand and catering to change-resistant institutional cultures on the other.

A unifying thread of our research and analysis suggests that effective responses reside substantially from within the corridors of higher education and emerge by devoting attention to problems that administrators and faculty can control rather than obsessing over those beyond their capacity to influence. Our language is direct rather than nuanced.

The primary audience for our book includes members of boards of trustees, institutional leaders, faculty, and public officials responsible for educational policy. Our audience also includes graduate school faculty and their students in higher education management programs. Our substantive chapters begin with hypothetical simulations of higher education institutions intended to share elements of context to help guide the interpretive capacities of an informed general public. These simulations are intended to be suggestive of systemic problems rather than portraying realities of any singular institution, leader, or student.

Our sources of information are varied. We rely upon a select literature review, research of select studies and reports by government agencies, educational and professional associations, foundations, policy think tanks, and consulting groups. This is supplemented by interviews and email correspondence with leaders of change within higher education. We accept full responsibility for analysis of data.

Acknowledgments

Many people provided meaningful feedback, criticisms, and suggestions to our book. We are grateful to them and wish to acknowledge their important contributions. The following individuals provided content contributions:

- Angela Baldasare, assistant provost for academic affairs, University of Arizona
- Denise Cuthbert, dean, School of Graduate Research, Royal Melbourne Institute of Technology
- Thomas Detre (dec.), former senior executive vice chancellor, Health Sciences, University of Pittsburgh, and CEO of UPMC
- Brian Donnelly, deputy director, Early College Initiatives, City University of New York
- James Earle, assistant chancellor for business, University of Pittsburgh
- Kurt Ewen, presidential fellow, Valencia College
- Ann Friebel, associate dean for academic affairs, La Guardia Community College
- Stephen P. Heyneman, emeritus professor, Vanderbilt University
- George Huber, former chief legal officer, UPMC
- Dick Jewell, retired president, Grove City College
- Sally Johnstone, vice president for academic advancement, Western Governors University
- Paul LeBlanc, president, Southern New Hampshire University
- Wanhua Ma, professor, Peking University, China
- James V. Maher, provost emeritus, University of Pittsburgh
- Paul J. McNulty, president, Grove City College
- Felix W. Ortiz, chairman and CEO, Viridis Learning
- David Raney, president and CEO, Nuventive

- Philip Regier, executive vice president and dean, Arizona State EdPlus
- Frederick Reif, professor emeritus of physics, Carnegie Mellon University
- Rick Shearer, director, Penn State World Campus Learning Design
- Charles Thornburgh, president and CEO, Civitas Learning

Other significant contributions came from the following individuals who provided helpful comments by reviewing drafts of the manuscript over the past couple of years:

- Livingston Alexander, president, University of Pittsburgh, Bradford Campus
- George R. Boggs, principal emeritus, Palomar Community College, and retired president, American Association of Community Colleges
- Jared L. Cohen, president emeritus, Carnegie Mellon University
- Kevin Corcoran, strategy director, Lumina Foundation
- Dan Derrico, retired interim chancellor and vice chancellor for administration, Alamo Community College District
- James Earle, assistant vice chancellor for business, University of Pittsburgh
- Rufus Glasper, president, League for Innovations, and retired president, Maricopa Community College District
- John N. Hawkins, co-director of the Asia-Pacific Higher Education Research Partnership (APHERP), East-West Center; professor emeritus, University of California, Los Angeles
- Sean Hughes, professor emeritus, University of Pittsburgh
- John E. Roueche, president, Roueche Graduate Center, National American University
- John C. Weidman III, professor of higher and international development education, University of Pittsburgh
- Jo Victoria Goodman and Sarah Hansen provided editorial and proofreading support that was much appreciated

Chapter 1

Strategic Transformation in Higher Education

Leadership, Guiding Values, and the Need for Change

Public expectation [handwritten]

The changing nature of higher education continues to challenge leaders at all levels. Higher education administrators are faced with new challenges that did not exist in previous eras. Even with all these challenges, demands continue to grow from higher education internal and external stakeholders.

Public expectations are at an all-time high, where tuition costs often outpace the average citizen's ability to afford sending their children to a quality college or university. Student debt upon graduation too often surpasses their ability to pay back loans acquired during their higher education experience. Most governments are cutting back on financing higher education, forcing higher education leaders to seek new revenue streams. Employers from all areas of industry are tired of hiring recent graduates, a group with obvious skills gap (Hawkins and Neubauer 2015). While this generalization does not apply universally, its presence is disturbing.

How do higher education leaders deal with these urgent and pressing challenges? What strategies are most successful in overcoming these challenges? Will the problems facing higher education continue, and if so, how can higher education administrators best work to overcome these problems? How can leaders deal with the many current challenges, as well as the undoubtedly many that will surface in the future? How can higher education institutions continue to compete in local, national, and international arenas? These are some of the questions that are addressed in this book.

BUILDING A CASE FOR STRATEGIC LEADERSHIP

In the midst of this changing higher education landscape, there is a need for strong and strategic leadership. Leadership is fundamental to ensuring that higher education continues to provide quality graduates, cutting-edge

highcost, [handwritten]

1

research, and, increasingly, exceptional customer service. Strategic leadership in higher education is based upon a set of personal characteristics and core values developed over the course of one's lifetime. These characteristics and core values serve as a moral compass to guide leaders in all that they do (Covey 1989).

Often, higher education leaders pattern their individual characteristics and values after positive leader role models they encountered in their past. In this way, leadership is often modeled by the many exceptional leader and mentor examples individuals have had the opportunity to meet and learn from (Kalungu-Banda 2006; Kerr 2001).

Higher education leaders should also be grounded on a set of core values. The following six core values are deemed essential for successful higher education leadership.

1. ***High Morals and Ethics.*** Moral and ethical leadership is the first-listed core value of higher education leadership for a reason—it is the foundation that students, teachers, and administrators can mutually build upon to achieve sustainable success (Brown and Treviño 2006; Greenleaf 2009). Ultimately, consistent moral and ethical leadership helps establish organizational virtue, positive reputation, and high performance (Cameron et al. 2004).

2. ***Innovation and Creativity.*** Successful higher education leaders encourage innovative thought, teaching pedagogies, and practices. Leaders should come prepared to offer meaningful solutions to help overcome challenges within organizations. Innovation is at the heart of cutting-edge research and teaching practices that are often required to best meet the unique challenges and needs of an increasingly diverse and changing field of education. Enabling leaders helps establish an institutional culture and atmosphere that helps innovation flourish in many varieties, including disruptive innovation (Christensen and Eyring 2011; Christensen et al. 2011).

3. ***Community Engagement and Service.*** Leaders should ideally be engaged and serve in the communities associated with their higher education assignments. This includes encouraging faculty members and students to do the same within their respective areas of expertise and personal and professional networks. Reaching out and engaging others provides leaders with an ability to build meaningful local, national, and international networks in a strategic way. It also enables leaders to better balance their many responsibilities by partnering with others (Jacob et al. 2015; Patterson et al. 1999).

4. ***Good Governance.*** Leadership should adhere to the principles of sound governance—organizational behavior based on appropriate theory and practice, sufficient information flow, transparency, and accountability.

These principles should serve as a standard of excellence in all areas of our instruction, research, and practice. Successful higher education leaders encourage strategic planning, recordkeeping, and setting goals (Hitt et al. 2013). Periodic progress evaluations set a standard of accountability for given goals and assignments.

5. ***Reflective Practice.*** It is important for higher education leaders to take time to reflect on various areas that are essential to help improve their organization. One of the greatest weaknesses of leaders is that they are often too busy to take the time necessary to evaluate and improve on what they have learned (Griessman 1994). Everyone makes mistakes, and it is important to learn from these mistakes. Good governance is a reciprocal and reflective leadership practice that includes important evaluation and feedback loops to help learn from our mistakes and find ways for continual improvement. Effective verbal and written communication skills are also needed as a reflective leader and in team environments through attentive listening, consensus building, motivating, negotiation, conflict resolution, and persuasion.

6. ***Team Work and Synergy.*** It is important for higher education leaders to strive to establish an organizational atmosphere that encourages each team member to become the best that they can (Patterson et al. 2002). We all have different strengths and talents, and together we can achieve much more than if we go at it alone. Synergy is an essential ingredient to any high-performing team (Covey 2013). There are often many ways to accomplish any given task in higher education. Effective leadership includes an ability to reach out to and be willing to work with those who may have differing opinions and perspectives than we do (Miles and Snow 1994).

Among the many characteristics we consider important in higher education leadership, the following eight are perhaps most essential:

1. ***Integrity.*** Honesty remains among the most important foundational characteristics of leaders in every field, especially in higher education. Sometimes it is difficult to do the right thing. Higher education leaders must remain steady when it comes to abiding by government laws and regulations and to setting the example for others to follow. While contexts, challenges, and relationships continuously change, integrity is something that should never be compromised. The most successful leaders are true to themselves and have substance; they are genuine and able to draw from their unique personality strengths (Bennis 1989).

2. ***Dependable.*** Being fully committed to one's institution, assignment, and responsibilities is a second fundamental characteristic. Higher education

leaders must be dependable. This is essential, whether it be related to your job, personal area of expertise, or in relation to community service opportunities. Regardless of the circumstance, it is important to approach each assignment with dedication and a willingness to see it through to the end. Commitment to others is a crucial element in team development, and is especially important for leaders to model so that others will feel like they are part of a high-performing team. When difficulties arise, and they often do in higher education contexts, leaders remain steady and can be looked to for guidance and as exemplars.

3. *Excellence.* Successful higher education leaders strive for excellence in several key areas and set an expectation for others to do the same. It is virtually impossible to achieve exceptional performance without first having a goal to do so, and this pertains to all areas of instruction, research, and community engagement. Strategic planning is an essential and ongoing process to achieve sustained excellence in higher education.

4. *Humble.* Successful higher education leaders are humble. Maintaining a constant desire to learn is fundamental in education and in higher education leadership. Learning can and should come from many sources, including through personal study, and perhaps most importantly from others. Being able to listen to others helps leaders better understand their perspectives and needs. Learning at the individual, group, and institutional levels is an ongoing process; leaders need to help forge an atmosphere and culture where this learning is continuous (Duke 2002; Senge 1990).

5. *Empathetic.* It is essential for leaders to learn about and love those they lead. This can only be achieved by showing empathy to others, and it includes getting to know them and truly understanding the diverse circumstances and needs that they have. When solid and trusting relationships are established by team members of an organization, there are tremendous opportunities for personal and collective growth.

6. *Empowering.* In a collaborative way, effective leaders help establish a higher education organizational mission and vision and effectively communicate them to others. The most effective leaders give others opportunities to participate in carrying forward leadership initiatives, including the implementation of a shared mission and vision for their respective units. No matter how talented the leader is, they cannot and should not do everything themselves. They proactively seek out and include others in decision-making processes. This inclusive, collaborative, and shared-governance approach motivates others to help share the leadership load and creates a greater sense of buy-in, ownership, and commitment (Blanchard et al. 1999).

7. *Results Based.* In order to obtain excellence in higher education, leaders should set a standard of expecting quality efforts from all within

their organization. Generally speaking, quality inputs lead to quality results. A results-based management approach is a best leadership practice, which includes establishing an atmosphere of progress reporting, continual improvement, and reflection that enables leaders to identify and report on areas of self- and organizational improvement.

8. Establishing a results-based culture within a higher education unit—which could be institution wide or pertinent to a smaller unit within a higher education institution (HEI)—ultimately leads toward establishing a foundation where the four principles of good governance (coordination, transparency, information flow, and accountability) can flourish. When higher education results are measured, results improve. When higher education results are measured and reported, "the rate of improvement accelerates" (Monson 1970).

9. **Prudence.** The post–global financial crisis era (post–2007–2008) has only amplified the need for greater fiscal prudence in all areas of higher education leadership. The most successful higher education leaders are strategically prudent with their time and money management and in judgment areas where decisions are impactful and long lasting.

The Higher Education Leadership Wheel visually displays each of the core values and essential characteristics of successful higher education leaders (see Figure 1.1).

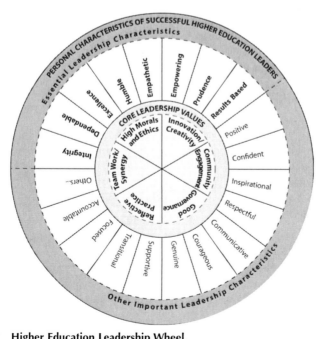

Figure 1.1 **Higher Education Leadership Wheel.**

We also provide an additional set of important characteristics common among the most successful higher education leaders. There is also a space for other characteristics that may be important or essential, depending on the leadership position. These core values and leadership characteristics are foundational to strategic leadership in higher education. In many ways, they serve as a guide when leaders are faced with new challenges and don't necessarily have a blueprint to follow.

Remaining adaptable to changing circumstances, contexts, and the various needs of a diverse student body, faculty, administrators, staff members, and the many additional stakeholders we engage with on a regular basis is key to a strategic leadership approach. Successful higher education leaders always come prepared with a number of eclectic leadership approaches to best meet the needs of diverse challenges, situations, and contexts.

OVERVIEW AND STRUCTURE OF THIS BOOK

Is a higher education degree less relevant than in the past? It certainly is less affordable in the United States and in most countries. Aggregate student debt has reached the tipping point. Tuition pricing in the United States has increased in multiples of inflation for the past three decades. The quality of a college education is increasingly suspect as institutional missions and curriculum blur, and liberal arts graduates struggle to gain employment in professions.

Many institutions fail to undertake meaningful student-centric transformation. Public education policy is mired in silos that treat K-12, community college and four-year college, and university education as disconnected enterprises. Most countries place great value on a competitive workforce, but few offer cost-effective solutions to close their skills gap (Portnoi et al. 2010). Are contemporary educational and business models of higher education sustainable? If not, who will change them? How? And for what purpose?

In this book, we examine the space where the quality, cost, and effectiveness of higher education converge in the United States and other countries. We evaluate the value propositions offered by distinct sectors of higher education and provide background evidence supportive of a case for systemic institutional reforms. We feature several good and best practices and institutional exemplars of innovation and effectiveness in the United States and abroad. We draw attention to lessons we can learn from the past and examine the potential of more recent educational and business models.

We address concerns relating to the gap between workplace competencies needed for countries to compete in a global marketplace and the perceived shortcomings of postsecondary degree graduates. Differentiation is made through side-by-side comparisons of quality and cost of higher education while drawing upon lessons that can be learned from other countries. Many of the chapters offer somewhat of a practitioner's guide to reform of educational policy by local and national governments while posing choices and potential solutions to complex institutional problems.

There are winners and losers in higher education. We assess the consequences for failure to keep pace with necessary change and respond to challenges. The book includes multiple perspectives of threats and opportunities and proposes strategic and tactical opportunities to reinvent higher education in ways that better serve students, employers, and the greater community well-being.

The first section of our book describes a competitive, global socioeconomic context, with a comparative assessment of student and employer learning expectations. This is followed by an evidence-based case for systemic reform of educational and business models. Prevailing educational and business models are described and examined for strengths and weaknesses. Public funding models and accreditation standards are also addressed. Several case study exemplars outline lessons learned from those who demonstratively excel through quality, tuition containment, and innovation. Business and quality control models that have served other mature industries well are also interwoven throughout the book, highlighting their potential applicability to higher education. Finally, we explore the leadership attributes needed to drive reform from within higher education and at the policy levels in governments.

Among the most pressing issues higher education leaders face include being able to provide quality postsecondary education; increasing access and equity, especially among the most disadvantaged groups (Bigalke and Zurbuchen 2014); recognizing and celebrating diversity; keeping tuition and fees from spiraling out of control; limiting student debt; and ensuring graduates are prepared to enter the job market in an increasingly competitive and globalized workforce. Effective leadership is central to addressing each of these issues. While leadership styles may differ, and foreign contexts and cultures make fiducial lines of comparison sometimes difficult, the Higher Education Leadership Wheel transcends international boundaries. All leaders need to be guided by an internal compass of ethics, core values, and essential leadership characteristics.

REFERENCES

Bennis, Warren. 1989. *On Becoming a Leader*. Reading, MA: Perseus Books.
Bigalke, Terrance W., and Mary S. Zurbuchen. 2014. *Leadership for Social Justice in Higher Education*. New York: Palgrave Macmillan.

Blanchard, Ken, John P. Carlos, and Alan Randolph. *The 3 Keys to Empowerment: Release the Power Within People for Astonishing Results*. San Francisco: Berrett-Koehler Publishers.

Brown, Michael E., and Linda K. Treviño. 2006. "Ethical Leadership: A Review and Future Directions." *The Leadership Quarterly* 17 (6): 595–616.

Cameron, Kim S., David Bright, and Arran Caza. 2004. "Exploring the Relationships between Organizational Virtuousness and Performance." *American Behavioral Scientist* 47 (6): 766–790.

Christensen, Clayton M., and Henry J. Eyring. 2011. *The Innovative University: Changing the DNA of Higher Education from the Inside Out*. New York: John Wiley & Sons.

Christensen, Clayton M., Michael B. Horn, Louis Caldera, and Louis Soares. 2011. *Disrupting College: How Disruptive Innovation Can Deliver Quality and Affordability to Postsecondary Education*. Washington, DC; Mountain View, CA: Center for American Progress and Innosight Institute.

Covey, Stephen R. 1989. *Principle-Centered Leadership*. New York: Simon & Schuster.

Covey, Stephen R. 2013. *The 7 Habits of Highly Effective People: Powerful Lessons in Personal Change*. New York: Simon & Schuster.

Duke, Christopher. 2002. *Managing the Learning University*. Buckingham, UK; Philadelphia, PA: The Society for Research into Higher Education and Open University Press.

Greenleaf, Robert K. 2009. *Servant Leadership: A Journey into the Nature of Legitimate Power and Greatness*. Mahwah, NJ: Paulist Press.

Greenleaf, Robert K. 2009. *The Institution as Servant*. Westfield, IN: Greenleaf Center for Servant Leadership.

Greissman, B. Eugene. 1994. *Time Tactics of Very Successful People*. New York: McGraw-Hill.

Hawkins, John N., and Deane Neubauer. 2015. "Twenty-First Century Work Skills and Competencies." In *Technology and Workplace Skills for the Twenty-First Century: Asia Pacific Universities in the Globalized Economy*, edited by Deane Neubauer and Kamila Ghazali (pp. 9–23). New York: Palgrave Macmillan.

Hitt, Michael A., R. Duane Ireland, and Robert E. Hoskisson. 2013. *Strategic Management: Concepts: Competitiveness and Globalization*. Independence, KY: Cengage Learning.

Jacob, W. James, Sutin, Stewart E., Weidman, John C., and Yeager, John L. (Eds.) 2015. *Community Engagement in Higher Education: Policy Reforms and Practice*. Boston, Taipei, London, Rotterdam: Sense Publishers.

Kalungu-Banda, Martin. 2006. *Leading like Madiba: Leadership Lessons from Nelson Mandela*. Claremont, South Africa: Juta and Company Ltd.

Kerr, Clark. 2001. *The Uses of the University*. Cambridge, MA: Harvard University Press.

Miles, Raymond E., and Charles C. Snow. 1994. *Fit, Failure and the Hall of Fame: How Companies Succeed or Fail*. New York: The Free Press.

Monson, Thomas S. 1970. "In Conference Report." *Ensign* November: 170.

Patterson, Kerry, Joseph Grenny, Ron McMillan, and Al Switzler. 1999. *The Balancing Act: Mastering the Competing Demands of Leadership*. Provo, UT: Vitality Alliance.

Patterson, Kerry, Joseph Grenny, Ron McMillan, and Al Switzler. 2002. *Crucial Conversations: Tools for Talking When Stakes are High*. New York: McGraw-Hill.

Portnoi, Laura M., Val D. Rust, and Sylvia S. Bagley, Eds. 2010. *Higher Education, Policy, and the Global Competition Phenomenon*. New York: Palgrave Macmillan.

Senge, Peter M. *The Fifth Discipline: The Art and Science of the Learning Organization*. New York: Currency Doubleday.

Chapter 2

Global Competition to Close the Skills Gap

Many Chinese youth are like 16-year-old Zhang Wei from Xi'an, Shaanxi Province, China. All his life, Zhang has dreamed of graduating from high school, passing the gaokao (高考, higher education exam), and attending a good university. In the back of his mind, his dream since childhood has been to be able to attend one of the leading universities in China, like Peking University, Tsinghua University, or, perhaps even, the local Shaanxi Normal University. If things go well in this dream, Zhang also has thought of a distant dream of continuing his higher education overseas, perhaps in Australia, Germany, or the United States.

As the only child in his family, Zhang's parents also have high hopes for their son. Zhang's father works as a police officer and his mother as a civil servant. They have worked hard all their lives, but they are not wealthy and are nearing retirement. There is no way that they will be able to save enough money to help Zhang accomplish his higher education dreams without needs-based financial aid.

After one semester of exceptional performance, Zhang will be eligible for a merit-based scholarship. But the realities often differ from the dreams of millions of Chinese children. The reality is that the majority of young men like Zhang will end up at a modest higher education institution (HEI), including vocational HEIs that help students graduate with a skillset leading toward a specific career path, but their opportunities for upward mobility in society will for the most part be stagnated. There is no question that higher education opportunities continue to increase. Yet, the reality is that most Chinese high school students like Zhang don't have the resources to attend top HEIs in China.

One of the greatest challenges higher education administrators face is the ability to internationalize their institutions. This was the challenge

11

Dr. Andrea Taylor-Magleby faced at the onset of her tenure as dean of the School of Business at Mountain State University. She had little to build on in terms of a strategic schoolwide international focus, but this is one of the reasons she was selected above other candidates. Dr. Taylor-Mableby learned that several faculty members were involved with some very interesting individual research and service-learning projects overseas. She decided to reach out to these faculty members and bring them together as part of a schoolwide taskforce to help internationalize the School of Business.

Realizing that they were not able to have a significant impact in many regions, she charged the team to develop a strategic plan to focus on three strategic countries that could help build on existing faculty and administrator relationships and also provide an avenue for other interested faculty members and students to get involved in these identified regions. Four faculty members had long-term relationships in Western Europe, so Switzerland was identified as a strategic focus country. Other faculty members had traveled to and had conducted research studies in Mexico, which became a second priority country.

Recognizing that they needed a footprint in Asia, Dr. Taylor-Mableby suggested that China be made a third priority, in which she had cultivated a strong network over the years. With these three target countries as the initial focus, Dr. Taylor-Mableby led the development of an international strategic plan with goals to increase enrollments from each of the target countries, establish memorandums of understanding with a few comparable universities (and, where appropriate, aspirational universities), and support faculty members in their desire to expand research, study abroad, and service-learning opportunities in these respective regions.

Dr. Taylor-Mableby's approach is strategic, with clearly identified geographic targets and enrollment goals. By involving and supporting faculty members, students, and alumni from the onset in the planning and development phase of the international strategic plan, she will most likely have buy-in and greater ownership when the plan is implemented throughout the duration of her term as dean. This is a pattern that will most likely lead to a fruitful and sustainable international initiative for her School of Business.

Global trends in higher education deal with major policy and practice issues relevant to help graduates obtain and maintain twenty-first-century skills. Financing, competition, quality assurance, and providing higher education opportunities to the masses are among the top issues worldwide. This chapter poses questions about the purposes and priorities of higher education as seen through the lenses of government officials, employers, university leaders, faculty members, and students. Several examples are provided from various case countries, including the United States and the so-called BRICS countries.[1]

SIMILAR GOALS, DIFFERING VIEWS

There are as many differing perspectives on how higher education should be offered as there are people who have a stake in how it is administered. This difference of opinions among stakeholders often leads to dissonance in political and community arenas. But differing views, and diversity in general, can also be a strength.

Let's take a look at some of the various perspectives of the following key stakeholder groups: government officials, employers, university leaders, board of trustees members, faculty members, students, community members, and accrediting agency leaders. Government officials are concerned about the growing financial strain higher education places on increasingly limited public funds.

Other areas of public finance seem to crowd out the need to focus on supporting higher education. Population aging among many Group of Twenty (G20) countries, including Australia, Germany, Japan, Korea, Taiwan, and the United States, shifts limited financial resources away from public higher education in support of rising health care costs and other welfare needs (Chia 2012; Higo and Khan 2014). Government leaders are concerned with the rising financial implications of supporting elite and mass higher education options for their citizenry (Lee 2014; Guri-Rosenblit 2012; Altbach, Gumport, and Berdahl 2011).

Policy makers and government planners are also often involved in the establishment of principles of good governance, quality assurance, and keeping costs to a manageable level. Another common challenge within predominantly democratic societies is that the amount and direction of public funding afforded to HEIs depends on which political party is in power.

Higher education is a highly contested political debate issue in many countries. Many of the most hotly contested issues have to deal with the financing of higher education and whether it is offered by public or private means. The BRICS countries have emerged in many ways as global leaders competing with HEIs in the United States and Europe. But BRICS higher education systems still have many significant shortcomings, especially in reference to quality assurance and social justice issues of access and equity (Altbach 2012).

Costs of quality higher education in BRICS countries consistently increased during the first decade in the twenty-first century. The amount of funding each country could invest per student decreased during this period (see Figure 2.1). And while access to mass higher education was achieved in virtually every BRICS country during the past 20 years, most higher education opportunities were available at low-quality mediocre institutions. Costs to attend the top-ranked universities consistently rose, making them less accessible to those from remote locations and with less financial means

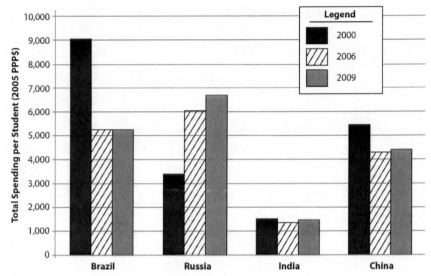

Figure 2.1 Total of Private Plus Public Spending in Higher Education per Student for Brazil, Russia, India, and China, 2000–2009.

(Carnoy et al. 2014; Li and Yang 2013). A global trend mirrors what the BRICS countries experienced in recent decades—there has been a consistent rise of student fees to help offset increasing costs of higher education at all levels (Sanyal and Johnstone 2011; Tilak 2013; Mok 2012).

Employers are constantly on the outlook for exceptional talent and qualified employees. The natural fit between industry and higher education is especially appropriate in some fields, but not as much in others. This is why schools of business, law, education, and engineering have made such strong inroads into higher education–industry partnerships. These partnerships include granting internship and apprenticeship opportunities for current students, serving on higher education advisory boards, and, of course, providing fulltime employment to graduates.

Too often, however, there is a mismatch between what higher education graduates can produce in terms of a skills set and what employers need and expect. Some of the shortcomings reported by many employers include lack of sufficient communication skills, ability to work as a member of a team, and the ability to work out complex problems (see Fischer 2014). Internships can help offset some of these graduate skill shortcomings, but curriculum shortcoming are at least the perceived norm for much of society and many employers. In order to help overcome this shortcoming, higher education administrators need to take a serious look at better aligning the curriculum with government, market, and industry standards.

The establishment of industry advisory councils (IACs)[2] within higher education departments, schools, and entire universities is a trend that has met with success in many countries. IACs can be established within single departments, schools, or faculties that can help higher education administrators, faculty members, and students network with leaders of industry in their respective disciplines. Larger IACs can represent consortia of HEIs at local, national, and international levels.

Some of the most effective IACs include activities for council members to review the curriculum on a regular basis to ensure that it remains current with industry trends and needs. IAC members can also recommend industry experts who can be called upon from time to time to help provide instruction or guest lecturers and serve on curriculum review panels. IAC members should work to establish meaningful internship programs that help link HEIs to employers in local and, where appropriate, national and international settings. IACs can become a cornerstone for higher education success in helping to identify and bridge the global skills gap.[3] (we have)

Higher education leaders often have to work closely with other stakeholder groups. Senior higher education administrators are constantly in public settings representing their respective institutions. Leaders who are best able to convey the message that the business aspects of higher education are taken seriously—especially when public taxes are used to help finance their HEIs— generally lead with a unified strategic vision and mission. Successful leaders also adhere to the four principles of higher education good governance, which include information flow, coordination, transparency, and accountability (Jacob and Rust 2010). Principles of good governance are fundamental in order to help other stakeholders understand higher education administrators' points of view.

The governance model for higher education is subject to wide variation by country, region, or state, whether ownership is public or private sector, and agreement in certain instances to open decision-making to a broader internal constituency. The ultimate differentiator is a function of who controls decision-making over appointments to boards of trustees, hiring and retaining leaders, approval of institutional strategies, and annual operating and capital budgets, and defining policies and procedures at the highest levels.

In some countries, such as China, the government sustains substantial and direct oversight and controls, and connectivity is evident between national socioeconomic goals and institutional priorities. By comparison, much of public higher education in the United States retains varying levels of institutional autonomy. Control by boards of trustees, boards of regents, and senior administrators varies widely by state, region, and at the institutional level.

In these situations, fidelity to national, state, or regional socioeconomic goals may be found in institutional mission statements and through an examination of educational priorities. As such, the correlation between public higher education in the United States and desirable economic outcomes is often less precise. In some instances, some public institutions have even acknowledged the role of faculty or labor unions in participative decision-making through processes known as "shared governance." In short, descriptors of governance do not lend themselves to sweeping generalizations.

Faculty members comprise very complex stakeholder group. In many countries, it is increasingly difficult for faculty members to secure a tenure-streamline of work. There has been a trend toward the inclusion of more part-time and adjunct faculty members. One of the greatest challenges many developing countries confront is having a sufficient number of qualified faculty members for their respective departments. National strategic goals to train thousands (and in some cases tens of thousands) of individuals with PhDs or other comparable doctoral degrees is a common theme echoed among many emerging economy countries.

The long-term impact of this strategic investment will help position their countries' higher education sectors so that they are more comparable with international standards of excellence in terms of faculty qualifications. But realities also weigh into this strategic planning process, because many who participate in these government-sponsored faculty training initiatives do not remain in the countries in which they obtained their doctorate degrees. This brain drain phenomenon is not new, but it highlights that many developing and emerging economy countries continue to struggle to recruit and retain the top talent within their potential faculty teaching pools because they can often find higher wages in other areas of employment or overseas.

Perhaps, the most important stakeholder group is students. Globally, higher education demand remains high. But enrollment trends differ depending upon the country context. For instance, the higher education subsector in several countries has leveled off; in some cases, demand in all education subsectors, including higher education, has decreased due to aging populations. This trend of decreasing enrollments is happening, for example, in countries like Japan, Korea, Taiwan, and, to some extent, the United States.

Similarly, certain disciplines have come under increased scrutiny as to the merits and overall economic value that a student can receive from obtaining a degree in a given field. This is why we see an increasing trend where many HEIs continue to consolidate schools, departments, and even degree programs. Students ultimately have to obtain a job following graduation, so it is particularly important for them to select a degree program that can help them find meaningful employment.

In addition to the formal curriculum that has been traditionally offered to students, it has become increasingly important for students to strengthen other work skills that can help them compete for and excel at their eventual jobs. Some of these skills include basic literacy and numeracy skills, critical thinking, cultural expression, and an ability to implement what they have learned in real-life settings. It is also essential for a graduate to have good social skills and to be able to work as a member of a team. Finally, it is essential for graduates to be able to network and leverage social media in a way that will best help them obtain a job in a career track.

Public views regarding higher education also stretch across a spectrum. Views are often linked to perceived costs and quality of higher education. Tuition and other higher education-related costs continue to escalate. This is a trend within the United States and across the world (Johnstone 2014). The fact that many graduates complete their degrees only after incurring substantial debt to help them finance their degrees is a topic of heated debate, and is often addressed by scholars and the mass media (Altbach, Gumport, and Berdahl 2011; Brown and Carasso 2013).

It is also used as a political platform by many politicians. Quality of instruction ranges from a public-perceived elite higher education training to those that barely meet the standards of most businesses and organizations. The United States has a strong public higher education sector, with many universities that rank among the top 100 world-class universities. In other countries, government school universities are normally top ranked within their respective countries.

The United States and the United Kingdom also have an unusually strong private higher education sector, including those that place in the top 10 world-class rankings (Shanghai Jiao Tong University 2015; *Times Higher Education* 2015). Online-only providers of higher education are usually perceived in the most negative public light. The criticisms are often justified, in that the public perceives online-only higher education offerings as overly laden with theory and often have little merit when it comes to application and practice.[4] But times and technologies are changing the way in which coursework is being delivered, including through blended or hybrid delivery or through massive open online courses (MOOCs). Some of these offerings are as good, if not better, than what can be offered through traditional delivery mediums (Moore, Dickson-Deane, and Galyen 2011; Allen and Seaman 2013).

In many cases, HEIs are the center of the economy for some cities and towns. This is especially the case in small college or university towns, but is also important in large, industrial hubs where clusters of HEIs exist to help build a triple-helix synergy between universities, industry, and government (Leydesdorff 2013; Jacob et al. 2015). Many community members have close and endearing affinity with local HEIs. College sports are huge in the United States, but not as much in other countries. HEIs often serve as role model organizations in community outreach, adult education, and service-learning opportunities. They are responsible for training the next generation of workers in the public and private sectors.

Even with all the goodwill higher education has and continues to garner, there has been a growing dissatisfaction among the general public in several countries[5] with some elements of the system that are in many ways viewed as archaic or underperforming. The argument that the education tenure system is out of date and needs reform is gaining momentum, especially in the wake of the global financial crisis of 2007. There are various scenarios regarding the traditional faculty tenure system within higher education.

While many tenured faculty members continue to make substantial contributions to their home institutions, a relative few choose to simply meet the bare minimum teaching and research requirements without fear of retribution or losing their jobs. The scenario where a professor reaches tenure and essentially enters a semiretirement mode for the next 30+ years is a situation that we have all at least heard of, if not seen playing out in real life. Unless a faculty member commits a serious crime, it is virtually impossible to remove a nonperforming or underperforming tenured faculty member.

To offset this growing sentiment, HEIs are increasingly implementing ways to reward productive faculty members and limit the growth potential of those who do not perform. Salary raises are increasingly linked to annual performance reviews. Several countries have established a mandatory retirement age for faculty members that helps prevent an excessively long tenure system. This required retirement policy exists for faculty members at public HEIs in China, India, Japan, Korea, South Africa, and Taiwan (Guri-Rosenblit 2012; González, Liu, and Shu 2012; Udjo and Erasmus 2014; Altbach et al. 2013). But generally speaking, there are no such retirement age requirements at private HEIs worldwide, and often the most renowned and respected faculty members who are required to retire at public HEIs will find employment for an additional five or more years in the private sector. _Why - demand_

Finally, accrediting agency leaders are important stakeholders who in many ways serve as guardians to ensure that national and international standards are achieved and maintained in training and practice. This includes quality assurance and accreditation standards that are based upon the principles of good governance. Accrediting agencies often have some of the most experienced leaders of industry and academe who are able to help identify and bridge gaps in curriculum, instruction, and assessment needs.

In the United States, accrediting agencies are nongovernmental organizations that remain at a distance from government oversight.[6] The European Association for Quality Assurance in Higher Education (ENQA) serves as an umbrella organization to ensure quality assurance across all countries in Europe and elsewhere that have formally endorsed the Bologna Process. Other countries, like Australia, China, and Saudi Arabia, have highly centralized accrediting agencies. Several discipline-specific accrediting agencies—such as the Accreditation Board for Engineering and Technology (ABET), the Association to Advance Collegiate Schools of Business (AACSB), and the National Council for Accreditation of Teacher Education (NCATE)—provide national and international standards of excellence for engineering, science, and education programs. Failure to include accrediting agency leaders in strategic planning initiatives often leads to gaps in being able to meet and maintain standards of excellence in teaching, research, service, and community outreach initiatives.

EDUCATION AND THE GLOBAL SKILLS GAP

Numerous political leaders, employers, educational foundations, students and families of students, and countless leaders from all levels and sectors of education in the United States and many countries share concerns about access, affordability, and beneficial results of obtaining higher education degrees. Barriers to degree attainment and skill enhancement pose material obstacles to job creation, the competitiveness of national and global economies, and sustainable economic growth. Declining medium household income in many countries—a common barometer of a widening skills gap between employer needs and the quality and depth of the workforce—causes concern for consumption-driven economies.

We live in an era of heightened global competition for jobs and for revenue from sales and procurement. Advanced communications, reduced barriers to movement of goods and services across national boundaries, and operational technologies have irrevocably integrated commercial, labor and capital markets, with the consequence that jobs, products, and support services increasingly flow to nations offering the most competitive mix of quality, price, and productivity. Breakthrough technologies and changing market conditions render certain occupational skill sets obsolete and create high demand for others with shocking speed. In this context, a nation's economic growth increasingly relies upon the talents of its workforce and the effectiveness of institutions of learning in meeting those needs.

Let us consider workforce skills and employee needs from a broader perspective. In the most immediate sense, a gap persists between certain high-demand regional occupational needs and awareness of those needs among students and unemployed or underemployed adults. Fairly or unfairly, traditional vocational high schools often carry the stigma of offering alternative education for losers. High school college counselors are often biased toward four-year colleges rather than community colleges or craft skill academies that offer associate degrees or certificate programs in a wide array of trade skills.

Recently, the head of the Carnegie Mellon University Robotics Institute informed us that there is a need for qualified technicians who are able to service and repair their robots. Seen through this lens, we have yet to develop sufficient remedies for bridging the worlds between employer needs and labor supply.

A closer inspection of workforce needs extends beyond technical qualifications alone. Intangible competencies matter. In competitive domestic and global markets, employers require highly productive, self-motivated, inventive, collaborative, and adaptive employees capable of self-management, setting their own goals, and consistently performing at high levels of competence.

Anthony P. Carnevale and Nicole Smith (2014) very effectively articulate the intangible skills and abilities sought by employers. They include such important outcomes as listening, critical thinking, reading comprehension, written and spoken expression, social perceptiveness, problem solving, and both inductive and deductive reasoning. To this, Tony Wagner (2015) adds such variables as collaboration, agility, initiative and entrepreneurship, and accessing and analyzing information.

Wagner, a former K-12 educator and school principal, understands that development of these abilities should begin during the developmental years of students, with higher education further enhancing these competencies. During the early 1900s, Abraham Flexner (1923) proposed ways to reenvision modern medical education in the United States. Several of his recommendations were subsequently adopted by many leading schools of medicine.

Flexner believed that a relevant curriculum was essential, and subsequently authored a think piece on "a modern school." At the heart of his concept for a new secondary school in New York City, Flexner envisioned a learned person as someone "trained to know, to care about and to understand the world he lives in, both the physical and the social world . . . interpret phenomena, and a comprehension of and sympathy with current industry, current science and current politics" (p. 3).

The United States and several G20 economies are advancing from a "knowledge-age" economy to a "performance age" economy in which degrees set minimum standards, while sustainable employment, promotion, and prosperity rely more upon talents not normally measured by transcripts. Our own experiences during many years of business leadership reinforce the salient observations drawn by Carnevale, Wagner, and Flexner. Meeting minimum career standards may position one to be hired, but employers seek those who own highly sought-after "soft" skills. For example, there is a need for employees who require little supervision, are curious, have a knack for finding solutions, and who inspire confidence and collaboration among their peers.

A closer examination of socioeconomic and demographic issues raises still further concerns. Attrition from high schools and higher education is alarmingly high. Now the United States faces retirement of its post–World War II baby boomer generation. To make matters worse, annual population growth declined to 0.87 percent by 2009, the lowest percent of growth in the past 54 years (U.S. Census Bureau 2012, p. 8). Between declining population growth rates, projected retirements, and restrictive immigration laws, the P-20 educational systems will have to perform at optimal levels to sustain job creation and economic growth.

With an aggregate population of about 198 million persons 25 years and older, under 40 percent has an associates, bachelors, or advanced degree (U.S. Census Bureau 2011, p. 150). Worse yet, a study of 2011 test scores by the educational testing service ACT reflects that only 25 percent of high school graduates were deemed college ready in English, reading, mathematics, and science combined (ACT 2013, p. 3).

Let's consider how well the United States is positioned to meet skills gap challenges. Economic history informs us that the United States and other leading and emergent economies went through transformations from high labor content industries to those that added value in the form of greater productivity, inventiveness, lower cost per unit of output, and increasingly sophisticated products and services. How well positioned is the US workforce to meet these rigorous global demands?

Lester Thurow (1992), a prominent economist and dean of the Sloan School of Management at MIT at the time of writing *Head to Head*, compared US primary and secondary school education to those of other major economic powers and cited concerns about lesser numbers of school days, fewer hours of learning per day, and lesser demands for at-home study. Michael E. Porter (1990) made the case for sustainably high productivity standards at a national level in order to sustain a competitive position in global markets.

Porter expressed concerns about high rates of functional illiteracy, low education standards, lack of a strong system for vocational education, and low levels of corporate training in the United States. Various companies and industries that succeeded in recent years alert us to the growing gap between what employers need from their workers, and the current pool of available workers (Slywotzky 1996). The oft-cited *Tough Choices or Tough Times* report by the National Center on Education and the Economy (NCEE 2007) called for educational standards and curriculum to meet "today's needs and tomorrow's requirements" (p. xxv).

A human resource crisis or a widening skills gap in many countries can be a harbinger of opportunity as well as risk. Optimists will envision opportunities for improvement in closing the indigenous skills gap from within and develop plans accordingly. As the prior narrative relates, the challenges are often more subtle and complex than will be remediated by simply increasing high school and college graduation rates. Notwithstanding signs of progress, the jury is still out in terms of the capacity to drive systemic reforms through the P-20 educational system.

GLOBAL COMPETITION THEMES

There are many topics that are important to each stakeholder group and others that are relevant to only one or a few. Other themes are cross-cutting and tend to impact all groups regardless of their differences. Mobility is a cross-cutting higher education issue that has captured virtually all stakeholder groups. There are multiple types of mobility, including *degree mobility, student mobility, and faculty mobility*.

By degree mobility, we refer to a graduate's ability to secure a job in industry based on the qualifications of their degree. For example, does a degree in engineering, software engineering, or medicine from a US university meet the required standards for a graduate to work in Brazil, China, Germany, India, or Indonesia, or vice versa?

Student mobility enables individuals currently enrolled in a university degree program to be able to take classes for a semester or year at another university and have those credits articulate or count toward their degree at their home institution. The Bologna Process, the Erasmus Programme, and the Lisbon Recognition Convention have helped establish and meet the needs of the greater European Higher Education Area in terms of helping students transition in a cross-border fashion between HEIs.

This increased mobility and standardization of the overall higher education curriculum has been met with both acclaim and disdain, depending on who you talk to. It has not solved the issue of immigration trends, yet there is a recognized minimum quality standard that must be met in order to achieve recognition as a Bologna Process member country. Similar efforts were led by Australia in 2006 through the establishment of the Brisbane Communiqué countries within the Asia-Pacific Region concerned about higher education standards and quality assurance (Chao 2011).

Faculty mobility enables faculty members at all levels (lecturers, instructors, professors) to be able to work in more than one location. It means that HEI administrators in one country or geographic region recognize faculty members from another country or region who are qualified to teach at their institution. Visiting scholars, joint appointments at multiple HEIs, and even study abroad ventures are all examples of faculty mobility.

Another cross-cutting theme is the hypersensitivity over university rankings at national, regional, and international levels. The ranking trend is often touted as a marketing strategy by university administrators and advertising campaigns. Billboards, websites, and online television ads often promote university and program rankings to advertise reputation status and attract the top students. The reality is that the methodologies established by many ranking organizations and systems are unique and often cater to subjective criteria such as reputation, number of significant achievements (e.g., Nobel Prize Laureates), publications in leading journals, and amount of research funding.

The three most notable international rankings of world-class universities are the Shanghai Jiao Tong University's Academic Ranking of World Universities, London *Times Higher Education* World University Rankings, and Quacquarelli Symonds World University Rankings. Many countries also have national or regional ranking systems, such as those produced on an annual basis by *U.S. News and World Report* in the United States and the Leiden Ranking for top European universities.

Quality higher education is not always aligned with higher education ranking systems. In large higher education systems like those in Canada, China, Germany, India, and the United States, the difference between the training received by students at a program in the top 20-ranked schools or programs is often minimal. But the prestige factor is an important one that often resonates within job interviews and recruiting circles.

There is no question that brand-name recognition from prominent HEIs is a key factor when graduates are seeking employment. This is especially the case within one to five years of graduation, but much less so afterward. While brand-name recognition continues to help those who graduate from world-class universities, there is generally a much heavier weight given to actual job performance, experience, and skills set postgraduation.

In theory, the move to a predominantly knowledge-based economy often favors countries with well-developed higher education systems such as Germany, Taiwan, and the United States. Each of these countries possesses large numbers of degree- and certificate-granting community colleges, vocational colleges, and universities. But the reality is that many jobs are becoming more and more competitive.

This is another competition theme and trend—graduates are expected to have a higher education level for most entry-level positions today than what was required in past generations. Fueling this raising of the bar is the growing perception of many employers that higher education graduates are severely unprepared or at best underprepared for what lies ahead for them in employment circles. While it was once an advantage for applicants to hold a bachelor's degree, master's degrees are now increasingly the standard entrance-level requirement in many fields and areas of employment.

The rise in minimum degree standards is an employment trend now commonplace in such countries as Japan, Korea, and Taiwan. The most competitive undergraduate degree programs are in education in these three East Asian countries. Graduating from a top-ranked or highly regarded university helps recent graduates obtain first-year teaching assignments in government schools, but often these limited positions are now being offered to those with master's degrees.

Decreasing enrollment trends among primary and secondary students only exacerbate the need to obtain a graduate degree prior to securing sustainable employment as a teacher in these countries. A similar trend exists in larger countries throughout the world. However, graduates can generally find employment in these larger countries with minimal degree and certification requirements if they are willing to take a position in rural or economically disadvantaged locations in the respective countries.

In emerging economy contexts, there is a tremendous need to strengthen postsecondary school infrastructure. This continues to be a priority in most BRICS countries and elsewhere (Ferreira 2013; Kariwo, Gounko, and Nungu 2014). Global trends indicate an increase in overall education enrollments and attainment of students at all levels, from preschool to obtaining a higher education degree. This surge in demand for higher levels of education emphasizes the need for all countries to recognize the important role higher education can and will play in developing economies and building local human capital and capacity.

While the brain drain exodus of top talent is not new to many countries, there are some ways that concerted efforts can help alleviate and in some cases reverse the trend. It begins with creating sustainable jobs. There also needs to be a concerted effort by all levels of government to help recruit and retain the top talent in order to avoid the global pulling forces that ultimately lead to brain drain in virtually every field. Economic incentives and job security are important deciding factors for recent higher education graduates who studied abroad when they consider whether to return to their home country for employment.

Certain fields are more competitive than others, and there is a shortage of workers in various areas of specialization that require hiring expatriates to help fill the vacant positions. Despite the growing competition for many job areas, there remain shortages in others. For instance, in much of Western Europe, Japan, Korea, Taiwan, and the United States, there is a current and projected shortage of workers throughout the health care industry.

Meanwhile, concerns have emerged in leading economy countries like the United States as to whether their educational systems are capable of yielding the quantity and quality of highly skilled labor needed to compete in a global economy. The improved output of highly skilled workers in other emerging economies provides a challenge to more traditional global leaders like the United States and much of Europe.

Economic growth in countries like Brazil, China, Japan, Korea, Taiwan, and Vietnam was initially driven by labor-intensive low-wage unsophisticated manufacturing but has transitioned to more sophisticated production of lower labor-content goods requiring more inventive, highly skilled, and lower labor content fabrication. This transition in the workforce highlights the shifts that have and continue to take place in postsecondary training settings globally. HEIs that refuse to change with the industry shifts and current and future needs will find it increasingly difficult to compete with other HEIs that adapt.

CONCLUDING OBSERVATIONS

Competition highlights some of the weaknesses and skills gaps of higher education globally as well. Among the most prominent questions that all stakeholders deal with to one degree or another is an obsession with output measures, such as graduation rates and test scores. There is often inadequate attention to inputs and structural reforms requisite to yielding desired outcomes in higher education and an overemphasis on outputs and test scores.

Does passing a test equate to being able to perform well in real-life scenarios? Can higher education theoretical training transition into practice? In many higher education disciplines, industry-standard tests differ from one global region to another, thus highlighting limitations on mobility as well as applicability.

Whether it is in accounting, business finance, education teaching certification, medical doctor credentials, or engineering certifications, standards differ from country to country. Being able to overcome these skills gaps and industry-standards differences is an essential curricular ingredient that should constitute the higher education training of all current and future graduates. Only through a more globalized curriculum can these skills gaps be bridged and overcome.

NOTES

1. Brazil, Russia, India, China, and South Africa constitute the five BRICS countries. Higher education has exploded in most of these countries in recent years. The two largest higher education systems are in China and India, and both countries are struggling to deal with inevitable growth issues such as quality, governance, equity, and access.

2. There are multiple names that exist for what we term "industry advisory councils" (IACs), including industry advisory committees, industry advisory boards, curriculum review committees, private-public industry advisory councils to name a few.

IACs include any organized council, committee, or board that includes representation from industry as well as faculty members and/or leaders of higher education. This may include private and/or public industry members on the council.

3. Examples of successful IACs include the Public Relations Institute of Australia (PRIA), the Ontario Brain Institute, and Iowa State University's Industrial Engineering IAC. Since the 1980s, PRIA and its National Education Committee have played an important advisory and accrediting role in shaping public relations curricula within Australian higher education since the 1980s (Fitch 2014). The Ontario Brain Institute established a network of advisory committees, including a Science Advisory Committee, Industry Advisory Committee, Patient Advisory Committee, Evaluation Advisory Committee, and International Advisory Committee to help with such areas as evaluation and informatics and to ensure OBI meets international standards of excellence (Stuss 2014). In order to best prepare students for work in the field, Iowa State University established an IAC for its Industrial Engineering Program. This IAC includes key stakeholders at all levels, including "professional societies and other relevant organizations such as the Institute of Industrial Engineers (IIE) and ABET" (Min, Jackman, and Gemmill 2013).

4. Online courses, degrees, and institutions have their place in higher education, but there are also many shortcomings with online-only offerings. Some of these shortcomings can be overcome if carefully managed and adhered to through appropriate support staff, adequately trained and prepared instructors, and an ability to meet the various needs of students from many diverse points of view. Some of the most challenging issues that online-only higher education offerings include understanding how to best meet the needs of learners with different learning styles, from different geographic locations, and with differing technology capacities. Some online-only students will have optimal access to their online coursework with high-speed Internet connections on a regular basis and from their residences. Others will not have such access and opportunity. Drop-out rates are generally higher in online-only degree programs. Student dissatisfaction is often higher in online-only formats compared to having more direct contact with instructors. There also continues to be a negative stigma associated with degrees earned from online-only institutions compared with those from higher education institutions that incorporate more traditional mediums of curriculum delivery (see, for instance, Power and Morven-Gould 2011, Wright 2014).

5. Rising tuition costs in Indonesia created a strong resistance from both the general public and afterward the Supreme Court that declared charging tuition unconstitutional (Jacob et al. 2012). In the post-2007 global financial crisis era, many state-level governments slashed funding for higher education. Without significant policy change, it is highly unlikely that this funding will return to its pre-2007 levels. This financial constraint on higher education led many policy makers and media outlets to target some traditional areas of higher education such as the tenure system and rising tuition costs that too often outpace annual cost of living and inflation rates. Most US states are requiring greater accountability from higher education leaders, including an increased demand for performance-based funding rather than unlimited and unchecked state appropriations (Geiger 2010; Dougherty and Reddy 2013; Miao 2012).

6. In the United States, six accrediting organizations are recognized by the Council for Higher Education Accreditation (2015): Middle States Commission on Higher Education; New England Association of Schools and Colleges–Commission on Institutions of Higher Education (NEASC–CIHE); North Central Association of Colleges and Schools–The Higher Learning Commission (NCA–HLC); Southern Association of Colleges and Schools (SACS) and Commission on Colleges; Western Association of Schools and Colleges–Accrediting Commission for Community and Junior Colleges (WASC–ACCJC); and Western Association of Schools and Colleges–Accrediting Commission for Senior Colleges and Universities (WASC–ACSCU).

REFERENCES

ACT. 2013. *The Reality of College Readiness 2013*. Iowa City, IA: ACT.

Allen, I. Elaine, and Jeff Seaman. 2013. *Changing Course: Ten Years of Tracking Online Education in the United States*. Babson Park, MA: Babson Survey Research Group, Pearson, and Sloan Consortium.

Altbach, Philip G. 2012. "The Prospects for the BRICs: The New Academic Superpowers?" *Economic & Political Weekly* 47 (43).

Altbach, Philip G., Gregory Androushchak, Yaroslav Kuzminov, Maria Yudkevich, and Liz Reisberg. 2013. *The Global Future of Higher Education and the Academic Profession: The BRICs and the United States*. New York: Palgrave Macmillan.

Altbach, Philip G., Patricia J. Gumport, and Robert O. Berdahl. 2011. *American Higher Education in the Twenty-First Century: Social, Political, and Economic Challenges*. Baltimore: Johns Hopkins University Press.

Brown, Roger, and Helen Carasso. 2013. *Everything for Sale?: The Marketisation of UK Higher Education*. Milton Park, UK; New York: Routledge.

Carnevale, Anthony P., and Nicole Smith. 2014. *Workplace Basics: The Skills Employees Need and Employers Want*. Washington, DC: Center on Education and the Workforce, Georgetown University.

Carnoy, Martin, Isak Froumin, Prashant K Loyalka, and Jandhyala B. G. Tilak. 2014. "The Concept of Public Goods, the State, and Higher Education Finance: A View from the BRICs." *Higher Education* 68 (3): 359–378. doi: 10.1007/s10734-014-9717-1.

Chao, Roger Y. 2011. "Reflections on the Bologna Process: The Making of an Asia Pacific Higher Education Area." *European Journal of Higher Education* 1 (2–3): 102–118. doi: 10.1080/21568235.2011.629040.

Chia, Siow Yue. 2012. "Changing Global and Regional Economic Environment and Challenges Facing East Asia." In *Moving Toward a New Development Model for East Asia: The Role of Domestic Policy and Regional Cooperation*, edited by Y. Zhang, F. Kimura and S. Oum, 1–26. Jakarta: Economic Research Institute for ASEAN and East Asia (ERIA).

Dougherty, Kevin J., and Vikash Reddy. 2013. Performance Funding for Higher Education: What are the Mechanisms? What are the Impacts? *ASHE Higher Education Report: Volume 39*, No. 2.

Ferreira, Elisa Helena Xiol Y. 2013. "Improving Public Secondary Education in Brazil: Opening Doors and Breaking the Cycle." MA, Political Science, Simon Fraser University.

Fischer, Karin. 2014. The Employment Mismatch: A College Degree Sorts Job Applicants, but Employers Wish it Meant More. *The Chronicle of Higher Education*.

Fitch, Kate. 2014. "Professionalisation and public relations education: Industry accreditation of Australian university courses in the early 1990s." *Public Relations Review* 40 (4): 623–631. doi: http://dx.doi.org/10.1016/j.pubrev.2014.02.015

Flexner, Abraham. 1916. *A Modern School*. New York: General Education Board.

Geiger, Roger L. 2010. "Impact of the Financial Crisis on Higher Education in the United States." *International Higher Education* 59: 9–11.

González, Cristina, Yamin Liu, and Xiaoling Shu. 2012. The Faculty Promotion and Merit System in China and the United States: The Cases of Wuhan University and the University of California, Davis. In *Research & Occasional Paper Series*. Berkeley, CA: Center for Studies in Higher Education, University of California, Berkeley.

Guri-Rosenblit, Sarah. 2012. Opening Up Access to Higher Education: Implications and Challenges. In *Freedom, Equity, University*. Raanana, Israel: Research Institute for Policy, Political Economy and Society, Open University of Israel.

Higo, Masa, and Hafiz T. A. Khan. 2014. "Global Population Aging: Unequal Distribution of Risks in Later Life Between Developed and Developing Countries." *Global Social Policy*: 1–21. doi: 10.1177/1468018114543157.

Jacob, W. James, and Val D. Rust. 2010. "Principles of Good Governance: A Review of Key Themes Identified at the 7th International Workshop on Higher Education Reforms." *Comparative and International Higher Education* 2 (2): 31–32.

Jacob, W. James, Stewart E. Sutin, John C. Weidman, and John L. Yeager. 2015. "Community Engagement in Higher Education: International and Local Perspectives." In *Community Engagement in Higher Education*, edited by W. James Jacob, Stewart E. Sutin, John C. Weidman and John L. Yeager, 1–29. New York: Sense Publishers.

Jacob, W. James, Yuanyuan Wang, Tracy Lynn Pelkowski, Ravik Karsidi, and Agus D. Priyanto. 2012. "Higher Education in Indonesia: A Trends Analysis of Current Challenges and Opportunities." In *Reform of University Governance: Policy, Fads, and Experience in International Perspective* edited by William Bruneau and Hans G. Schuetze, 225–240. New York: Palgrave Macmillan.

Johnstone, D. Bruce. 2014. "Tuition Fees, Student Loans, and Other Manifestations of Cost Sharing: Variations and Misconceptions." In *The Forefront of International Higher Education*, edited by Alma Maldonado-Maldonado and Roberta Malee Bassett, 235–244. Dordrecht, Netherlands: Springer.

Kariwo, Michael, Tatiana Gounko, and Musembi Nungu, Eds. 2014. *A Comparative Analysis of Higher Education Systems*: Sense Publishers.

Lee, Jack T. 2014. "Education Hubs and Talent Development: Policymaking and Implementation Challenges." *Higher Education* 68 (6): 807–823.

Leydesdorff, Loet. 2013. "Triple Helix of University-Industry-Government Relations." In *Encyclopedia of Creativity, Invention, Innovation and Entrepreneurship*, edited by Elias G. Carayannis, 1844–1851. Springer New York.

Li, Mei, and Rui Yang. 2013. "Interrogating Institutionalized Establishments: Urban–Rural Inequalities in China's Higher Education." *Asia Pacific Education Review* 14 (3): 315–323. doi: 10.1007/s12564-013-9262-0.

Miao, Kysie. 2012. Performance-Based Funding of Higher Education: A Detailed Look at Best Practices in 6 States. Washington, DC: Center for American Progress.

Min, K. Jo, John Jackman, and Doug Gemmill. 2013. "Assessment and Evaluation of Objectives and Outcomes for Continuous Improvement of an Industrial Engineering Program." *International Journal of Engineering Education* 29 (2): 520–532.

Mok, Ka Ho. 2012. "Bringing the State Back In: Restoring the Role of the State in Chinese Higher Education." *European Journal of Education* 47 (2): 228–241. doi: 10.1111/j.1465-3435.2012.01520.x.

Moore, Joi L., Camille Dickson-Deane, and Krista Galyen. 2011. "e-Learning, Online Learning, and Distance Learning Environments: Are They the Same?" *The Internet and Higher Education* 14 (2): 129–135. doi: http://dx.doi.org/10.1016/j.iheduc.2010.10.001

National Center on Education and the Economy (NCEE). 2007. *Tough Choices or Tough Times*. The Report of the New Commission on the Skills of the American Workforce. San Francisco, CA: John Wiley & Sons, Inc.

Porter, Michael E. 1990. *The Competitive Advantage of Nations.* New York: Free Press.

Power, Thomas Michael, and Anthony Morven-Gould. 2011. "Head of Gold, Feet of Clay: The Online Learning Paradox." *The International Review of Research in Open and Distributed Learning* 12 (2).

Sanyal, Bikas C., and D. Bruce Johnstone. 2011. "International Trends in the Public and Private Financing of Higher Education." *PROSPECTS* 41 (1): 157–175. doi: 10.1007/s11125-011-9180-z.

Shanghai Jiao Tong University. 2015. Academic Ranking of World Universities, 2015. Shanghai: Center for World-Class Universities, Shanghai Jiao Tong University.

Slywotzsky, Adrian J. 1996. *Value Migration: How to Think Several Moves Ahead of the Competition.* Boston, MA: Harvard Business School Press.

Stuss, Donald T. 2014. "The Ontario Brain Institute: Completing the Circle." *Canadian Journal of Neurological Sciences / Journal Canadien des Sciences Neurologiques* 41 (6): 683–693. doi: doi:10.1017/cjn.2014.36.

Thurow, Lester. 1992. *Head to Head: The Coming Economic Battle Among Japan, Europe, and America.* New York: William Morrow & Co.

Tilak, Jandhyala B. G. 2013. "Higher Education in the BRIC Member-Countries: Comparative Patterns and Policies." *Economic and Political Weekly* 48 (14): 41–47.

Times Higher Education. 2015. "World University Rankings, 2015–2016." Accessed 29 January 2015. http://www.timeshigereducation.co.uk

Udjo, Eric O., and Barney Erasmus. 2014. "Impact of Retirement Age Policy on the Workforce of a Higher Education Institution in South Africa." *Politics & Policy* 42 (5): 744–768. doi: 10.1111/polp.12092.

U.S. Census Bureau. 2011. *Statistical Abstract of the United States: 2011.* Washington, DC: U.S. Census Bureau.

U.S. Census Bureau. 2012. *Statistical Abstract of the United States: 2012.* Washington, DC: U.S. Census Bureau.

Wagner, Tony. 2015. *Tony Wagner's Seven Survival Skills*. Cambridge, MA: Innovation Lab, Harvard University. Available online at: http://www.tonywagner.com/7-survival; accessed on 11 November 2015.

Wright, M. Keith. 2014. "The Trouble With Online Undergraduate Business Degrees In Traditional Regional Universities." *Journal of College Teaching & Learning* 11 (1): 13–24.

Chapter 3

The Case for Changing the Business Model of Higher Education

Let's begin with two illustrative fictitious stories to sharpen our senses. In the first instance, high school student, Alf Hendricks, considers college alternatives. Alf's father, Harry Hendricks, is a financial planner and his mother, Jane Hendricks, is a registered nurse. Harry and Jane saved money to help finance the college education of their three children, contributing US$10,000 for each year of undergraduate education of each child.

Alf wants to be a teacher, and is impressed by the walking tour at a small regional liberal arts college that offers a major in his field. The net price of tuition, fees, room and board is US$28,000 in the first year. Alf calculates that other expenses will total US$3,000 annually. But he did not anticipate annual increases in tuition pricing and fees, nor did he consider that starting pay for teachers with a bachelor's degree averaged US$32,000 in his hometown. He did, however, work part-time during the summer to help defray some costs.

The bottom line is that Alf graduated in four years with aggregate student debt of US$50,000, and his monthly take-home pay after tax and other deductions was US$2,000. He struggles now to make monthly payments on his student loans and still have enough money to cover apartment rent, transportation, and other expenses. Alf reflects upon the choices he made and wonders what he might have done differently.

Our second example offers an institutional perspective. Valley Institute of Technology (VIT) is devoted to higher education and is located in a Midwestern state. Originally founded as a public "normal" or teacher's college, VIT eventually broadened its curriculum and added professional graduate schools. Thirty years ago, VIT faculty and administration elected to seek university status, added a research agenda to the institutional mission, offered a PhD in select fields, and eventually grew to 18,000 full-time students.

Times were good. New buildings were built, financed partially by long-term loans. Enrollment growth was robust. State subsidies increased and totaled 70 percent of the annual operating budget. VIT assumed more debt to fund new construction. No contingency plans were made for rainy days. The 2008–2009 economic crisis abruptly changed VIT's financial world. State funding for VIT dropped 30 percent from 2007 to 2014. Tuition increased by 26 percent over the same years.

Many potential students found tuition unaffordable, were less willing to assume debt to finance a college education, and enrolled in community colleges for the first two years of undergraduate education. Enrollment declined at VIT by 7 percent in 2014 from its peak levels in 2006. VIT's annual financial statements for the school year 2013–2014 reflect operating losses. VIT's president and board of trustees worry about the institution's financial outlook.

When viewed through the lens of Alf Hendricks or VIT's leadership, the prevailing business model of higher education no longer works. The legacy model is revenue-dependent, and sustained by enrollment growth, tuition increases, state and local subsidies for public higher education, and access to endowment monies to cover operating expenses. This formula is unsustainable when enrollment declines, fewer students are willing to finance their education through debt-based financial aid, public funding declines, and tuition increases in excess of inflation price lead students to make other educational choices.

This is the new harsh reality of higher education. Nonelite, high-cost private and public colleges are most at risk. Community colleges and public four-year universities suffer when state and local government subsidies decline. Many for-profit organizations are struggling amid media reports of high cost, student drop-out rates, questionable employment results for graduates, and increasing pressure from the federal government. High-cost operating environments render higher education financially more vulnerable. Institutional financial sustainability is no longer assured. This is the new normal.[1]

Except for well-endowed world-class institutions, which largely serve the offspring of affluent families, the rest of higher education is scrambling for solutions. This trend is largely exacerbated in developing country contexts. Examining shards from this broken model causes uneasiness. There are consequences for institutions that fail to adapt to a paradigm change. Fragile institutions will not survive financially unless thoughtful strategic and comprehensive solutions emerge.

Similarly, dire consequences await national economies and employers whose workers lack skills required to compete. Developed economies rely upon value-added products and services, which becomes problematic when higher education becomes less accessible and affordable. Emerging economies rely upon higher education to support a migration of product output from low-cost high-labor content to more sophisticated and better-compensated jobs. Although a quality education remains among the top priorities of expanding higher education systems worldwide (Teichler 2014), an effective business model is now a matter of both institutional survival and national competitiveness. In short, the issues are intertwined between a viable and affordable higher education business model, the skills gap, and sustainable economic growth.

FOLLOW THE MONEY: AN OVERVIEW OF HIGHER EDUCATION FINANCING IN THE UNITED STATES

To better understand why the business model ~~of many~~ *College ready*
let's examine our environment after the glob~~al financial crisis~~
In the United States, most states reduced fu~~nding~~ *Government funding*
tion. Enrollment at many of the less compet~~itive colleges began to decline~~
Student concerns mounted about financing ~~college education through debt~~
amid uncertain postgraduation employment prospects. Total outstanding student debt neared US$1.2 trillion by school year 2013 (Consumer Finance Protection Bureau 2013). A closer examination of data allows us to better understand the vulnerability of a tuition- and public subsidy–dependant business model.

Government Funding of Higher Education

The legal basis for public education is found in Article 10 of the Constitution of the United States, which cedes authority to the states except for those specifically reserved for the federal government. Education was not among the functions assigned to the federal government. Accordingly, education oversight and funding was largely left to the purview of state and local government. Notwithstanding grants to encourage certain forms of research and certain other behaviors, and federal government financial aid to college students, state and local governments subsidize operating and capital budgets in public education. A closer examination of funding trends and the outlook for the future informs our analysis.

Public subsidies to higher education reveal a lack of predictability and a trend toward generally lower budget allocations to higher education during recent decades. Local and state government funding per full-time equivalent (FTE) student declined in 2012 to its lowest level in 25 years from an average of US$8,497 per student in 1987 to US$5,188 in 2012 in inflation-adjusted dollars (SHEEO 2013). Student enrollment during the academic year

2013–2014 was up 13 percent over 2007 numbers, which further exacerbated the trend toward gradual defunding of public higher education on a per student basis (SHEEO 2013).

In 1988, state and local funding of public higher education exceeded tuition dollars per student by 3.2 times. By 2013–2014, that ratio had fallen to 1.1 times, and state funding of higher education declined by an average 23 percent relative to pre-2008 recession levels (Mitchell, Palacios and Leachman 2014). In other words, the combination of annual tuition and room and board in public higher education in 22 states had reached one-third of median household income by 2013 (Hiltonsmith and Draut 2014).

Generalizations about public funding for higher education can be misleading. Public education in some states fares better than others. Among the hardest hit between 2008 and 2013 were Arizona (down 50 percent), New Hampshire (down 49.9 percent), Oregon (down 44 percent), Louisiana (down 42 percent), and Florida (down 40 percent). On the other hand, North Carolina and New York, each down by an estimated 15 percent, fared better over the same time frame (Oliff et al. 2014).

More recently, the governors of Indiana, New Hampshire, and Florida proposed budget increases for public higher education (Schatz 2013). In fiscal year (FY) 2012, aggregate state government funding for public higher education operating and capital budgets was US$81.3 billion, while net tuition revenues totaled US$61.8 billion (SHEEO 2013). Since most state appropriations fund general operating budgets, the relationship between public subsidies and tuition pricing has been apparent. State-by-state and institution-by-institution analysis is required to identify how this translates into affordable tuition in public higher education.

Outlook for Public Funding of Higher Education

Many years ago, the first author instructed a course in the MBA program of the Katz Graduate School of Business at the University of Pittsburgh titled "Managing Risk for a Global Enterprise." This course was largely based upon professional experiences in the banking industry that included responsibilities for underwriting risk in foreign countries. We understood the importance of examining lead indicators and evaluated risks associated with country politics, economics, fiscal and monetary practices, industry and operating risks, law and the judiciary system, and industry and financial institution management capacity and infrastructure.

Analytics included assessments of prevailing and projected risks. Application of comprehensive risk analysis methodology enables one to appreciate the caution adopted by credit rating agencies toward higher education and their increasingly pessimistic mood. The prevailing highly partisan atmosphere and incapacity to constrain governmental expenditures renders many state and local governments unable to discharge basic fiduciary responsibilities. Our collective fiscal house is a mess, reflecting high dependency on debt to finance budget deficits and unaffordable spending practices. The trend imperils the outlook for improved funding of public higher education.

RETIREMENT BENEFITS OF STATE EMPLOYEES: MORE STATE FUNDING PROBLEMS AHEAD

Many states have limited financial capacity to fund benefit promises made to retiring workers. The Pew Center on the States tracks the gap between state retirement plan financial obligations, and monies set aside to fund those commitments. According to their analysis of 2010 data, only 11 states had funded 90 percent or more of future pension obligations, and retiree health care benefits were funded at a far lower level (The Pew Charitable Trusts 2012).

Eleven states had funded 65 percent or less of their pension obligations. *The Economist* reported in 2010 that as many as 16 states may have fully defunded pension plans between 2019 and 2039, citing a study by professors Joshua Raub (Northwestern University) and Robert Novy Marx (University of Rochester), who estimated state underfunding of pension obligations at US\$3.4 trillion and a negative gap at the municipal level totaling US\$574 billion ("American states' pension funds: A gold-plated burden" 2010).

Estimating funding gaps for future retirees is complicated. A lot depends on future return on assets (ROA) of current pension fund reserves, future corporate and individual state tax revenues collected, and the states' ability to curb spending. What we do know is worrisome. Most states assume ROA's of between 7.8 and 8 percent (Reilly 2010) on the funds already set aside for pensions, while most corporate pension plans assume a far more conservative 5 percent ROA (Corkery and Rapoport 2012). Stock market performance is unpredictable and historically volatile. Current yields on investment grade government and corporate bonds are well below 7 to 8 percent.

To further complicate matters, many pension plans are defined benefit rather than defined contributions, meaning that states are obliged to "top off" financial shortfalls that accrue from reserve retirement assets that fail to perform at the assumed benchmarks. The situation is far worse in some states than others. For example, as of 2012, adjusted net pension liabilities were 241 percent of state tax revenues in Illinois, 190 percent in Connecticut, and 137 percent in New Jersey, while Nebraska had the smallest gap at 7 percent ("Retirement benefits: Who pays the bill?" 2013).

The fiscal budgetary outlook in many states is worse yet when one considers additional, largely unaffordable promises to government employees.

Some states include cost-of-living increases and health, dental and vision plans, while allowing for early retirement and lump-sum payments of accrued and unused sick leave. On average, pre-funding of retiree health care benefits was a scary 3 percent (The Pew Charitable Trusts 2012). The *New York Times* excoriated the New York state legislature in these terms: "Ever eager to curry favor with powerful unions, [they] added sweeteners to pensions and allowed employees to stop making contributions [to their pension plans] after 10 years of service" ("State Workers and N.Y.'s Fiscal Crisis" 2011, p. 9L).

Pew estimated that underfunded pension liabilities had grown to US$915 billion by 2012, with another US$577 billion in underfunded health and other retirement benefits. When added to aggregate outstanding state debt of US$757 billion, total outstanding financial obligations exceeded US$2.2 trillion (The Pew Charitable Trusts 2014). According to other studies, under-funded state pension obligations may be much higher.

Let's consider the financial implications of state retirement plan reliance upon an 8 percent per annum ROA on pension fund assets invested in equity and bond markets. Prudential allocation of pension fund assets calls for diver-sification between equities, bonds, and other asset classes. Average annual performance of the Standard & Poors 500, an index often cited as a gauge of stock market performance, was below 8 percent on the average from 1990 to 2012. S&P 500 returned a lofty yield of above 25 percent in 2013. But one year alone does not move the aggregate average ROA enough.

Meanwhile, average annual yield on the 10-year US Treasury Bonds between 2002 and 2012 was 5.31 percent. The current yield is under 3 percent. Investment grade corporate bonds offered a slightly higher yield, but nowhere near the 8 percent benchmark. The long-term economic outlook predicted by many economists, the US Federal Reserve Bank, and the Inter-national Monetary Fund project slow and steady growth within a historically low-inflation environment.

Asset managers are divided in their opinions as to the implications of this scenario for stock market and bond yields. Many believe that yield expecta-tions should be adjusted downward. In the past, some pension funds and university endowment funds allocated portions of their portfolios to higher-risk investments such as hedge funds and emerging market portfolios, many of which suffered substantial losses in the wake of the 2008–2009 economic shocks. To make matters worse, several hedge fund managers were crooks who had fabricated hedge fund performance numbers. In summation, it is questionable whether the 8 percent ROA per annum on pension assets already under management is realistic, and underfunding of retirement plans will remain a source of great concern in many states.

The fiscal hole created by underfunded state and local retirement benefits is a moving target, and varies from one state to another. Yet, the overall financial pressures on state governments to ante up financial resources to pay government pensioners in the future are not in doubt. The only questions relate to timing and the full impact on various state budgets from failing to act sooner and more responsibly. The implications for public higher education are clear. Many states will be hard pressed to fund higher education at even current levels once the full impact of underfunded retirement benefits requires year-to-year increases in annual state budgets. More fiscal troubles lie ahead.

Other State Budget Appropriations

Outlays for Medicaid constitute a growing component of state budgets. Medicaid provides critical health care coverage for a needy population. This commentary is not about what is moral, but about fiscal reality and the implications of Medicaid funding for public higher education. The cost of state and federal funding of Medicaid has grown significantly over the years. A recent report from the U.S. Department of Health and Human Services (USDHH) informs us that Medicaid appropriations averaged 0.5 percent of total federal and state spending in 1970 and increased by more than five times to 2.7 percent in FY 2014. Total state outlays for Medicaid are projected to grow from US$131 billion in 2010 to US$340 billion in 2020 (USDHH 2012).

Further, the National Association of State Budget Officers (NASBO) recently reported that Medicaid had become the largest line item of state budgets and had risen to an average of 24.4 percent (NASBO 2014). The estimated cost of Medicaid in California alone in 2013 was US$50.2 billion (Henry Kaiser Family Foundation 2013).

The competition for limited state financial resources will become keener between competing constituencies in the years ahead. The projected increase in state budget allocations to fund retirement benefits and Medicaid will have an inevitable impact upon appropriations to public higher education. Retirement benefits for state and local workers will consume an increasing share of annual budgets. Other calls for state funding include subsidies for primary and secondary school education, the cost of funding state correction facilities, and monies needed for infrastructure.

This situation is compounded by existing budget deficits and the high debt levels of many state governments. Some states are better positioned financially than others. Some governmental leaders may look more favorably upon higher education as an essential component of economic growth and may find ways to sustain subsidies. Others may continue down the path of defunding public higher education as pressures to allocate monies for growth of other purposes. On the whole, we are pessimistic about the outlook for future funding of public higher education in many states.

IS HIGHER EDUCATION AFFORDABLE?

A good starting point for our discussion begins with considering all out-of-pocket expenses incurred by students. Many colleges and universities charge a wide range of service fees. Some are mandated. Others are discretionary. Some fees, such as those applied to technology, cover expenses to support ongoing institutional investments in hardware, bandwidth, and software. Student health insurance fees help defray high-cost medical expenses. Student activity fees cover attendance at athletic events, use of student center facilities, and similar activities. Other direct costs include book acquisition or rental, computers, stationery supplies, room and board, and transportation.

Working adults think about lost wages while they attend college. International students often reflect on the high costs of covering tuition and living expenses and if and how their parents may be able to help cover this large investment. Those with young children consider costs for childcare. In short, when seen through the lens of the student, the all-in cost of a higher education degree substantially exceeds the cost of tuition.

Measures of affordability must consider the comprehensive costs of attending college with consumer purchasing power, their discretionary income and their confidence in the nation's economic outlook. Lower-, middle-, and upper-middle-income families are increasingly worried about affordability, even more so in the aftermath of the 2008–2009 economic recession. Stubbornly high rates of unemployment and underemployment persist and are currently a bit under 6 percent in the United States.

To make matters worse, the median household income (MHI) reached a high of US$56,987 per annum in 1999 and has since declined to US$51,017 in inflation-adjusted dollars in 2012 (U.S. Census Bureau, 2014). Worse yet, the College Board (2013) reports that real family income in the bottom quintile declined by 13 percent from 2002 to 2012. This is reflected in a 28 percent decline from 2002–2003 to 2011–2012 in family funding of students attending public two-year colleges, most of which are community colleges that largely serve students from lower-income families (Payea et al. 2013).

Millions of people worldwide read about higher education graduates weighed down by tuition-related debt service obligations, a situation more grave for those with debt who did not graduate. Disturbing rates of home foreclosures in the United States and news about higher education graduates unable to find jobs commensurate with their degrees and instill trauma-induced financial awareness less evident in the past. Inability to pay, compounded by an increasing reluctance to borrow, renders much of higher education vulnerable to enrollment declines and commensurate loss of revenues.

Higher Education Tuition Trends

Concerns about affordable postsecondary school education have been around for years. In the United States, the presidential commission on higher education, or the Truman Commission Report of 1947, called for free education through the first two years of college. The commission, chaired by George F. Zook, then president of the American Council on Education (ACE), was uneasy with perceptible inequalities of opportunity and socioeconomic barriers to education and professional advancement (Zook et al. 1947).

The so-called Spellings Commission Report of 2006, named for then U.S. Secretary of Education Margaret Spellings, who convened this study, cited "the seemingly inexorable increase in college costs which have outpaced inflation for the past two decades" (U.S. Department of Education 2006). Frustrated by the inability of higher education to contain tuition pricing, President Barack Obama has proposed a plan that would seemingly condition access to federal aid to such metrics as cost of tuition, graduation rates, and potential earning of graduates ("Reining in college tuition" 2012). As of this writing, final details remain a work in progress.

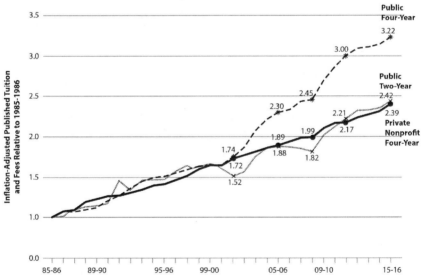

Figure 3.1 Inflation-Adjusted Published Tuition and Fees Relative to 1985–1986, 1985–1986 to 2015–2016 (1985–1986 = 1.0). *Notes:* Figure 3.1 shows published tuition and fees by sector, adjusted for inflation, relative to 1985–1986 published prices. For example, a value of 3.22 indicates that the tuition and fee price in the public four-year sector in 2015–2016 is 3.22 times as high as it was in 1985–1986, after adjusting for increases in the Consumer Price Index. Average tuition and fee prices reflect in-district charges for public two-year institutions and in-state charges for public four-year institutions. *Source:* Adapted by the authors from the College Board (2015, p. 16).

Directional signals from the federal government and many state govern-ments inform us that public funding and access to financial aid may be increasingly used as leverage to change certain behaviors of higher education. Federal assistance to higher education totaled an estimated US$155 billion in 2011, of which an estimated US$116 billion came in the form of federal direct student loans (U.S. Census 2012). Pell Grants awarded to low-income students totaled US$35 billion. The U.S. Department of Education sustains a website that ranks all sectors of education from highest to lowest tuition cost.

Several states have moved toward performance-based funding by which similar indicators would be used to add or reduce state subsidies to public community colleges and universities. Gone are the days when tuition price increases attracted little attention beyond the students and families who paid the bills. The federal and many state governments are defining the rules of engagement governing appropriations. Using College Board data, Table 3.1 offers insight into the public sector case for financial reforms regarding tuition and fees from 1975–1976 to 2015–2016.

Adding room and board fees to the mix over the same time frame raises still more concerns about an affordable college education. Data for private four-year nonprofits reflects a jump from an average all-in price of US$16,979 in 1973–1974 relative to US$40,917 in 2013–1914. Public four-year colleges rose from US$8,416 to US$18,391. Two-year public colleges are not included in this category since most community colleges are largely populated by com-muter students and do not offer dormitory facilities.

Here too, price averages are subject to wide variances from state to state and college to college. Some institutions apply tuition discounts by only charging full price to some students, and reallocate that money to lure others by offering merit or needs-based grants. Bluntly speaking, discounting may

Table 3.1   Increases of Annual Tuition and Fees in 2015 US Dollars: 1975–1976 to 2015–2016

	Private Nonprofit Four-Year	Dollar Variance	% Variance	Public Four-Year	Dollar Variance	% Variance	Public Two-Year	Dollar Variance	% Variance
1975–1976	$10,088			$2,387			$1,079		
1985–1986	$13,551	$3,463	34.3	$2,918	$531	22.2	$1,419	$340	31.5
1995–1996	$19,117	$9,029	89.5	$4,399	$2,012	84.3	$2,081	$1,002	92.9
2005–2006	$25,624	$15,536	154.0	$6,708	$4,321	181.0	$2,665	$1,586	147.0
2015–2016	$32,405	$22,317	221.2	$9,410	$7,023	294.2	$3,435	$2,356	218.4

Source: Calculations by the authors with data from the College Board (2015, p. 17).

be thought of as a form of income redistribution in which more affluent families pay full sticker price of tuition and subsidize others.

What Causes Higher Education Expenses to Rise?

An unsympathetic view holds that higher education pricing trends during the past half century are indicative of a culture of indifference, operational inefficiency, a lack of clarity of institutional mission and purposes, and incapacity to change. While these behaviors may be present to varying degrees on certain campuses, the facts reveal a more balanced picture. Reduced government subsidies for public higher education have caused institutions to seek revenues from other sources, often taking the form of rising tuition and fees.

In addition, certain drivers of increased expenses are not discretionary and represent the cost of doing business. Such expenses include campus security, technological infrastructure, compliance and reporting to governmental regulatory agencies, rising health care insurance premiums for full-time faculty and staff, repair and maintenance of aging physical facilities, services for students with disabilities, writing centers, and developmental education for students who enroll in but are not prepared for postsecondary-level work in math, writing, and/or reading.

The institutional mission may also cause expenses to increase. Research 1 universities, whose missions are wedded to knowledge creation, normally allow reduced instructional loads so that faculty can pursue research and publish studies in their respective fields. Community colleges and many four-year public colleges bear the additional costs to support remedial education for those who enroll but are not college ready in math, reading, and/or writing. While the lead author was serving as president of the Community College of Allegheny County, an estimated US$10 million, or about 10 percent of our annual operating budget, supported developmental education initiatives. Public higher education inherits problems not of their own creation and actively strives to help at-risk students overcome behavioral and learning gaps. From a financial standpoint, remedial or so-called developmental education is a cost of doing business borne by all students and public subsidies.

A closer inspection of higher education spending offers insights that inform our discussion. Studies by Delta Cost Project, funded by Lumina Foundation, provide important data about the changing composition of spending patterns in higher education. Expense outlays between 1999 and 2009 reveal that overall spending on instruction per FTE student reached a high point of 63.2 percent as a percent of total spending in 2004 and had declined to 49.9 percent by 2009.

This dramatic swing reflects larger class sections, a pronounced shift to less expensive adjunct faculty, and the growth of higher enrollment online courses. Student services climbed from 8.3 percent in 1999 to a high of 12.2 percent of total operating budgets by 2009, and spending on academic and institutional support and operations and maintenance increased from a low of 27.9 percent in 2004 to a 38 percent high in 2008 (Delta Cost Project 2011). Telling observations were subsequently drawn by Rita Kirshstein and Jane Wellman (2013, p. 14), lead researchers and analysts for Delta (both now with the American Institutes for Research):

> Getting a better handle on college costs requires a new focus on institutional spending, buttressed by analytics that allow institutions to look at spending in relation to outcomes (not just inputs) and that permit them to benchmark costs by examining them over time and in comparison to peers. . . . The higher education "industry" has long overlooked the spending side of the college cost equation.

Examination of spending data from the Delta studies raises further questions. Can faculty productivity increase without impairing the quality of instruction? A related issue suggested by Kirschstein and Wellman concerns the relationships between spending and student learning outcomes. Instruction aside, other subsurface drivers of operating expenses merit attention. Society is largely unimpressed by higher education's ability to contain costs. A recent article in *The Economist* declared: "Higher education suffers from Baumol's disease—the tendency of costs to soar in labour-intensive sectors with stagnant productivity" ("Creative Destruction" 2014). We know a lot about metrics to evaluate instructor productivity. How can we gauge administrative and support staff productivity?

Revenue growth is aspirational, while we own our expenses. As such, we need to examine the cost base of higher education in ways that are increasingly sophisticated and to question current practices. Opportunities abound to reduce overhead if we know the right questions. Some hidden costs are not contained in line-item budgets. Poorly focused or unrealistically broad mission statements fail to offer an institutional context to govern budget decisions.

Many institutions still attempt to be all things to all people. Inability to define one's reason for being comes at a cost. An ill-defined curriculum, or the diffusion of courses over time to meet faculty interests more than student needs, bear upon tuition costs without necessarily adding value to their education. Derek Bok (2006, p. 2), former president of Harvard, commented upon the adverse educational consequences of a diffused educational model by noting that "without a compelling, unifying purpose, universities are charged with allowing their curricula to degenerate into a vast smorgasbord of elective courses."

Former president of Cornell, Frank H. T. Rhodes (2001, p. 14), noted, "The American university remains an organizational enigma, whose loosely coupled structure and collegiality . . . defy the canons of management." Legacy and unnecessarily complex organizational structures, inefficient labor-intensive processes, excess middle management, refusal to delegate authority to align with accountability, and a reticence to think and act outside of the box bear upon the cost of doing business. None of the variables commented on are found in line-item budgets. Yet, they cause tuition pricing to rise and constrain beneficial educational results for students. Bluntly stated, fixation upon short-term tactical remedies such as reducing certain line-item expenses without tackling underlying strategic lapses comes at the risk of leaving basic infirmities untouched.

VIEWS OF INFORMED OBSERVERS

An increasing body of college presidents, their chief business officers, educators, and educational associations worry about institutional financial sustainability, and the ability of higher education to meet the expectations and needs of their constituents. *The Iron Triangle*, a classic study of higher education based largely on interviews with college presidents observed that higher education is "in the crosshairs of competing social needs and economic realities" (Immerwahr, Johnson, and Gasparra 2008).

A more recent study of community colleges by the American Association of Community Colleges called for "a budget reengineering dream team to help colleges design programs in a much smarter way while working within the budgets they have" (AACC 2012, p. 4). A 2014 poll of chief business officers in higher education conducted by Gallup revealed that 60 percent of those surveyed neither agree nor strongly agree that their institutional financial model is sustainable over the next 10 years (Inside Higher Ed 2014).

A similar survey of college and university presidents in 2013 revealed that 60 percent of respondents believe that budget shortfalls are already a problem (Inside Higher Ed 2013). A more recent survey of college and university presidents conducted by Witt/Kieffer (Goldstein, Miller and Courson 2014, p. 2), an executive search firm specializing in higher education, indicates a shared opinion among many presidents that "whether from financial crisis, global competition or disruptive technologies, higher education is irrevocably changing . . . the basic business model is broken."

A failing business model is no surprise to many who know higher education. However, there is less consensus about a new and more vibrant business model. There is also considerable concern about a rating system for higher education outlined in August 2013 by President Obama and Secretary of Education Arne Duncan, which has since given way to a College Scorecard.

The scorecard is an online website supported by the U.S. Department of Education as an information source for aspiring college students. It offers comparable financial and other information intended to help college-bound students make informed decisions. Molly Corbett Broad, president of the ACE, and Peter McPherson, president of the Association of Public and Land-Grant Colleges (APLU), expressed their reservations in open letters to the Department of Education about distilling complex fields of data into a one-size-fits-all scorecard (ACE 2014; APLU 2014).

A steady progression of reports, books, and other commentaries underscore worries about the declining affordability of a college degree. The National Commission on the Cost of Higher Education, comprised largely of college leaders, faculty, and research fellows, was chartered by former president Bill Clinton, former vice president Senate Al Gore, and former speaker of the House Newt Gingrich to study college costs and prices. Their 1998 report sustained the belief that "higher education remains an extraordinary value," yet expressed the concern that "most academic institutions have permitted a veil of obscurity to settle over their financial operations, and many have yet to take seriously basic strategies for reducing their costs and prices" (National Commission on the Cost of Higher Education 1998, p. 4).

A 2006 study of higher education performance at the state level awarded a grade of "C" to only Utah and California on the metric of affordability. No "A" or "B" grades were given (National Center for Public Policy and Higher Education 2006). Jeff Selingo (2013), longtime reporter and editor for the *Chronicle of Higher Education*, summed up the worries held by many in this way: "Higher education is clinging to tradition. Too few students are going to college, not enough are graduating, and the whole thing costs too much" (p. xi).

CONCLUDING OBSERVATIONS

Complex problems such as a faltering revenue-dependent business model in higher education require comprehensive planning, leaders who make tough decisions, collaboration among internal and external stakeholders, and a disposition to tackle sacred cows with an understanding that revenue and expense challenges are apt to intensify. The outlook for increasing financial support for public higher education is less than promising.

A business model reliant upon government funding and increasing tuition pricing is, for the most part, unsustainable. More students and their families worry about incurring debt as a means of financing their postsecondary edu-cation. These trends are unlikely to abate in the foreseeable future and will cause senior administrators and their boards of trustees to undertake fundamental change of institutional business models from within.

It is uncertain whether higher education is prepared to reinvent itself by building upon what works, redesigning what does not, and going about its business in ways that improve upon the quality of education, while rendering tuition affordable. Success will be achieved when institutional financial sustainability and affordable tuition pricing align. The stakes for failure to succeed at systemic reform of the higher education business model are high in terms of socioeconomic dislocation for millions of middle- and working-class families and the adverse economic consequences of incapacity to close the skills both qualitatively and quantitatively. Subsequent sections of this book afford treatment to successes achieved to date and will explore a pathway to better times.

NOTE

1. The two examples we provide at the beginning of this and subsequent chapters are commonplace for what many students and parents of students face regarding the financing of higher education in the US context. We recognize, however, that due to the geographic size and diversity of the United States, circumstance differ depending on the location (there is often great variance in each state and in between states), and it will also differ depending if students are considered residents, nonresidents, or international students. We also note the challenges single-parent households face in helping to finance higher education for their children. The situation is also quite different in other countries. We delve into the international and global perspective in more detail in chapter 4. Countries like Brazil, China, India, and other emerging market contexts within the G20, tuition will be substantially less that the cost of financing higher education in Australia, Canada, the United Kingdom, and the United States. However, based on the purchasing power parity comparisons of citizens in these countries, the cost of living is generally much lower than most places within the European Union and US contexts.

REFERENCES

American Association of Community Colleges (AACC). 2012. *Final Report of the 21st-Century Initiative Listening Tour*. Washington, DC: AACC.

American Council on Education (ACE). 2014. Letter to Richard Reeves, U.S. Department of Education. January 31, 2014. Washington, DC: ACE.

Association of Public Land-Grant Universities (APLU). 2014. Letter to Secretary of Education, the Honorable Arne Duncan. January 22, 2014. Washington, DC: APLU.

"American states' pension funds: A gold-plated burden." 2010, October 16. *The Economist*, 397, p. 95. Available online at: http://www.economist.com/node/17248984; accessed on 30 June 2016.

Bok, Derek. 2006. *Our Underachieving Colleges*. 2006. Princeton, NJ: Princeton University Press.

Chopra, Rohit. 2013. *Student Debt Swells, Federal Loans Now Top a Trillion*. July 17, 2013. Washington, DC: Consumer Financial Protection Bureau. Available online at: http://www.consumerfinance.gov/newsroom/student-debt-swells-federal-loans-now-top-a-trillion/; accessed on 11 November 2014.

College Board. 2015. *Trends in College Pricing 2015*. New York: College Board.

Corkery, Michael, and Michael Rapoport. 2012, June 23. "States Face Pressure on Pension Shortfalls." *Wall Street Journal*, p. A1.

"Creative destruction; Higher education." 2014, June 28. *The Economist*, 411, p. 11.

Delta Cost Project. 2011. *Trends in College Spending 1999–2009*. Washington, DC: Delta Cost Project.

Goldstein, Karen, Alice Miller, and Jane Courson. 2014. *Reinventing Leadership in Higher Education: A Confidential Survey of College Presidents*. Stanwix, PA: Witt/ Kieffer.

Henry J. Kaiser Family Foundation, The. 2013. *The Facts on Medicaid Spending: State Budget Shortfalls SFY 2013*. Menlo Park, CA: The Henry J. Kaiser Family Foundation.

Hiltonsmith, Robert, and Tamara Draut. 2014. *The Great Cost Shift Continues: State Higher Education Funding After the Recession*. New York: Demos. Available Online at: http://www.demos.org/publication/great-cost-shift-continues-state-higher-education-funding-after-recession; accessed on 30 June 2016.

Immerwahr, John, Jean Johnson, and Paul Gasparra. 2008. *The Iron Triangle: College Presidents Talk about Costs, Access, and Quality*. Washington, DC: National Center for Public Policy and Higher Education and Public Agenda.

Inside Higher Ed. 2014. *2014 Survey of College and University Business Officers*. Washington, DC: Gallup.

Inside Higher Ed. 2013. *2013 Survey of College and University Presidents*. Washington, DC: Gallup.

Kirshstein, Rita, and Jane Wellman. 2012. "Technology and the Broken Higher Education Cost Model: Insights from the Delta Cost Project." *EDUCAUSE Review* 47 (5). Available online at: http://www.deltacostproject.org/products/technology-and-broken-higher-education-cost-model-insights-delta-cost-project; accessed on 11 November 2014.

Mitchell, Michael, Vincent Palacios, and Michael Leachman. 2014. *States Are Still Funding Higher Education Below Pre-Recession Levels*. Washington, DC: Center on Budget & Policy Priorities. Available online at http://www.cbpp.org/cms/?fa=view&id=4135; accessed on 30 June 2016.

National Association of State Budget Officers (NASBO). 2014. *Fiscal Survey of States*. Washington, DC: NASBO.

National Center for Public Policy and Higher Education (NCPPHE). 2006. *Measuring Up 2006: The National Report Card on Higher Education*. Washington, DC: NCPPHE.

National Commission on the Cost of Higher Education (NCCHE). 1998. *Straight Talk about College Costs and Prices*. Washington, DC: NCCHE.

Oliff, Phil, Vincent Palacios, Ingrid Johnson, and Michael Leachman. 2013. *Recent Deep State Higher Education Cuts May Harm Students and the Economy for Years to Come*. Washington, DC: Center on Budget & Policy Priorities. Available online at: http://www.cbpp.org/cms/?fa=view&id=3927; accessed on 30 June 2016.

Payea, Kathleen, Sandy Baum, and Charles Kurose. 2013. *How Students and Parents Pay for College*. New York: College Board.

Pew Charitable Trusts, The. 2012. *The Widening Gap Update: States are $1.38 Trillion Short in Funding Retirement Systems*. Philadelphia, PA: The Pew Center on the States.

Pew Charitable Trusts, The. 2014. *Size of Long-Term Obligations Varies Across States*. Philadelphia, PA: The Pew Charitable Trusts.

Reilly, David. 2010, September 18. "Pension Gaps Loom Larger—Funds Stick to 'Unrealistic' Return Assumptions, Threatening Bigger Shortfalls." *Wall Street Journal*, p. A1.

"Reining in college tuition." 2012, February 4. *The New York Times*, p. A20.

"Retirement benefits: Who pays the bill? Pensioners are pushing many cities and states towards financial crisis." 2013, July 27. *The Economist*, p. 24. Available online at: http://www.economist.com/news/united-states/21582282-pensioners-are-pushing-many-cities-and-states-towards-financial-crisis-who-pays-bill; accessed on 30 June 2016.

Rhodes, Frank H. T. 2001. *The Creation of the Future*. Ithaca, NY: Cornell University Press.

Schatz, Amy. 2013, May 28. "States Raise College Budgets After Years of Deep Cuts." *Wall Street Journal*, p. A1.

Selingo, Jeff. 2013. *College Unbound: The Future of Higher Education and What It Means for Students*. Boston, MA: Houghton Mifflin Harcourt.

State Higher Education Executive Officers (SHEEO). 2014. *Education Finance FY 2013*. Boulder, CO: SHEEO. Available online at: http://www.edexcelencia.org; accessed on 11 November 2014.

"State Workers and N.Y.'s Fiscal Crisis." 2011, March 6. *The New York Times*, p. 9L.

Teichler, Ulrich. 2014. "Higher Education and the Future Social Order: Equality of Opportunity, Quality, Competitiveness?" In *The Future of the Post-Massified University at the Crossroads*, edited by Jung Cheol Shin and Ulrich Teichler (pp. 183–203). Dordrecht, Netherlands: Springer.

U.S. Census Bureau (USCB). 2014. *Quick Facts, 2014*. Table H-AR. Suitland, MD: USCB. 1. Available online at: http://www.census.gov; accessed on 11 November 2014.

USCB. 2012. *Statistical Abstracts, 2012*. Suitland, MD: USCB. 1. Available online at: http://www.census.gov; accessed on 11 November 2014.

U.S. Department of Education. 2006. *A Test of Leadership: Charting the Future of U.S. Higher Education*. Washington, DC: U.S. Department of Education.

U.S. Department of Health and Human Services (USDHH). 2012. *2011 Actuarial Report on the Financial Outlook for Medicaid*. Washington, DC: Office of the Actuary and Centers for Medicare and Medicaid Services.

Zook, George F. et al. 1947. *Higher Education for Democracy: A Report of the President's Commission on Higher Education. Vol. 1, Establishing the Goals*. New York: Harper & Brothers.

Chapter 4

Comparative Assessment of Government Policies, Practices, and Funding Models

In an era where the costs of higher education continue to rise, there is a huge demand to maintain enrollments. Where some countries' populations begin to age, as we see in South Korea, Taiwan, and parts of the United States (e.g., much of the Northeastern Region), enrollments are beginning to wane. One proactive approach to help offset this enrollment trend is to strategically examine nontraditional student groups to help stabilize enrollment. One of these approaches could be to attract a greater number of quality international students.

Dr. John Evergreen, vice provost for International Affairs at Central University, had such a vision. He began by establishing a small unit within the provost's office that helped coordinate the development of an institution-wide international strategic plan. This step was necessary, because it gave specific ownership for this important strategic initiative to a small group of capable administrators.

Next, he led the development of a five-year institution-wide strategic plan. He then fleshed out the guiding document into annual action plans that could be used as a guide for implementation, costs, and continual feedback. Each of the schools and departments was expected to develop annual action plans in alignment with the institution-wide international strategic plan. One goal was to help the university steadily increase international student enrollments by 5 percent each year over the next five-year period.

His approach could have focused on what many higher education institutions (HEIs) do in the United States—to continue to charge an exorbitant, nonresident tuition rate for international students—but he decided against this approach. Instead, he convinced the board of trustees to equalize tuition costs for all students, regardless of their residency location. This leveled the tuition rates across the board, including for international students. His approach was a gamble, but it worked.

Over time, the economies of scale enrollment approach that had worked for so long from a traditional, local student enrollments perspective began to also work with the university's new focus on recruiting both local and international students. But there was more to Dr. Evergreen's strategic international enrollment approach than just recruitment; it also included a shift in the treatment of international students at his university from being situated on the periphery to becoming central to all key areas of the institution.

This included having all university personnel (administrators, faculty, staff, students, and alumni) identify ways to help international students feel welcomed and seek out and obtain quality higher education services at all levels. This included a cultural shift so that student affairs, academics (through careful internationalization of the curriculum), enrollment management, and all other administrative support services focused on the unique needs international students have. Instead of remaining peripheral, the international component became a strategic core emphasis of Central University.

Growing up in Pasadena, California, Sofia Garcia has dreamed of attending the University of California, Los Angeles (UCLA) or the University of Southern California (USC) all her life. She is now in her senior year of high school and is faced with a tough decision. Realizing that she struggled through several high school courses and her SAT score will not permit her to secure a scholarship at either of these world-class universities, Sofia begins to consider applying to Pasadena City College (PCC). Only a few minutes' drive from her parents' home, Sofia can easily commute to and from PCC by bus. And, staying at home will also help her save money to help pay for her schooling.

This approach to begin one's higher education journey by attending a community college is traveled by millions of students each year in the United States and in other countries. The reality is that if Sofia really focuses on her studies and performs well, she will be able to transfer to either USC or UCLA, and save a lot of money in the process. And, if she transfers to one of these elite schools, her degree won't be from PCC but UCLA or USC.

Unfortunately, too many students who begin their higher education journey at a smaller HEI, like PCC, do not realize that they can move on if they choose to do so. Attending smaller HEIs like community colleges is also a smart move for foreign students studying in the United States for the first time. It allows them to familiarize themselves with US cultures, societal norms, and teaching styles that may differ from their homelands. It is also a smart move for speakers for whom English is a second language or a foreign language, because smaller HEIs and community colleges often provide a greater focus on instruction and smaller classes than the large, world-class universities do. After one or two years attending a smaller HEI, these students could follow Sofia's plan to transfer to a major university if they choose to do so.

In this chapter, we examine six case countries from within the G20: Australia, Brazil, China, India, Germany, and the United Kingdom. We have intentionally looked at countries from various global regions to depict similarities and variances that exist in these differing locations worldwide. Underpinning much of the success of these global leaders in higher education are national economies that help support higher education at various levels.

The six case countries constitute roughly a fourth of top 100 universities, often deemed to have world-class status, and 28.8 percent of the top universities in the leading global rankings (see Table 4.1).[1] Language of institutional instruction has often been a focus of critique of the major ranking systems, while research production in top academic journals is a key indicator of higher education prowess. Since most of the top-ranked academic journals are published in English, global higher education rankings inevitably give English-based instruction countries an advantage (Baty 2015).

Funding strategies and government-supported policies differ in each of the six countries examined in this chapter. Several countries capitalized on their capacity to provide English courses and degrees in English in the aftermath of the September 11, 2001, terrorist attacks in the United States and thus to serve

Table 4.1 Higher Education Institutions Included in World University Rankings among G20 Countries

	QS		ARWU		THE	
Country	*2011*	*2015–2016*	*2011*	*2015**	*2010–2011*	*2015–2016*
Argentina	0	0	0	0	0	0
Australia	8	7	4	4	5	6
Brazil	0	0	0	0	0	0
Canada	4	4	4	4	4	4
China	6	8	0	0	5	4
France	2	2	3	4	2	1
Germany	4	4	6	4	3	9
India	0	0	0	0	0	0
Indonesia	0	0	0	0	0	0
Italy	0	0	0	0	0	0
Japan	6	5	5	4	2	2
Mexico	0	0	0	0	0	0
Russia	0	0	1	1	0	0
Saudi Arabia	0	0	0	0	0	0
South Africa	0	0	0	0	0	0
South Korea	3	3	0	0	2	1
Turkey	0	0	0	0	0	0
United Kingdom	19	18	10	9	14	16
United States	31	30	53	51	53	39

Note: *Latest year available as of 30 June 2016.
Sources: Created by the authors with data from Quacquarelli Symonds (QS), Shanghai Jiao Tong University Academic Ranking of World Universities (ARWU), and *Times Higher Education* (*THE*) for the years noted.

as alternatives to study in the United States. Australia, India, and the United Kingdom were among the most important destination countries to help fill the vacuum created by the more stringent visa policies in the United States.

Top-level government support is a key element that has enabled some of the most successful higher education systems to best meet the needs of citizens as well as attracting others to participate in their higher education system from overseas.

AUSTRALIA

Widely recognized as being among the most prominent destinations for students throughout Oceania,[2] the Australian higher education system has been able to capitalize on its unique leadership role within and beyond this region. Three universities are ranked among the top 50 in the world, and several HEIs have established strong international relationships and an online presence with many Pacific island neighboring countries. Government policies, funding streams, and wide public support have helped position Australian higher education as a foundation for local and national economies and in successful outreach initiatives.

The Australian Qualifications Framework (AQF) (2013, p. 9) was established in 1995 "to underpin the national system of qualifications in Australia encompassing higher education, vocational education and training and schools." AQF remains as the comprehensive foundation legislation for Australia's education system and a bridge between P12 and higher education.

The Tertiary Education Quality and Standards Agency (TEQSA) was formally established in 2011 and oversees the accreditation and quality assurance of Australia's 173 HEIs.[3] TEQSA also administers several key elements of the *Education Services for Overseas Students Act 2000*, including the English Language Intensive Course for Overseas Students (ELICOS) through one of Australia's HEIs. Quality remains a key focus of Australian HEIs, boasting the most world-class universities to rank among the top global 100 of those universities that opened in the past 50 years, according to the *THE* Top 100 Under 50 2015 Rankings (Hare 2015, p. 5).

Australia's strategic geographic location, along with its relative consistent government support, has helped it become a leader in attracting international students. In proportion to its total higher education student enrollments, Australia leads the world in foreign student enrollments, with roughly 25 percent registering as overseas students. Outreach goes well beyond Australian shores, with 7 percent of all students enrolling from offshore locations (TEQSA 2015, p. 10).

The international inflow has its financial benefits as well, contributing to the Australian economy. Higher education is viewed by many policy makers and senior higher education administrators as a key export industry (Grattan Institute 2013). This proactive internationalization stance and move to managerial governance have also garnered a backlash among some scholars and practitioners (see for instance Meyers 2012; Harris 2014). But there is no doubt that Australia continues to serve as a trailblazer country in its internationalized higher education efforts, especially within the greater ASEAN and Oceanic regions.

BRAZIL

Brazil's latest National Education Plan (*Plano Nacional de Educação*) was approved on 25 June 2014, and it establishes 10 educational priorities and 20 corresponding goals to be achieved through 2024. This is a sector-wide plan; many of the corresponding priorities and goals can be related to higher education. The guiding policy emphasizes several social justice issues: equity, access, and sustainability. It also outlines the need for Brazil's HEIs to improve in overall quality at all levels, including in instruction, technology, and student skills preparation for career placement (Ministry of Education [BMEC] 2014).

Government leaders hope to "increase the gross enrolment ratio in higher education to 50% of the population aged 18–24, and the net enrolment ratio to 33%, by 2020" (UNESCO 2014, p. 19). The government also wants to build its higher education capacity to where it can sustain, awarding "60,000 master's degrees and 25,000 doctorate degrees" annually by the year 2020 (p. 19).

Higher education has traditionally been less emphasized and supported by policy makers and government planners. Brazil remains an active supporter of the UN's Education for All initiative, and this is generally demonstrated through emphasized government funding for primary and secondary education. Private higher education continues to be regulated by the government. Roughly 70 percent of all students enroll in a private HEI. Private HEIs can be established based on meeting the following two conditions: (1) complying with the general regulations concerning national education and (2) submitting to public authorities regarding institutional operation and evaluation (Bruno 2010, p. 194).

In 2005, the government initiated the *Programa Universidade para Todos* (PROUNI: University for All Program) in an effort to provide greater access to a greater number of Brazilians, especially focusing on students from low socioeconomic status backgrounds. While not mandatory, this funding model provides incentives to private HEIs to offer financial assistance in the form of scholarships to students in return for federal tax exemptions.

HEIs are required to extend PROUNI scholarships to at least 10 percent of their student body (de Araujo 2012; Maculan et al. 2006). Reflecting back on the past decade since PROUNI was first implemented nationwide, there is no question it has led to greater access and a strengthening of the private sector in the delivery of higher education services. But critics argue that providing such significant tax incentives to private HEIs often disadvantages investment in the public sector (Algebaile 2007; Somers et al. 2013).

Other issues that arise deal primarily with quality and student attainment, as the private sector remains much less regulated than do public HEIs. While access may have been increased through PROUNI since 2005, several questions remain for government planners and higher education administrators. Do students actually graduate and can these students obtain jobs at the end of their higher education experience?

In an effort to encourage higher quality, the BMEC requires PROUNI-participating HEIs to meet certain standards[4] or they will be rendered ineligible for PROUNI funding and accompanying tax exemptions. In 2007, the government launched the Program for Restructuring and Expanding Plans of Federal Universities (REUNI), which increases and enhances resources to federal HEIs to improve access, quality, and retention.

Access for the masses has been achieved in Brazil, supported largely through a robust private sector that has risen to meet the influx of student demands. Patricia Somers and colleagues (2013, p. 214) note how "[c]ompared to other countries with affirmative action programs, the criteria for qualifying (race, ethnicity, socioeconomic [status], public school attendance, handicap, and indigenous status) are more expansive" in Brazil than in other G20 countries. But the ongoing and larger challenge that remains has to deal with improving the quality of instruction, existing programs, degree offerings, and institutions. Raising the bar to meet international accreditation standards of higher education excellence is a next step for Brazilian HEIs in its sustained efforts to provide higher education for all.

CHINA

The manufacturing engine of the world is a title China has held for several decades. Only recently have financial projections indicated that the economic boom has begun to thaw. Central government intervention in the national economy is nothing new for China, and this centralized approach also extends into several public sectors, including education. Projects 985 and 211 are two prime examples of government interventions to help catapult its flagship universities onto the world stage.

These projects highlight top-level government commitment to provide financial support and autonomy, at least to the most prominent national HEIs. There is significantly less autonomy granted by the China Ministry of Education (CMOE) in terms of management and oversight of HEIs at the local and regional levels, however, and this governance limitation is often viewed as a deterrent to senior administrators being able to best meet the higher education needs of the masses throughout the country (Yaisawarng and Ng 2014; Jacob and Hawkins 2015). And, for a nation that has cherished education for millennia through long-embedded cultural values, repositioning higher education as a means for regaining world prominence remains a key priority for the government.

By 2020, the government hopes that at least 20 percent of its population will hold a bachelor's degree (China Ministry of Education 2010). Access and equity remain key initiatives at the policy level, though it is often difficult to realize among all areas of gender, ethnicity, and geographic region (Jacob 2004; Yeung 2013). There remains a great disparity between higher education opportunities for those from the Eastern region of the country compared to those from other regions, especially the remote, hinterland areas of the country like Xizang (Tibet), Xinjiang, and Nei Mongol (Inner Mongolia).

Also, the massification of higher education has also raised increasing concerns about unemployment and underemployment of higher education graduates (Li et al. 2014). In the 1990s and during the early part of the twenty-first century, Chinese who sought degrees overseas in the United States, Canada, Australia, Germany, France, and the United Kingdom could easily find jobs to help support the bourgeoning economy. But times have changed in many regards, and competition significantly increased. Opportunities still remain for higher education graduates, but are more promising if graduates are willing to take an initial job in a rural or remote location within the country. Wing Kit Chan (2015, p. 43) notes how important it is to understand the geographic context of the Chinese case among higher education graduates:

> When regional disparity is considered, the relative severity of graduate unemployment among developed regions can be explained as follows: university graduates may yet be in oversupply in relative terms, but the job market is experiencing an oversupply of well-educated labour in absolute term[s] because a large proportion of graduates from the hinterlands are looking for jobs in the coastal region. The hinterlands of China are significantly less developed than the coastal region in economic terms; thus, graduates view jobseeking and settling down in the latter as upward social mobility . . ., which is the fundamental drive of such a flow of well-educated migrants.

The inevitable stabilizing and eventual cooling off of the national economy and the rapid growth of higher education are projected to continue well into the future. This dialectical issue will only further exacerbate unemployment and equity issues among current and future Chinese graduates.

Outside of Hong Kong and Macau, government-curtailed private higher education is the norm within the Chinese context. Jing Lei (2012) identifies three types of private HEIs in China: (1) private HEIs not authorized to grant degrees and diplomas, which facilitate self-study programs as an alternative to traditional higher education and the national College Entrance Exam; (2) private HEIs authorized to grant degrees and diplomas, which provide certificates, associate's and bachelor's degrees; and (3) independent (also "second-tier" or "affiliate") HEIs that are attached to a public (usually prestigious) university. The independent private HEIs "are self-funded, but they use the public universities' names and thus are considered a core reputable substitute to non-public-university-affiliated private universities" (p. 276).

A select number of joint venture programs, departments, and even institutions have arisen in recent years, especially those partnering with world-class universities from other countries. Most notable of these include the East China Normal University and New York University initiative—NYU Shanghai; Carnegie Mellon University's partnership with Harbin Institute of Technology,[5] Nanjing University of Science and Technology,[6] Sun Yat-sen University,[7] and Tsinghua University;[8] Sichuan University and the University of Pittsburgh Swanson School of Engineering;[9] Wuhan University and Duke University—Duke Kunshan University; and the University of Michigan—Peking University Joint Institute. There appears to be room for expansion and additional partnerships in the near future, but these higher education institutional leaders will most likely have an upper hand over others that are just now entering the scene.

Higher education outreach initiatives continue to expand, especially with the CMOE-supported Hanban, or Confucius Institutes. Sometimes criticized because of a tendency to be one-sided, the Confucius Institutes have helped China forge lasting partnerships with leading HEIs across the globe.

GERMANY

German higher education has long been at the forefront of innovation and job creation within the European Union (EU) and in international circles. Along with three other countries in 1998, Germany helped conceptualize and support the Bologna Process,[10] which in many ways has standardized and strengthened higher education throughout the entire European Higher Education Area. It took time for German HEIs to adopt and buy-in to the Bologna Process; by 2015, nearly all HEIs have supported the initiative (Mause 2013).

As a result of this initiative, the European Credit Transfer System, International Diploma Supplement, and the European Qualification Framework were established (OECD 2009). German policy makers approved the *Framework Act for Higher Education* in 1999, which provides definitions, standards, and governance guidelines for all German HEIs. It was last amended in December 2004 and remains as a guide for both public and private HEIs.

Tuition fees were first introduced in some German states in 2006, but after significant political juggling, there were mixed results in the effectiveness of introducing these fees. Where implemented, students paid up to €500 per term or semester. Following the aftermath of the global financial crisis and gains among the political left, tuition fees were entirely abolished in 2014 (Kauder and Potrafke 2013). But the lack of tuition fees can also be a deterrent to having students complete their degrees on time, as students are given the opportunity to complete their postsecondary education at their own pace (see, for instance, Theune 2015). One of the strengths of the German higher education system is its ability to forge partnerships with international governments and HEIs, due largely to the relatively small cost of higher education compared to other leading destination countries for foreign students, namely the United States, Canada, and the United Kingdom.

In 2005, Germany launched the Excellence Initiative, which provides competitive funding designed to distinguish and generate schools of excellence, in many ways comparable to the US Ivy League for research and the Massachusetts Institute of Technology and the California Institute of Technology for science and engineering. The Excellence Initiative in many ways changed Germany's traditional egalitarian funding model to a more neoliberal, market-driven, and internationally competitive model, which has been both criticized and recognized as a nonfactor among scholars (Krücken et al. 2013; Olivares and Wetzel 2014). Funding for the second phase of the Initiative began in June 2012, allocating €2.4 billion to support 44 universities through 45 graduate schools, 43 clusters of excellence, and 11 institutional strategies over a five-year period (German Research Foundation 2015).

The German Ministry of Education and Research (2015) has implemented the *Horizon 2020 Framework Programme*, which will provide €70 billion toward research, innovation, and market delivery services from 2014 to 2020. It is a community engagement in higher education initiative to better link German and European HEIs with industry at local, national, and international levels. Currently, there is a joint initiative by the federal and state governments focused around three pillars of German higher education:

Pillar 1—program for the Admission of Additional University Entrants, to provide funding to better meet increasing demands for higher education. Pillar 2—program Allowances for Projects funded by the German Research Foundation where the federal government contributes 20 percent of research project costs to HEIs to assist in covering indirect costs. Pillar 3—Quality Pact for Teaching that offers government funding to improve the study conditions of 186 HEIs; increase staffing; provide training, mentoring, and advisory services to faculty; and encourage innovation.

Germany's long tradition of postsecondary apprenticeships continues through its Dual Apprenticeships initiative. Funded largely through the private industry sector, organizations hire graduates as trade apprentices. In this regard, students learn practical skills while completing their higher education degrees. The initiative also enables individuals to attend state-funded vocational schools (*Berufsakademie*) or accept an apprenticeship that consists entirely of on-the-job training. Germany's long history of institutional autonomy remains a key ingredient of the strength of the higher education system. This autonomy should continue, albeit with the ability to further engage communities, foster government support, and partner with industry in the private and public sectors (Welsh 2004).

Some scholars argue that the increased interplay between German HEIs and industry, especially private companies, has led to a new managerialism "within the higher education sector as an ideology [that] has not only altered the ways of planning, funding, evaluating research and teaching but has also had far-reaching implications for the formal organization of institutional management and administrative realms of universities" (Krücken et al. 2013, p. 419).

The German Academic Exchange Service (DAAD) remains an active player in helping to internationalize Germany's higher education system. Exchange program opportunities for German and foreign students will continue to remain a priority in their strategic initiatives through 2020. Also supported in this initiative are strategies to help Germany remain among the top five study abroad destination countries for foreign students and a leader within the European Higher Education Area (EHEA) (DAAD 2013). German higher education continues to play a prominent role in leading and supporting the EU's Lisbon Agenda (Weigmann 2015) and the *Europe 2020* Strategic Plan; the country is on target to surpass the EU target (40 percent) and reach its own national target of having at least 42 percent of 30–34-year-old Germans having completed tertiary or equivalent education by 2020.

INDIA

Unlike the other G20 countries, India's poverty level and sociocultural inequalities are unmatched. Yet, it remains a significant economic power in the region, and will soon have the largest education sector worldwide. Some of the greatest inequalities of education that exist within the Indian context deal with gender, social status (including the strata restrictions inherent in the traditional caste system), extreme poverty, and ethnicity (Barstow and Raj 2015; Maslak 2008).

Higher education has traditionally been only a luxury for the masses in India. And, while the massification of higher education has occurred in recent years, this has occurred simultaneously with the expansion of primary and secondary education; higher education enrollments have not kept pace. Several additional challenges have hindered progress in India's higher education, including high drop-out rates and low quality of instruction and skills acquisition (Altbach 2014).

Based on the former colonial model established by Great Britain, Indian higher education governance at independence was largely decentralized and vested at the state level. This has often pitted policy challenges and inconsistencies between the central and state-level governments in regulating higher education throughout the country. Since 1956, the Government of India has orchestrated its higher education system though the University Grants Commission (UGC), which issues five-year strategic plans to help guide growth and provide policy direction to all HEIs.

The UGC's 12th Five-Year Plan, 2012–2017 for higher education was titled *Inclusive and Qualitative Expansion of Higher Education*. This in many ways depicts the current focus on growth, while simultaneously recognizing the need for greater emphasis on quality. Of the 23 strategic points outlined in the 12th FYP, 9 focused on social justice issues of equity and access among all, females, those from low socioeconomic status backgrounds, and ethnic minorities; 3 on capacity building needs of faculty members, leaders, infrastructure, and technology; 7 that focus on quality improvements; and 4 that will help enable a culture of good governance practices at all levels.

The Ministry of Human Resource Development (MHRD) has engaged in several initiatives to improve higher education, including the *Rashtriya Uchchatar Shiksha Abhiyan* (RUSA: National Higher Education Mission). A centrally sponsored scheme launched in 2013, the Rashtriya Uchchatar Shiksha Abhiyan (RUSA) has eight primary objectives, including an emphasis on regulating the quality of HEIs at the national level, monitoring state governance of their respective higher education systems, as well as improving governance among HEIs and improving equity nationwide (MHRD 2015).

C. Padmanabhan (2014) notes that several elements of RUSA are incongruent with its depiction of higher education commercialization, noting how states may raise 50 percent of their matching funds through the private sector; the government will no longer provide for higher education, but merely regulate it; and public-private partnerships and viability gap funding are promoted models for higher education. Padmanabhan argues that developing a national system of higher education promotes market-based education while limiting regional and state contextualizing: "The whole programme looks like a coercive apparatus using conditional grants to wean state universities away from chalking out their unique trajectories of development."

The Federation of Indian Chambers of Commerce and Industry (FICCI) established the *Higher Education in India: Vision 2030* (Ernst & Young 2013) that provides policy recommendations and strategies to help India improve in several strategic areas. These include the capacity to train a skilled workforce of approximately 250 million, becoming a recognized leader in research and development, and a commitment to quality among all types of HEIs—including those which are research focused, career focused, and foundation institutions (p. 20).

Philip G. Altbach describes the state of higher education in India as "a sea of mediocrity, in which some islands of excellence can be found" (p. 505). Most HEIs face the dual challenge of producing more graduates than there are jobs in certain fields and not producing quality graduates for high-demand fields such as engineering and management. Following independence, higher education was fully controlled by the government until 1980.

Today there is an accelerating rate of growth of both HEIs and enrollments (Angom 2015). Martin Carnoy and Rafiq Dossani (2013) argue that economic globalization and the demand for increased access to higher education came into play in the 1980s, as "pressure from underprivileged groups for expansion was supplemented by pressures for expansion from the growing middle classes, who sought professional education as a response to globalization" (p. 606).

The massification of Indian higher education in recent years has resulted in an emphasis on educational outcomes, with coinciding pressures for evaluation and managerialism. Carnoy and Dossani further note that even though the central government promoted HEI autonomy and quality, in most cases the universities and state governments retained a large amount of regulatory control over the affiliated colleges. As a result, privatization has not resulted in increasing higher education quality:

> While some of the new private colleges, including those which are autonomous, offer a better quality of education than the best public colleges, most of the private colleges fare much worse, due to under-spending on infrastructure and increasing teaching loads, usually in violation of their affiliating university's standards. (p. 609)

Determining whether to offer government financial aid to students in the form of loans or grants is an issue that has challenged policy makers and planners for a long time. P. Geetha Rani (2014, p. 200) proposes a formula through which to link income with other social categories in order to more equitably determine when individuals should be eligible to receive educational grants rather than loans:

Financial need = cost of courses (e.g., tuition and fees + living and other expenses) **– ability of students' parents to contribute based on parental income net of parental liabilities**

The net of financial need = financial need—scholarships and concessions and a grant = net financial need—% of deprivation in financial need. Being able to implement a financial model like Rani's proposed equity equation is yet to be realized in India, but it is one that may prove more equitable for India and other countries to consider.

In a country that boasts the largest number of native English speakers on the earth, India has a bright future to play on the global higher education stage. The higher education foundation is still malleable at present, and it remains to be seen how soon India can capitalize on its greatest resource of virtually unlimited human resource potential. Partnering with other countries in a fashion similar to what China has done with a handful of world-class universities through 2015 is a strategy that is also being tested in India and may bode well as a starting point. But this direction will only provide a limited number of opportunities for an increasingly elite few (Rajkhowa 2013). How to increase and maintain quality alongside the extreme growth in this time of higher education massification is a challenge that will continue for many years to come.

UNITED KINGDOM

Like Germany, the United Kingdom helped spearhead the Bologna Process and has consistently led many higher education initiatives in the EHEA.[11] The Quality Assurance Agency helps monitor and advise HEIs nationwide on issues of standards, quality, and accreditation, which align with the Bologna Process's Framework for Qualification of the EHEA. Quality assurance within the UK higher education system has remained a "collaboration between self-regulation, the state and the market" (Brown 2013, p. 421).

Consistently outranking most other countries, the United Kingdom boasts an average of 14.3 percent of all world-class universities based on the three rankings depicted in Table 4.1 over the past five years. Oxford and Cambridge are the only two universities outside of the United States that consistently rank in the top 10. Much of the UK higher education legacy of success is built on institutional autonomy and an ability to generate excellence in research, innovation, and in meeting the needs of a diverse student body (Universities UK 2015).

Policy-based tuition fees have fluctuated in the United Kingdom in recent years. The *Higher Education Act 2004* allowed HEIs to raise tuition fees to a maximum of £3,000 annually, provided HEIs had an Office of Fair Access-approved access agreement. In 2009, the government commissioned a committee report on higher education funding, where the tuition cap was removed entirely. Then, in September 2012, the *Higher Education Act* was amended such that HEIs were capped at being able to charge up to £9,000 in annual tuition fees. This rise in tuition costs from what it was in 2004 came at the same time in which the government cut substantial funding to higher education, replacing grants with student loans as the primary source of financial assistance (Hubble 2015a). Access to government loans and grants is largely based upon students' household income (West et al. 2015).

The Department for Business, Innovation and Skills (2014) published a *National Strategy for Access and Student Success in Higher Education* with a vision to help "all those with the potential to benefit from higher education [so that they] have equal opportunity to participate and succeed, on a course and in an institution that best fit their potential, needs and ambitions for employment or further study" (p. 7). Roger Brown (2013, p. 431) describes the introduction of a recent voucher system for undergraduate teaching in the United Kingdom:

> From 2012–13 most university teaching is being funded entirely from tuition fees, with direct institutional subsidies confined to a small number of priority areas including medicine, science and engineering, and modern languages. By mimicking as closely as possible a "real" market where consumers choose with their own resources, voucher systems are seen by some economists as the best means of giving consumers leverage over publicly funded services.

An overemphasis on market-oriented outcomes is a caution some scholars compare to a rise in the managerial HEI in the UK context. Alan Cribb and Sharon Gewirtz (2013, p. 344), for instance, argue that

> it would appear that the university as an institution with a distinctive rationality and social purpose . . . has been replaced with the idea of the university as a generic large-scale social organization—what we are calling a hollowed-out university—that can increasingly be seen less as a community of learners and more as a social site that can be engineered to serve any social function. The increased emphasis on marketing and corporate identity and a concern with institutional competition and success, and gloss and spin all make the university look, feel and act like countless other non-educational corporate institutions.

Government research funding for projects is administered through the United Kingdom's research councils; funding for research infrastructure initiatives is administered by the United Kingdom's three Higher Education Funding Councils in England, Scotland, and Wales and the Department for Employment and Learning in Northern Ireland. Research funding allotments are largely based on a metrics-based Research Excellence Framework (REF) that took several years to develop and was launched in January 2014.

The REF provides assessment outcomes guidance on what is required of HEIs requesting research funds, and is based on the following three criteria: the output quality of their research (65 percent), impact on the economy and society in general (20 percent), and the overall research environment (15 percent). Decisions are made by expert review panels consisting of content area experts related to the respective disciplines applying for research funding (REF 2011, p. 6).

In addition to being eligible for much-needed research funding, HEIs that perform well on REF assessments also gain (or maintain) exemplary reputations and an ability to attract quality students. "Conversely a poor result in the assessment can see institutional funding reduced and in some cases this can lead to departmental restructuring or closures" (Hubble 2015b, p. 4).

CONCLUDING OBSERVATIONS

In this chapter, we have offered a concise understanding of how higher education is funded within Australia, Brazil, China, Germany, India, and the United Kingdom by examining the connectivity between government funding priorities, education policies, and the important social justice issues of access to and affordability of higher education. Data informs us that approximately three out of four college and university students in the United States are enrolled in public institutions and that governments subsidize higher education in other countries to varying degrees. This remains consistent in each of the six case countries we examined in this chapter, though the approaches and funding schemes differ in many areas in each context.

In several country circumstances, we highlight the advantages and disadvantages of government-planned higher education relative to those characterized by institutional autonomy. Socioeconomic needs and the ways in which the case countries have responded through public education policy, postsecondary education priorities, and financial subsidies to higher education were discussed.

NOTES

1. Shanghai Jiao Tong University's Academic Ranking of World Universities (ARWU), Quacquarelli Symonds (QS), and *Times Higher Education* (*THE*) are considered by many as the leading global ranking systems of higher education institutions.

2. While we focus on the prominence of the Australian higher education influence throughout Oceania, we want to recognize the important status and role higher education in New Zealand has also played in this region.

3. TEQSA was formally established with the passing of the *Tertiary Education Quality and Standards Agency Act 2011*. The *TEQSA Act* has been amended eight times, most recently on 13 December 2014.

4. The standards require PROUNI-participating private HEIs to satisfactorily pass National Assessment of Higher Education System (SINAES) evaluations, the National Student Performance Exam (ENADE), and other evaluations (for more information, see Somers et al. 2013).

5. This is a five-year, joint-training program that will offer students degrees from both CMU and HIT.

6. Partnership that offers students a master of science degree in robotics technology.

7. Multiple initiatives between CMU and SYSU include the establishment of the Joint Institute of Engineering, Shunde International Joint Research Institute, and a joint graduate engineering program.

8. This program offers participating students a dual master's degree in computer science from CMU and Tsinghua University.

9. The Sichuan University-Pittsburgh Institute was forged in April 2013 and establishes a joint engineering institute between the two universities.

10. Twenty-five countries joined Germany, France, Italy, and the United Kingdom as inaugural signatories of the Bologna Process. As of December 2015, 47 countries and the European Commission are member signatories, along with eight consultative member organizations, including UNESCO (EHEA 2015).

11. The United Kingdom's participation in the Bologna Process is headed by the High Level Policy Forum, which includes representatives of the Department for Business, Innovation and Skills; the Scottish Government; the Welsh Assembly Government; the Higher Education Funding Councils for England, Scotland and Wales; the Quality Assurance Agency; Universities UK; GuildHE; and the National Recognition Information Centre for the United Kingdom.

REFERENCES

Algebaile, M. E. B. 2007. "Expansion of Higher Education: Traces of Selective Inclusion in the Brazilian Educational Case." ["Expansão da educação superior: Traços de uma inclusão seletiva no cenário educational brasileiro"]. In *Education and Public Policy: Topics for Debate [Educação e políticas públicas: Tópicos para o debate]*, edited by C. G. Vieitez, and R. E. M. Barone. Araraquara, SP: Junqueira & Marin.

Altbach, Philip G. 2014. "India's Higher Education Challenges." *Asia Pacific Education Review* 15 (4): 503–510.

Angom, Sangeeta. 2015. "Private Higher Education in India: A Study of Two Private Universities." *Higher Education for the Future* 2 (1): 92–111.

Australian Qualifications Framework Council. 2013. *Australian Qualifications Framework.* 2nd Edition. Canberra: Australian Qualifications Framework Council, 2013. Available online at: http://www.aqf.edu.au/wp-content/ uploads/2013/05/AQF-2nd-Edition-January-2013.pdf; accessed on 21 March 2015.

Barstow, David, and Suhasini Raj. 2015. "Caste Quotas in India Come Under Attack." *New York Times*, August 31, p. A1.

Baty, Phil. 2015. *World University Rankings blog: Treating countries fairly*. London: THE. Available online at: https://www.timeshighereducation.co.uk/blog/world-uni-versity-rankings-blog-treating-countries-fairly; accessed on 29 August 2015.

Brown, Roger. 2013. "Mutuality Meets the Market: Analysing Changes in the Control of Quality Assurance in United Kingdom Higher Education 1992–2012." *Higher Education Quarterly* 67 (4): 420–437.

Bruno, Lúcia. 2010. "Evaluation of Higher Education in Brazil: Rationale and Goals." In *International Educational Governance*, edited by S. Karin Amos (pp. 193–216). International Perspectives on Education and Society No. 12. Bradford, UK: Emerald Publishing Group Ltd.

Carnoy, Martin, and Rafiq Dossani. 2013. "Goals and Governance of Higher Education in India." *Higher Education* 65 (5): 595–612.

Chan, Wing Kit. 2015. "Higher Education and Graduate Employment in China: Challenges for Sustainable Development." *Higher Education Policy* 28: 35–53.

Cribb, Alan, and Sharon Gewirtz. 2013. "The Hollowed-Out University? A Critical Analysis of Changing Institutional and Academic Norms in UK Higher Education." *Discourse: Studies in the Cultural Politics of Education* 34 (3): 338–350.

de Araujo, Abrahao Andre. 2012. "Access to Higher Education in Brazil with Reference to Prouni." *Higher Education Studies* 2 (1): 32–37.

Department for Business, Innovation and Skills. 2014. *National Strategy for Access and Student Success in Higher Education*. London: Department for Business, Innovation and Skills.

Ernst & Young LLP. 2013. *Higher Education in India: Vision 2030*. Kolkata, India: Earnst & Young LLP. Available online at: http://www.ey.com/Publication/vwLU-Assets/Higher-education-in-India-Vision-2030/$FILE/EY-Higher-education-in-India-Vision-2030.pdf; accessed on 15 April 2015.

European Commission. 2015. *Europe 2020*. Brussels, Belgium: European Commission. Available online at: http://ec.europa.eu/europe2020; accessed on 29 August 2015.

European Higher Education Area (EHEA). 2015. *Participating Countries and Organisations*. Yerevan, Armenia: EHEA.

German Academic Exchange Service (DAAD). 2013. *Strategy DAAD 2020*. Bonn, Germany: DAAD.

German Research Foundation (DFG). 2015. *Excellence Initiative*. Bonn, Germany: DFG.

Government of Australia. 2014. *Tertiary Education Quality and Standards Agency Act 2011*. Compilation No. 8. Canberra: Government of Australia.

Hare, Julie. 2015. "Australia leads world on young-gun unis." *The Australian*, April 30, p. 5.

Harris, Bede. 2014. "Corporatisation, Managerialism, and the Death of the University Ideal in Australia." *Journal of Politics and Law* 7 (2): 63–80.

Hubble, Sue. 2015a. *Higher Education Tuition Fees in England—Party Policies 2015*. London: House of Commons Library.

Hubble, Sue. 2015b. *2014 Research Excellence Framework*. London: House of Commons Library.

Jacob, W. James. 2004. *Marketization, Demarketization, and Remarketization: The Impact of the Economic Market on Higher Education in China*. PhD dissertation, University of California, Los Angeles.

Jacob, W. James, and John N. Hawkins. 2015. "Trends in Chinese Higher Education: Opportunities and Challenges." In *Higher Education Reform: Looking Back – Looking Forward*, edited by Pavel Zgaga and Hans G. Schuetze. Boston, Rotterdam, Taipei: Sense Publishers.

Kauder, Björn, and Niklas Potrafke. "Government Ideology and Tuition Fee Policy: Evidence from the German States." *CESifo Economic Studies* 59 (4): 628–649.

Krücken, Georg, Albrecht Blümel, and Katharina Kloke. 2013. "The Managerial Turn in Higher Education? On the Interplay of Organizational and Occupational Change in German Academia." *Minerva* 51 (4): 417–442.

Lei, Jing. 2012. "Striving for Survival and Success: Chinese Private Higher Education in the Twenty-First Century." *On the Horizon* 20 (4): 274–283.

Li, Shi, John Whalley, and Chunbing Xing. 2014. "China's Higher Education Expansion and Unemployment of College Graduates." *China Economic Review* 30: 567–582.

Maculan, N., Celso C. Ribeiro, and F. Haddad. 2009. "Program PROUNI: Changing the Panorama of Access to Higher Education in Brazil." *IAU Horizons* 12 (2).

Maslak, Mary Anne. 2008. "Using Enrollment and Attainment in Formal Education to Understand the Case of India." In *Inequality in Education: Comparative and International Perspectives*, edited by Donald B. Holsinger and W. James Jacob (pp. 240–260). Dordrecht, the Netherlands: Comparative Education Research Center and Springer.

Mause, Karsten. 2013. "With Bologna in Mind and the Sword in the Hand: The German Bachelor/Master Reform Reconsidered." *Higher Education Policy* 26: 325–347.

Meyers, Donald. 2012. *Australian Universities: A Portrait of Decline*. Available online at: http://www.australianuniversities.id.au/; accessed on 25 August 2015.

Ministry of Education, Brazil (BMEC). 2014. *Planning for the Next Decade: Understanding the 20 Goals of the National Education Plan* [*Planejando a Próxima Década: Conhecendo as 20 Metas do Plano Nacional de Educação*]. Brasilia: BMEC.

Ministry of Education, China (CMOE). 2010. *National Plan for Medium and Long-Term Education Reform and Development* (2010–2020). Beijing, CMOE.

Ministry of Education and Research. 2015. *Horizon 2020—The European Research Framework Programme*. Bonn, Germany: Ministry of Education and Research.

Ministry of Human Resource Development (MHRD). 2015. *Rashtriya Uchchatar Shiksha Abhiyan (RUSA)*. New Delhi, India: MHRD. Available online at: http://mhrd.gov.in/rusa; accessed on 15 May 2015.

Norton, Andrew. 2013. *Mapping Australian Higher Education, 2013 Version*. Carlton, VIC: Grattan Institute.

Organisation for Economic Co-operation and Development (OECD). 2009. *Higher Education to 2030*. Volume 2: Globalisation. Paris: Centre for Educational Research and Innovation, OECD.

Padmanabhan, C. 2014. "A Mission Rebuffing a Vision: Rashtriya Ucchatar Shiksha Abhiyan." *Economic & Political Weekly* 49 (14).

Quacquarelli Symonds (QS). 2011 and 2015. *World University Rankings*. New York: QS.

Rajkhowa, Gautam. 2013. "Cross Border Higher Education in India: Challenges and Opportunities." *International Journal of Organizational Analysis* 21 (3): 471–484.

Rani, P. Geetha. 2014. "Education Loans and Financing Higher Education in India: Addressing Equity." *Higher Education for the Future* 1 (2): 183–210.

Research Excellence Framework (REF). 2011. *Assessment Framework and Guidance on Submissions*. REF 02.2011. Bristol, UK: REF.

Shanghai Jiao Tong University. 2011 and 2015. *Academic Ranking of World Universities*. Shanghai: Center for World-Class Universities, Shanghai Jiao Tong University.

Somers, Patricia, Marilia Morosini, Miriam Pan, and James E. Cofer, Sr. 2013. "Brazil's Radical Approach to Expanding Access for Underrepresented College Students." In *Fairness in Access to Higher Education in a Global Perspective: Reconciling Excellence, Efficiency, and Justice*, edited by Heinz-Dieter Meyer, Edward P. St. John, Maia Chankseliani, and Lina Uribe (pp. 203–221). Boston, Rotterdam, Taipei: Sense Publishers.

Tertiary Education Quality and Standards Agency (TEQSA). 2015a. *Statistics Report on TEQSA Registered Higher Education Providers*. Melbourne, VIC: TEQSA.

TEQSA. 2015b. *TEQSA's role and functions*. Melbourne, VIC: TEQSA. Available online at: http://www.teqsa.gov.au/about/; accessed on 24 August 2015.

Theune, Katja. 2015. "The Working Status of Students and Time to Degree at German Universities." *Higher Education*. doi: 10.1007/s10734-015-9864-z.

Times Higher Education (THE). 2011 and 2015. *World University Rankings*. London: THE.

Universities UK. 2015. *Quality, Equity, Sustainability: The Future of Higher Education Regulation*. Report of the Universities UK Regulation Task and Finish Group. London: Universities UK.

UNESCO. 2014. *BRICS: Building Education for the Future: Priorities for National Development and International Cooperation*. Paris: UNESCO.

Weigmann, Katrin. 2015. "Lessons Learned in Germany." *EMBO Reports* 16 (2): 142–146.

Welsh, Helga. 2004. "Higher Education in Germany: Reform in Incremental Steps." *European Journal of Education* 3 (39): 359–375.

West, Anne, Roberts, Jonathan, Lewis, Jane, and Philip Noden. 2015. "Paying for Higher Education in England: Funding Policy and Families." *British Journal of Educational Studies* 63 (1): 23–45.

Yaisawarng, Suthathip, and Ying Chu Ng. 2014. "The Impact of Higher Education Reform on Research Performance of Chinese Universities." *China Economic Review* 31: 94–105.

Yeung, Wei-Jun Jean. 2013. "Higher Education Expansion and Social Stratification in China." *Chinese Sociological Review* 45 (4): 54–80.

Chapter 5

A Global Perspective of Learning Outcomes, Assessments, and the Skills Gap

We continue our journey by returning to the fictitious case of Alf Hendricks, and differing ways to appraise his situation. Alf graduated with honors from an accredited non-flagship public university in four years with a degree in secondary education and a career objective of teaching history at high school. He completed requisite courses for an education major, along with a minor in history. Alf graduated cum laude.

Within a month of graduation, Alf received state certification in teaching and found a job as a history instructor at his high school alma mater. He was pleased with his progress, and he was not alone. His achievements met outcomes by which his college, state, and federal department of education officials measure success by graduating in four years and landing a job in his chosen field in a timely manner. Logic suggests that Alf, his university, its regional accreditation association, and public officials should declare "mission accomplished." Not so fast.

Further inquiry will more completely determine whether Alf's "win" holds up under closer inspection. First-year instruction assignments called for him to teach courses in US History, European History, World History, and Geography and World Cultures. Although Alf had co-majored in history, he had only 21 total credit hours in courses directly or indirectly related to his course load. As a result, he lacked the content knowledge across this wide array of subjects. Worse yet, he discovered that his writing, communication, organization, information literacy, and problem-solving skills were inadequate.

Alf was unable to effectively critique student writing assignments. He could neither relate to disruptive, and at times disrespectful, students nor their parents. Coming from a university where 90-minute class sessions were the norm, he found it difficult to manage content delivery in 50 minutes.

*In addition, history and English faculty were held jointly accountable for
student performance on statewide Common Core Standards (CCS) exams in
reading and writing. Within three years of employment, Alf had begun to think
about career alternatives as he scrambled to perform in an environment for
which he had not been prepared. The high school principal observed a gap
between the skills, knowledge, and behaviors teachers need to succeed and
the preparation offered by certain teacher education programs. Alf was not an
exception. He evaluated Alf unsatisfactory in year three and did not recommend him for tenure. What's wrong with this picture?*

*Alf's predicament causes one to reflect upon disparities that may arise
between employer expectations and ways that institutional and program
effectiveness are measured. As it happens, faculty at the state university had
not revised their curriculum and pedagogy to meet increasing demands and
challenges of the teaching profession. The regional accreditation association
evaluated institutional effectiveness in accordance with its standards, but
lacked the resources to examine all programs.*

*The paperwork submitted to the accreditation association by his uni-
versity suggested that all programs met prevailing standards. The state
department of education had not revamped certification requirements to
assure that public school teachers were fully prepared in terms of content expertise, classroom management, use of instructional technology,
and student engagement techniques. More students were visual learners,
were entranced by social media, and did not respond well to traditional
lecture format. Ongoing professional development programs for teachers were out of touch with prevailing needs and did not address the challenges at hand. The causal factors behind Alf's problems were many.*

The above illustration is by no means representative of higher education.
On the contrary, many of the most highly regarded liberal arts and research
universities around the world are located in the United States. Numerous
career-oriented community colleges sustain close and collaborative relationships with local employers who hire their graduates, and curriculum
relevance is deemed mission critical. Instead, the underlying questions relate
more to how *an educated person* is characterized in socioeconomic terms,
who defines those traits, what the role of educators is in adding value to the
learning processes of their students, and how the results can be measured.

On the other hand, the fictional story of Alf does pose a basis for inquiry
about curriculum and instructional pedagogy, and how well prepared university graduates are to enter the workplace or perform with proficiency in
graduate school. One might also question the utility of certain output indicators such as preuniversity standardized test results, postsecondary school
graduation rates or job placements. In other words, a confluence of input

variables materially influences the quality of the learning process and the educational and behavioral growth of students. They include curriculum design, instructional quality and pedagogy, academic and student services support, and systemic integration of instructional technology. Problems arise anytime skill sets required by employers, university curriculum, educational policy, and practice lack alignment.

AN EDUCATED PERSON AND STUDENT LEARNING OUTCOMES

Let us now consider the elusive subject of an *educated person*. Ancient Greek philosophers such as Socrates, Aristotle, and Plato reportedly developed the abilities of their followers to think, question, and contest ideas through debate. The pyramids in Egypt, Roman aqueducts, Mayan temples, Stonehenge, and the Great Wall of China were designed by brilliant visionaries and inventors. Their creations served a purpose.

Confucius expounded upon wisdom, virtuous, and moral behavior. Christopher Columbus, Galileo, and Copernicus were all daring thinkers, doers, and risk takers. Brunelleschi lacked formal training as an architect, yet designed the magnificent dome for Florence's Santa Maria del Fiore cathedral. He also invented the equipment and construction techniques to mount the dome on top of the cathedral.

Nearer to our time, Charles William Elliot transformed Harvard, just as Abraham Flexner had a profound influence upon the way medical education is delivered in the United States and the need to develop clinical skills. Today's geniuses are often found in technological innovation. All shared a capacity to think and translate vision and analysis to action. So we query whether educational systems define educators or whether educators define their systems.

To have demonstrative capacity to expand one's range of knowledge and to think and find ways of applying or articulating the results of one's effort are inherent characteristics of an educated person. Some may find expression as *reflective thinkers* who process their interactions and acquired knowledge, analyze what transpired, and draw conclusions consistent with their findings. Inventors and others at the leading edge of breakthrough research or idea generation somehow discover what others cannot. They are *original thinkers.*

Still others are *critical thinkers,* or persons who are intellectually disciplined. Their observations are informed by independent evaluation of evidence presented in written or verbal presentations, and they are able to identify the relative strengths and weaknesses of ideas, actions, and information presented. Their thinking processes extend beyond summations.

This talent can be nurtured by educators and is integral to one's ability to solve problems.

Our discussion of an educated person is further informed by the views of accomplished educators, employers, educational associations, and those familiar with educational processes. Some ponder societal and institutional shortcomings of the educational processes. Frederick Reif (2008, p. 3), a retired professor of physics from Carnegie Mellon University, observes "we rarely think much about thinking."

A business survey in the United Kingdom concluded that schools turn out pupils "who simply do not have the relevant skills or personal qualities" as measured by math, ability to craft basic business letters, perform effectively in teams, and communicate well with their customers (Wolf 2012, p. 117).

An employer survey conducted by Hart Research Associates (2013) for the Association of American Colleges and Universities (AACU) in 2013 reveals a desire for colleges to focus attention upon developing graduates capable of innovation, critical thinking, effective two-way communications, applying analytical reasoning skills, solving complex problems, translating know-how to "real-world" settings, and functioning as team members in diverse settings. Sean Hughes (2015), a friend and former colleague on the School of Education faculty at the University of Pittsburgh, expressed concerns about university graduates who are "schooled but not educated."

The challenges facing higher education are more daunting yet when one considers that an ACT benchmarking testing of the college readiness of high school graduates informs us that only 28 percent of those evaluated were deemed college ready in English, reading, math, and science (ACT 2015, p. 4). Some question the motivation, behaviors, and performance standards that first-year college students set for themselves (Rosenbaum 2001). These results are alarming and pose dire socioeconomic implications at the national, employer, and household levels. A highly productive and well-compensated workforce is the locomotive that drives the competitiveness of a consumption-driven national economy.

Student learning outcomes may evolve at the institutional, program, or academic discipline levels and are further informed by the insights offered by leading scholars. Some cite needs for persons with an aptitude for quantitative analysis, problem solving and an ability to perform in workplaces subject to continuous change and who are informationally literate. For example, Tony Wagner (2010, p. 14), a member of the Harvard Graduate School of Education faculty, calls for students with abilities to think critically, solve problems, collaborate "across networks," adapt to change, initiate, communicate effectively in writing and verbally, access and analyze information, and demonstrate curiosity.

Wagner refers to these attributes as "seven survival skills" and believes that development of these competencies must begin during K-12 (p. 13). A recent study by *The Economist* Intelligence Unit (2014, p. 3), which was sponsored by the Lumina Foundation, cited "overwhelming consensus" among employers that college graduates lack many of these skills.

During my tenure as president of the Community College of Allegheny County (CCAC), our faculty agreed upon general education goals that, among other characteristics, identified a student's learning attainment as one who acquires the following:

- A broad range of knowledge upon which to make value judgments
- The skills to locate valid information and comprehend that information
- The ability to critically analyze and synthesize efficiently valid information
- The ability to listen carefully and to communicate effectively (CCAC 2015)

These general education goals became a centerpiece for curriculum planning and eventual modifications of course syllabi and instructional pedagogy. They also offered a vision for integration of a foundational liberal arts curriculum with practical career degree and certificate programs. Many of these goals are remarkably similar to those embraced by Tony Wagner.

Based upon our collective experiences in higher education and industry, we often asked business and labor union leaders about skills desired from higher education graduates. Most cite the need for graduates who are professionally trained to the standards of the industry, but they also value so-called soft skills or intangibles not necessarily reflected in grades or diplomas.

Their views aligned with those expressed by Tony Wagner, CCAC faculty, and the articulation of desirable learning outcomes by the AACU, which include inquiry analysis, quantitative literacy, problem solving, multicultural interactions, teamwork, civic knowledge and engagement, ethical reasoning and action, and foundations skills for lifelong learning (AACU 2008). This suggests that technical training requires some reasonable integration of skill set development offered by a liberal arts curriculum.

This raises questions about curriculum characteristics, courses, and instructional interactions likely to yield such results and about how institutions and programs can better plan and deliver high-quality, relevant student learning outcomes. When one considers the types of personal skills and behaviors desired of employees, a broader exposure to a liberal arts curriculum in social sciences, humanities, math, and sciences offers further opportunities for undergraduates to develop skills valued by employers.

As it happens, both the authors were history majors in undergraduate school and are well aware of the lasting value derived from courses and faculty who developed our capacities to question assumptions, think critically and reflectively, tolerate ambiguity, respect contested ideas, examine current circumstances within a broader socioeconomic, political, and cultural context, and communicate effectively in written and verbal form.

One may argue that the United States suffers as much from both a soft or performance skills gap as from a diploma gap. Put another way, what happens if the United States reaches its stated goal, for 60 percent of adults aged 25 or above to hold a community college or bachelor's degree, yet degree holders lack the soft skills needed by employers for them to sustainably compete in an increasingly competitive global market.

The skills gap will be closed in proportion not only to higher levels of degree attainment but also in relation to the demonstrative intangible competencies of community college and university graduates in the workplace. In this sense, foundational skills position accountants, machinists, registered nurses, lawyers, bankers, licensed electricians, computer software engineers, and others to meet the increasingly complex expectations of employers, their colleagues, and their customers.

CURRICULUM CHARACTERISTICS AND QUALITY CONTROLS

Growth in knowledge acquisition and personal behaviors speak to the value proposition of higher education. Frank Rhodes, retired president of Cornell University, observed: "The university's core business is learning, and the most basic part of learning is the education of undergraduates" (Rhodes 2011, p. 84). Life and employability skills matter, and higher education plays a vital role in the developing of those talents.

An increasing body of informed observers is concerned about skills development in higher education. Some question whether higher education, in the aggregate, consistently meets these expectations. Rita Roy, chief executive officer (CEO) of MasterCard Foundation, noted, "It is very obvious after meeting with people in the world of education that formal education seldom speaks to the world of employment."

Roy went on to expand upon the pivotal role higher education can and should play in connecting the world of learning to the workplace (Sharma 2014). The United Kingdom's Higher Education Statistics Agency has long reported on employability outcomes as an important metric by which to measure success at public institutions (Purcell 2014). Tom Donahue, president and CEO of the US Chamber of Commerce called for business leaders to collaborate with educators, phrasing his concerns as "among the many factors that influence the success of business and the strength of our overall economy, few matter more than human capital" (Institute for a Competitive Workforce 2012, p. 2).

In our broader construct, education policies and institutional priorities have a shared responsibility to prepare postsecondary school graduates to narrow the performance gap and recognize that diploma acquisition per se may well undershoot the mark. On the opinion page of *The Wall Street Journal*, Jim Clifton and Mitch Daniels (2013), former governor of Indiana and the current president of Purdue University, noted the opinion shared by many business executives that holding a college degree does not necessarily equate with graduate preparedness to perform in the workplace.

Others observe the dichotomy between hours that students spend online and with their cell phones, and their information literacy (Bannerline 2009). In fairness, many universities, colleges and community colleges and their programs perform these functions quite well, but societies evolve and so too must curriculum in order to retain its vitality.

Who "owns" the curriculum in higher education? Faculty, deans, and department chairs play a vital role in articulating student learning outcomes for the schools, programs, and disciplines in which they reside. The provost or chief academic officer has a critical multifunctional role in providing essential academic leadership, inspiration, resources, guidance, and process management oversight in support of quality assurance for the students.

These responsibilities are usually shared with deans, department chairs, and program directors. In the final analysis, all share accountability for providing a relevant student-centric learning environment. Prudence suggests that formal or informal feedback mechanisms from program graduates and their employers will offer insights not otherwise obtainable. To the extent that battle lines are drawn over power and control rather than an enduring commitment to a focused and value-added student-centric curriculum, students are likely to be underserved.

AN EXEMPLAR OF CHANGE: HIGHER EDUCATION MANAGEMENT PROGRAM AT UNIVERSITY OF PITTSBURGH

Curriculum changes and process management in our graduate Higher Education Management program in the School of Education at the University of Pittsburgh (Pitt) illustrate an approach to shared responsibility for the benefit of our students. The dean of our school challenged our faculty to consider changes to both our curriculum and delivery systems for our master's and educational doctoral degrees. Our faculty agreed that employability and an enhanced prospect for successful careers of our graduates in higher education would guide curriculum modifications.

While committed to the research mission of our university, we agreed upon our program mission, vision, values, overarching curriculum characteristics, and courses for distinctive tracks in student affairs and management. Knowledge acquisition and development of agreed-upon student learning outcomes influenced our planning.

Our planning mode was collegial, inclusive, and outreaching. We actively sought advice on desirable learning outcomes from senior representatives of community colleges, universities, education associations, and executive search firms. We held focus groups meetings and conference calls and conducted individual interviews. Our advisory team included community college and university presidents, deans of academic and student affairs, provosts, senior business officers, and an athletic director. Participants included national and regional representation. We drew upon reports from leading educational associations to supplement our understanding of curriculum needs. Our faculty committed to ongoing curriculum planning and redesign. In summation, our faculty made a conscious decision to be market- rather than product-driven in redefining our core curriculum.

The initial end results of our planning efforts came in various forms. Henceforth, we would require structured internships of our graduates. New courses were created, and others were modified. Some courses were dropped altogether, while others were redesigned and elevated to our educational doctoral program.

Until our proposed changes occurred, masters, EdD, and PhD students enrolled in like courses. Our faculty agreed that a "one-size-fits-all" approach no longer served the interests of our students. We further agreed that the wide array of challenges facing higher education called for future leaders with an enhanced capacity to perform with distinction as student affairs professionals and in administration.

Our EdD program affords special attention to strategic enterprise management and academic leadership within a more broadly redesigned schoolwide curriculum that is cohort based. The revised curriculum is designed for mid- and advanced-career professionals and is offered in a hybrid delivery model that includes face time and online classes. As important, the redesigned educational doctoral program provides forums for student discourse across areas of concentration.

Modifications of curriculum and delivery models occurred within a positive reinforcement environment. Redesign required high levels of collaborative planning among faculty. The changes were actively encouraged and supported by the dean of our School of Education. Approvals occurred within an existing shared-governance model, and ultimately received approval from our university provost.

Lessons learned from our case study inform our discussion of what can be achieved when processes, academic leaders, and faculty agree to serve the interests of students. Processes have not been an impediment to reform.

Deliberations and planning remain labor intensive, student centric, market oriented, and committed to continuous improvement. Tenured and tenure stream faculty, at least in our case, have not been change resistant.

We were driven by a shared determination to present greater value for students in our degree program. University and School of Education administrators understood our desires, were supportive, and respected the role of faculty. Neither individual research agendas nor tenure nor school or university bureaucracy were insurmountable obstacles to change. We reconciled concerns for academic rigor, the research interests of our faculty, and the discernible needs of our students.

ACCREDITATION AND CONTINUOUS QUALITY IMPROVEMENT

A retrospective and reflective view from the mountaintop raises as many questions as it does answers:

• Are some faculty inclined to discount the concerns expressed by employers and public officials, while others value such connectivity?
• What causes some to associate and others to disengage?
• How should institutions, programs, and academic disciplines measure success?
• Do some public officials propose to quantify institutional effectiveness and accountability in ways that may distort an understanding of performance?
• Are public officials too concerned with a limited number of indicators?
• On the other hand, are accreditation associations too focused upon internal processes without sufficient consideration of quantifiable output metrics?

A closer look at challenges facing accreditation in higher education will prove instructive.

Calls for reform of accreditation are mounting from institutional leaders and some education associations. This is especially noteworthy since regional and professional accreditation associations count upon membership dues and administrator and faculty volunteers to conduct institutional evaluations. Accreditors call upon member institutions to define their own student learning outcomes and then to examine processes, data, and planning in accordance with predetermined evaluation standards.

Some informed observers now call for a national system that defines the parameters by which to measure student learning aligned with employer expectations (Dwyer et al. 2006). Mary Corbett Broad, former president of the American Council on Higher Education (ACE), opined: "Voluntary accreditation has served higher education well in this country for more than a century . . . but in an era of global competition and increased demand for public accountability, we must ensure that accreditation is more than adequately discharging its public responsibility" (ACE 2012, p. 5).

ACE also notes that the *Higher Education Act* of 1965 inextricably linked accreditation to access to federal student aid, which effectively placed accreditation associations under the vigilance of the U.S. Department of Education. An estimated US$180 billion per annum contribution to higher education through student financial aid and tax benefits affords the federal government a voice in quality assurance and oversight (Dannenberg and Barry 2014, p. i).

A retrospective on the evolution of accreditation in the United States merits attention. Institutional, school, and program accreditation in the United States evolved as a peer review process, independent from governmental controls at the state or federal levels. Six major regional accreditation associations are responsible for institutional accreditation for their member institutions, namely Middle States Commission on Higher Education, Southern Association of Colleges and Schools, New England Association of Schools and Colleges, North Central Association of Colleges and Schools, Northwest Commission on Colleges and Universities, and Western Association of Schools and Colleges.

Another organization, Council for Higher Education Accreditation (CHEA), supports regional and professional accreditation associations in the performance of their duties. CHEA's mission is to "promote academic quality through formal recognition of higher education accrediting bodies . . . and to advance self-regulation through accreditation" (CHEA 2012). Accreditation associations offer the public assurances of academic quality, institutional effectiveness, and their financial and resource viability. CHEA regional and professional accreditation associations are supported by membership fees and volunteers from their members to perform their functions and supplement the work done by their full-time staff.

A closer study of accreditation standards proves informative. Although relatively modest differences of evaluation criteria can be found among the associations, the recently updated standards published by Middle States Commission on Higher Education (MSCHE) help us to better understand major institutional performance metrics that draw attention. A brief synopsis of those standards calls for the following:

1. A clear statement of institutional mission and purpose, plus supportive goals and actions
2. Evidence of ethics, integrity, and commitment to institutional mission, purposes, and policies

3. Academic rigor at all levels, and learning experiences consistent with higher education
4. Student admission, retention, experiences and completion that foster student success
5. Assessment of student learning and achievement based upon clearly stated educational goals
6. Applied planning and adequate resources supportive of mission and goals
7. Governance and administration in support of institutional mission, purposes and goals and devoid of conflict of interest or interference with day-to-day operations of the institution (MSCHE 2014).

Each standard includes very specific operational definitions and elaboration of assessable evaluative criteria. MSCHE's language is complete and unambiguous throughout. A review of the other five major regional accreditation associations finds very similar standards and language.

A balanced view of accreditation associations supports the view that, on the whole, they have performed well and discharge their fiduciary responsibilities effectively. Differences exist, however, between an assurance of institutional quality as opposed to performance guarantees. Just as one hopes that a qualified home inspector will detect flaws for a home buyer prior to finalizing a contract, a relatively brief study is unlikely to detect all malfunctions. Yet, times and expectations change. Just as external stakeholder expectations of institutional effectiveness grow exponentially, accreditation associations are increasingly subject to criticism for being too "soft" on their members. Some argue that peer evaluations are inherently and favorably biased and call for greater transparency and accountability.

Personal professional experiences are inherently self-limiting, yet can offer insight into the otherwise largely private world of accreditation. The first author participated in an MSCHE accreditation while at CCAC and a Southern Association of Colleges and Schools (SACS) accreditation while serving as vice chair of a college board of trustees. These experiences found accreditation processes, inquiries, and observations to be rigorous, thoughtful, and fair. Self-studies, a prerequisite of accreditor visitation, offer faculty and administrators alike an opportunity to reflect upon what works, what can improve, and an opportunity to tender recommendations accordingly. This suggests that the deeper value of accreditation can be a consequence of internal reality checks more than the final act of reaccreditation.

Accreditation associations have a long-standing concern for evaluation of student learning outcomes and institutional effectiveness. Yet, they are increasingly subject to unrelenting criticism by public officials and more private concerns from their member institutions. This causes heightened concerns about the potential for *regulatory creep* by federal and state officials desirous of invasive and more direct oversight.

A debate over regulatory and oversight turf will benefit from a broader consideration of regulatory context. Just as public accounting firms and some federal and state regulatory bodies are subject to criticism for being "too client and industry friendly," so too are accreditation commissions vulnerable to criticism. Are there occasional lapses in their processes? Perhaps. Is there a pronounced tendency to sugarcoat their concerns in official correspondence with member institutions? Maybe sometimes. Are they inherently conservative and inclined to be suspicious of change? Are those charged with oversight unfairly expected to champion reform?

Regulatory or institutional oversight is complex stuff. During the recent tenure of U.S. Secretary of Education Arnie Duncan, the U.S. Department of Education queried how certain institutions can be reaccredited while remaining financially fragile. A more deliberate and balanced study should consider how banking regulators, who in theory are far better equipped to evaluate the financial condition of national and state chartered banks, repeatedly missed opportunities to preemptively reign in worrisome lending, bond trading, and asset management practices.

A more cerebral approach suggests that the skill sets that accreditation agencies tap going forward need to expand in proportion to changes within the industry. The sad reality is that the fund accounting standards used by external auditors to examine and opine upon the financial statements of their clients offers a literal burial ground to mask issues of potential illiquidity and institutional debt. As for critics of accreditors from federal and state government, perhaps those who live in glass houses should be reluctant to throw stones.

A GLOBAL OVERVIEW OF ACCREDITATION PRACTICES

Accreditation of higher education varies from country to country. When national accreditation organizations exist, they are generally at the central government level, such as in Germany, Saudi Arabia, Sri Lanka, Taiwan, and the United Kingdom. This central government link helps provide government oversight, but it can also prove to be a hindrance to quality, autonomy, and innovation.

CHEA and the six regional accrediting agencies in the United States remain independent from central government oversight, which has long been a strength that underpins the US higher education system. This independence has helped the United States to build strong connections to industry that in many ways ensure quality standards based on industry standards of excellence. Several higher education institutions outside of the United States have sought and obtained accreditation from one of the US accrediting agencies listed above. This is often a reputation builder for international accredited HEIs in recruitment and grants procurement efforts.

In some specialized training areas such as engineering, psychology, and medicine, there are independent accrediting agencies that have in recent years helped set international standards for these respective fields. Examples include ABET[1] and the American Psychology Association,[2] which are both headquartered in the United States. The Bologna Process within the European Union and beyond includes an emphasis on higher education accreditation standards (Saarinen and Ala-Vähälä 2007) and is adhered to by 48 governments as of December 2015.

CONCLUDING OBSERVATIONS

The broader socioeconomic, political, demographic, and technological global and national context has been altered dramatically and irreversibly. Sustainable economic growth is of paramount importance to countries, employers, and employees alike. Development of human capital that is effective, is productive, and possesses multiple competencies and which adapts to rapidly changing conditions are building blocks for economic growth. G20 countries and emerging market economies share these concerns. Government officials and employers feel a sense of urgency for prudential changes from traditional higher education and hold faculty and administrators accountable.

As mentioned, US and state government officials call for marked increases in higher education degree completion and insist upon results that are transparent and supportive of economic growth. The United States suffers from quantitative and qualitative underperformance at all levels of education except for highly regarded public and private schools, public and private research universities, and elite private colleges.

In the United States, the federal and many state government officials have effectively informed accreditation associations that they will either change their ways or risk marginalization. An overarching question remains. Will degree attainment per se close the skills gap, or shall higher education meet student learning aspirations that further enhance their life and employment competencies? Or, should leaders in higher education, public policy decision-makers, and employers endeavor to form common cause around closing the performance gap?

The good news is that much is known about what needs to be done and processes that work to assure that higher education graduates *an educated person.* Higher education earns high marks for knowledge creation, but has much to learn about converting know-how toward continuous improvement of human capital. Just ask an unemployed Alf Hendricks.

NOTES

1. The Accreditation Board for Engineering and Technology (ABET) has a long history of accrediting engineering, computing, applied science, and engineering technology education that dates back to the 1930s. ABET has grown to accredit thousands of programs at some 700 higher education institutions in 28 countries (ABET 2015).

2. Founded in 1892, the APA has grown to become the world's largest body of academic and practitioner psychologists. Its mission includes the advancement of psychological knowledge, promotion of research, and establishment of standards of ethics, conduct, education, and achievement (APA 2015).

REFERENCES

ABET. 2015. *History.* Baltimore, MD: ABET. Available online at: www.abet.org; accessed on 1 September 2015.

ACT. 2013. *The Reality of College Readiness.* Iowa City, IA: ACT. Available online at: http://www.act.org/readinessreality/13/pdf/Reality-of-College-Readiness-2013. pdf; accessed on 1 September 2015.

ACT. 2015. *The Condition of College & Career Readiness 2015.* Iowa City, IA: ACT. Available online at: http://www.act.org/research/policymakers/cccr15; accessed on 26 January 2016.

American Council on Education (ACE). 2012. *Assuring Academic Quality in the 21st Century: Self-Regulation in a New Era.* Available online at: http://www.acenet.edu/ news-room/Documents/Accreditation-TaskForce-revised-070512.pdf; accessed on 1 September 2015.

American Psychological Association (APA). 2015. *About APA.* Washington, DC: APA. Available online at: www.apa.org; accessed on 1 September 2015.

Association of American Colleges and Universities (AACU). 2008. *Our Student's Best Work: A Framework for Accountability Worthy of Our Mission.* Washington, DC: AACU.

Bauerline, Mark. 2009. *The Dumbest Generation: How the Digital Age Stupefies Young Americans and Jeopardizes Our Future.* New York: Jeremy P. Tarcher/ Penguin.

Clifton, Jim, and Mitch Daniels. 2013. "A Real Measure of Higher Ed Success." *Wall Street Journal*, December 17, p. A17.

Community College of Allegheny County (CCAC). 2005. *General Education Learning Goals.* Pittsburgh, PA: CCAC. Available online at: www.ccac.edu; accessed on 1 September 2015.

Dannenberg, Michael, and Mary Nguyen Barry. 2014. "Tough Love: Bottom-Line Quality Standards for Colleges." Washington, DC: The Education Trust.

Dwyer, Carol A, Catherine M. Millett, and David G. Payne. 2006. *A Culture of Evidence: Postsecondary Assessment and Learning Outcomes. Educational Testing Service.* Princeton, NJ: ETS.

Eaton, Judith S. 2012. *An Overview of U.S. Accreditation.*" Washington, DC: Council for Higher Education Accreditation.

The Economist Intelligence Unit. 2014. "Closing the Skills Gap: Companies and Colleges Collaborating for Change." London: *The Economist* Intelligence Unit.

Hart Research Associates. 2013. "It Takes More than a Major: Employer Priorities for College Learning and Student Success." Washington, DC: Association of American Colleges and Universities. Available online at: https://www.aacu.org; accessed on 10 April 2013.

Hughes, Sean. 2015. Discussion with Stewart E. Sutin at his home, Pittsburgh, PA, 12 November 2015. Hughes is Professor Emeritus at the University of Pittsburgh.

Institute for a Competitive Workplace. 2012. *Education Reform Playbook.* Washington, DC: Institute for a Competitive Workplace.

Middle States Commission on Higher Education (MSCHE). 2014. *Standards for Accreditation and Requirements of Affiliation.* Philadelphia, PA: MSCHE.

Purcell, Wendy. 2014, June 13. "Essay Says Colleges and Universities Should be Judged by Employability." *Inside Higher Ed.* Available online at: http://insidehighered.com; accessed on 1 September 2015.

Reif, Frederick. 2008. *Applying Cognitive Science to Education.* Cambridge: MIT Press.

Rhodes, Frank H. T. 2001. *The Role of the American University: The Creation of the Future.* Ithaca, NY: Cornell University Press.

Rosenbaum, James. 2001. *Beyond College For All: Career Paths for the Forgotten Half.* Albany NY: Russell Sage Foundation.

Saarinen, Taina, and Timo Ala-Vähälä. 2007. "Accreditation, the Bologna Process and National Reactions: Accreditation as Concept and Action." *Higher Education in Europe* 32 (4): 333–345.

Sharma, Yojana. 2014, December 19. "Universities and Employability—Preparing for Work." *University World News*, Global Edition, No. 348, pp. 1–3.

Soares, Louis, and Laura W. Perna. 2014. *Readiness for the Learning Economy: Insights from OECD's Survey of Adult Skills on Workforce Readiness and Preparation.* Issue Brief. Washington, DC: ACE & Center for Policy Research and Strategy.

Wager, Tony. 2010. *The Global Achievement Gap: Why Even Our Best Schools Don't Teach the New Survival Skills Our Children Need—And What We Can Do about It.* New York: Basic Books.

Wolf, Alison. 2002. *Does Education Matter: Myths About Education and Economic Growth.* London: Penguin.

Chapter 6

A Practitioner's Guide to Systemic Reform and Increasing Financial Effectiveness

Dr. J.P. Friendly was named president and chief executive officer (CEO) of the State University of Peninsula at Erie (SUPE) in 2004. Full-time undergraduate student enrollment at the time of his inauguration was 6,256, with an additional 950 graduate students enrolled in a wide range of professional and liberal arts degree programs. Eighty-five percent of its students were Pennsylvania residents, with most of the remaining students coming from Eastern Ohio and other Midwestern states. Six-year graduation rates averaged 54 percent.

Originally founded in 1895 as a Normal College to prepare primary and secondary school teachers, SUPE gradually broadened its program offerings and curriculum and became an official state-supported university in 1956. Its majors in education, business administration, nursing, pharmacy, science, and math had achieved some measure of distinction within their service region. Approximately 40 percent of its revenues came from state budget allocations, with most of the remainder dependent upon student tuition and fees.

Shortly after becoming president, Dr. Friendly expanded the institutional mission to embrace research and added new doctoral programs in nine academic and professional disciplines. His proposals were approved by the board of trustees, the system chancellor, and shared governance in the form of consent from the university senate. The president had formerly been the provost of SUPE for eight years and had envisioned these initiatives as a centerpiece of an ambitious educational agenda to recruit nationally acclaimed research faculty.

Dr. Friendly believed that SUPE's 725-acre campus 20 miles east of Erie could readily accommodate 10,000 undergraduates and 2,500 graduate students by 2014. School deans and department chairs in select fields were encouraged to hire more research tenure stream faculty, and were allocated funds for that purpose.

In an effort to "play in the big leagues," Dr. Friendly and his leadership team developed a facilities master plan to showcase the university. The board of trustees, with encouragement from the system chancellor, approved a bond issue in 2006 to incur US$375 million of long-term debt for the purpose of building two new dormitories, modernizing and expanding the student union, adding a new academic building, and renovating an old recreation hall into a state-of-the-art gymnasium and physical fitness center.

Dr. Friendly committed to lead a US$150 million capital campaign, with most of the funds dedicated to facility construction, modernization, and student scholarships. Based upon existing multiyear financial plans for the state university system, Dr. Friendly further assumed that state funding for public universities would be sustained at prevailing levels, and that enrollment growth would generate incremental revenues to service institutional debt and the costs of hiring more research faculty.

The financial consequences of Dr. Friendly's decisions meant that institutional expenses would rise by 11.5 percent in two years relative to the annual operating and capital budgets approved for 2006. This resulted from new faculty hires consistent with the expanded university research mission, staff hired in advance of anticipated enrollment increases, lease payments on acquired technology and equipment, and new construction expenses. The board of trustees and the system chancellor had known Dr. Friendly for many years, and his sound academic leadership had earned their confidence and support.

Financial plans did not cover contingencies in the eventuality that Dr. Friendly's favorable revenue assumptions failed to materialize. SUPE's chief financial officer (CFO), George Shidlowski, privately cautioned Dr. Friendly about potential adverse consequences of significant expense increases should revenue growth assumption not materialize. He was also concerned about rising operating costs such as the cost-of-living increases in union contracts, the lack of a financial contingency plan, and rising costs to maintain aging facilities. In public forums, however, Mr. Shidlowski was supportive of his president.

The downturn in the national and regional economy in 2008–2009 could not have come at a worse time for SUPE. Unemployment in Western Pennsylvania climbed to 11.6 percent. Mortgage loan defaults and uncertainties of postgraduation employment caused many students and their parents to defer plans to enroll in college. Pennsylvania's state budget suffered from declining revenues as tax dollars from personal income and corporate sources were reduced. Between 2008 and 2013, state funding for four-year public colleges was reduced by over 30 percent in inflation-adjusted dollars.

To make matters worse, SUPE's undergraduate student enrollment decreased by 4 percent in 2013–2014 to 6,005 from its 2006 peak. In sum, the financial outlook for budget deficits had become a source of grave concern for

Dr. Friendly, his board of trustees, and the system chancellor. Sustainability of the institutional financial model was in doubt. What choices were available to SUPE's president and its board of trustees?

INSTITUTIONAL FINANCIAL MANAGEMENT

The scenario presented in our hypothetical university illustrates financial challenges facing an increasing number of community colleges, liberal arts colleges, and public and private colleges and universities in the United States as public subsidies and enrollments decline. The recent announcement to close Sweet Briar College, which was afterward temporarily rescinded by the intervention of the attorney general of the Commonwealth of Virginia, reminds us of the financial crisis facing a growing number of higher education institutions.

Only 14 percent of the chief business officers (our book uses the title of chief financial officer, or CFO) surveyed in 2015 by Gallup (2015, p. 9) for *Inside Higher Ed* strongly agree that their institutions' current financial model is sustainable over the next ten years. That still leaves a majority of those surveyed with various degrees of uncertainty. This chapter examines strategic and tactical approaches toward improving institutional business models.

EVIDENCE-BASED BUDGETS AND FINANCIAL PLANNING

The old adage "hope for the best but plan for the worst" applies to institutional financial planning. Data analysis is of paramount importance. In the broadest sense, examination of financial data should occur on two levels, namely through annual operating and capital budgets and through medium-term financial planning. Both must assure institutional financial sustainability, while allocating constrained financial resources to short- and medium-term education and student support priorities.

Annual operating and capital budgets and medium-term financial plans are indispensable tools to calibrate and manage financial resources. Assumptions must be identified, commented upon, and questioned. Trend analysis of the prior three-year revenues and expenses should identify sources of concern. Multiyear financial plans offer important perspective to decisions relating to approval of annual operating and capital budgets by board members and institutional leadership.

The review processes will benefit from creating and stress-testing multiple revenue generation and expense containment scenarios. Projections should quantify the anticipated results from redesign of the institutional business model through generating more revenues from nontraditional sources and containment of discretionary operating expenses. Year-over-year incremental line-item budget creation processes do not afford depth of analysis to materially alter an institutional business model.

Data Analytics, Budgets, and Financial Planning Practices

The CFO plays a mission-critical role in evidence-based financial management and planning. Sound practice calls for the CFO to annually provide a detailed analysis of the prevailing institution's financial condition and the medium-term outlook, along with annual operating and capital budgets. This data is subject to review and approval by the president and board of trustees. Annual budgets and medium-term financial projections should include integrative plans to

1. align financial resources with institutional and functional priorities,
2. increase sustainable revenues from nontraditional sources,
3. reduce operating expenses through improving operating efficiencies,
4. sustain balanced budgets,
5. generate cash flow to effect payments for short- and long-term liabilities,
6. keep institutional short- and long-term debt within levels that can be serviced by projected cash flow, and
7. include financial provisions for contingencies in the event of adverse unpredictable events.

Stand-alone annual and capital budget proposals do not offer sufficient context for either the president or the board of trustees to make informed decisions.

Annual budget creation and financial plans offer opportunities to rethink and reenvision academic, student services, and other priorities and redesign the institutional business model. Out-of-the-box thinking should be encouraged as opposed to year-to-year budget incrementalism in which line-item revenues from the prior year are modified by some amount for the new year. A more radical approach might include periodic application of so-called zero-based budgets, which approaches costs and revenues as if a *de novo* institution were being launched. Beware. The potential utility of the zero-based budget approach rests more with idea creation, whereas actual implementation of a zero-based budget rigor may cause the cure to be worse than the sum of underlying problems.

Some institutions appear to use comparatively primitive tools to contain costs. In these cases, line-item budget management is often the primary driver of financial remedies. This approach encourages greater faculty productivity and lower costs in the short run by increasing the size of course section enrollment and hiring more adjunct faculty. The ranks of secretaries and certain support staff may be reduced. Salaries may be occasionally frozen or incremental increases for nonunionized staff may be restrained. Positions vacated by retirement or departures may not be filled for a while, or ever. Travel and entertainment budgets may be reduced. Allocations for repair and maintenance can be temporarily restricted. In some cases, academic departments are closed or merged. Many of these measures, however important in the short term, are often unsustainable over time.

Process management offers important ways to assure that the integrity of budgets and financial plans and that both arise within an environment that encourages broad participation and contesting of ideas. The CFO should send financial challenges or targets ahead of time to all participants as a way of stimulating debate and to infuse financial realities into budget preparation and financial planning at all levels of the institution. *Budget hearing*

Use of budget hearings allows senior administrators an opportunity to identify priorities consistent with the institutional mission and enduring goals and to quantify their resource needs. All should be encouraged to offer revenue generation and expense containment initiatives as evidence of their ability to organically generate financial resources internally to support additional expenses elsewhere.

This process calls for questioning of underlying assumptions, and stress-testing multiple scenarios will help determine the probability of certain outcomes. For example, suppose a vice president of Academic and Student Affairs proposes incremental spending predicated upon increasing revenues from enrollment growth, one might question the plans of action intended to assure improving student retention and increasing admissions. The CFO and vice president should also agree upon a contingency plan in the event that enrollment growth and related revenue growth does not materialize.

INDICATORS OF FINANCIAL CONDITION

A rigorous process calls for additional data examination to assure institutional sustainability. This requires probing beneath budget line items and quantifying any significant gaps that may appear between sources and uses of cash. Solvency is a function of paying bills as they come due. Hence, distinguishing between short- and long-term assets and liabilities, or so-called liquidity analysis, is key to understanding an institutions' financial condition.

What are short-term assets and liabilities and why do they matter? Short-term assets include such items as cash, investments due to mature within

12 months, and accounts receivable from tuition, fees, and room and board, which are likely to convert to cash within a year. Short-term liabilities include accounts payable, credit card debt, mortgage payments, insurance premiums, utility bills, current portion of long-term bank or bond debt, lease payments, vendor or trade obligations, payroll, and other items due and payable within 12 months.

Short-term liabilities require proportionate sums of short-term assets to sustain operations and solvency. A rule of thumb is that short-term assets on the balance sheet should exceed short-term liabilities by a reasonable margin, and may be thought of as constituting the working capital position. In addition, institutional balance sheet net assets should exceed total liabilities by a reasonable margin, or what we might think of as institutional debt to worth or leverage. A highly leveraged institution is one where total liabilities exceed net assets, thereby placing excessive pressures on cash generation.

Accounting Practices, Assessing Financial Condition, and the Chief Financial Officer

The importance of the CFO in analyzing the actual and projected financial condition of an institution, reporting on same, and acting as a change agent cannot be overstated. In some cases, such as analysis of institutional financial statements, the role of CFO is more nuanced. The role of the CFO as institutional guide and mentor to enhance the financial literacy of the president, other senior administrators, board members, faculty, and other staff should not be undervalued.

Fund accounting can be confusing, even for those with a reasonable financial and accounting background. It provides the standards by which educational institutions present their financial statements. The standard accounting practices applicable to fund accounting differ in certain important respects from how other industries present their financial statements. For example, in fund accounting total assets and liabilities may be grouped together, with no differentiation between short- and long-term maturities. In addition, fund accounting does not provide an income statement per se.

Instead, revenues and expenses are quantified by category. To the extent that accumulated revenues exceed total expenses, the financial statements reflect an addition to net assets in that amount. The reverse is true should total expenses exceed total revenues. Hence, fund accounting does not use such terms as operating gains or losses. Net assets may be thought of as the higher education accounting proxy for net worth.

In order to interpret current financial data and model future projections, the CFO must probe beneath the numbers and offer thoughtful and understandable narratives to key stakeholders of factors that cause financial outcomes.

Adequacy of cash flow and excess of short-term assets over short-term liabilities (e.g., working capital) are of pivotal importance to assure institutional solvency and a sustainable business model. Likewise, debt-to-worth ratio (e.g., net assets) merits attention. Net assets should exceed total liabilities by a reasonable margin in order to assure that debt service payments do not imperil solvency.

Of particular interest are bank and bond indebtedness relative to debt service capacity. How much debt is too much? How many colleges and universities borrow at high levels with the hope of increasing student enrollment through building newly constructed dorms? Higher levels of debt should be accompanied by realistic plans to reduce those obligations, and contingency plans in the event that expenses rise above forecast levels and/or revenues fail to meet expectations.

Certain financial statement indicators such as liquidity, working capital, cash flow analysis, and leverage or debt-to-worth ratios help explain the financial condition of a college or university. Rating agencies, banks, and, increasingly, the U.S. Department of Education, apply these and other tools when examining and reporting on the financial condition of colleges and universities. The CFO is tasked with providing full, timely, and accurate reports, commenting upon what stakeholders need to know to meet their fiduciary responsibilities and offering choices to act upon.

Management reporting to the president, other senior administrators, and the board of trustees by the CFO should occur at least quarterly and include comments on key financial indicators, positive or negative budget variances, and the financial outlook. An objective and thoughtful study of current financial conditions and the future outlook should afford leaders timing and opportunity needed to make important adjustment to spending practices.

Communications Plans and Emergency Measures

Undisclosed institutional financial challenges or crises represent opportunities lost. The president, CFO, and other members of the president's cabinet are obliged to develop and implement a communication plan that calls for sharing information with their board of trustees on a timely basis, and afterward with other stakeholders. The president and CFO should dimension the financial challenges facing the institution for stakeholders and the likely consequences of failing to act. In the event of an imminent crisis, senior administrators are obliged to assume a lead role to quantify the problem, ascertain the underlying causes, and propose a financial intervention plan.

The leadership team bears primary responsibility to design an emergency plan for review and approval by the board. Respect for the norms of shared governance and labor union contractual obligations merit attention.

But depending upon the immediacy and extent of financial destabilization, shared-governance processes may need to be temporarily suspended, especially on actions relating to administrative costs. While every effort should be made to invite faculty collaboration in problem solving, some difficult decisions may render broad institutional support difficult to achieve and traditional vetting processes too slow. Notwithstanding this important qualifier, when times and conditions permit, it is prudent to share information with internal constituents and to invite their comments and suggestions.

In tandem with short-term measures, administrators and other internal stakeholders are well advised to codevelop a longer-term, more strategic, and comprehensive intervention plan to assure ongoing institutional sustainability. In short, it is incumbent upon the president to be the institutional voice and to openly communicate the case for reform with honesty, integrity, and a sense of urgency as a precursor of pursuing remedial actions, while enacting changes as may be required. This is consistent with the need for the president and senior leaders to be grounded in core values and essential leadership characteristics as reflected in the Higher Education Leadership Wheel introduced in chapter 1.

Boards of trustees bear primary fiduciary responsibility to assure institutional sustainability. The president, CFO, and other senior administrators are accountable to the board and have the duty of acting and planning in ways that inspire confidence. Presidents count upon board members for support, especially when difficult personnel and other related financial decisions are required. Boards may anticipate adverse actions from faculty, other employees, and even administrators who are adversely affected by interventions. They are well advised to plan ahead in the eventuality of countervailing actions such as letters to newspapers, public demonstrations, and/or faculty votes of no confidence. Declining morale may be anticipated, merit attention, and should not be dismissed as "collateral damage."

Imminent Problems and Institutional Responses

When concerns arise about the financial condition of a college, the CEO and president's cabinet recommend emergency measures for approval by the board of trustees. Their initial task is to identify revenue-generating and expense containment options that can be acted upon quickly. The financial and other consequences of these measures should be quantified. This allows leadership to determine anticipated cash flow shortfalls that remain after the emergency actions are implemented.

Leadership is counted upon to identify emergency measures and assign execution responsibilities to appropriate administrators. By acting upon so-called low-hanging fruit, leadership and the board offer a proof statement of their determination to remediate financial challenges. Information should alert internal constituents to the underlying causes of the financial squeeze and to the fact that "tough times require tough decisions." This requires quantifying the financial problems at hand and the likely impact of adopting emergency measures as required to address the difficulties.

The intent of a short-term action plan is to accomplish as much as possible as soon as possible, while recognizing that enduring solutions often require more time, effort, and comprehensive solutions. Of paramount importance is the need to appreciate that short-term "fixes" such as temporary freezes of salary, hiring freezes, and deferring repairs and maintenance are unsustainable over time. Other actions, such as reducing travel budgets and holding off on costly new construction, can be retained for longer periods of time.

Very often, emergency measures begin by examining all line items in an institutional operating budget and making case-by-case decisions. Actions begin with contracting certain discretionary expenses, with all options subject to review and approval by the president and the board of trustees. In doing so, the president and other senior administrators must be cognizant that their own direct costs and actions are subject to scrutiny by a potentially hostile audience.

Financial intervention plans should recognize the importance of sound leadership, reflective decision-making, collaborative problem solving, fostering an awareness of institutional context, and determining to chart a course for institutional survival. This presupposes that institutional leaders believe the following:

1. Appeals for a publicly funded rescue plan are not likely to be successful
2. Material increases in tuition and fees are apt to result in still lower enrollment
3. Raising funds through additional bank borrowings or bond issues will not mitigate underlying causes of disequilibrium
4. Short-term emergency measures are insufficient to mitigate financial woes
5. Institutional financial and short-term remedies will only "buy time" before launching more comprehensive, strategic, and systemic reforms

This calls upon leaders to plan strategically and undertake all necessary measures required to implement annual operating plans.

STRATEGIC RESPONSES FOR A SUSTAINABLE BUSINESS MODEL

Strategic responses are requisite for much of traditional higher education amid ongoing external financial and educational challenges. Prerequisites to systemic reforms include (1) leadership recognition that the sum of day-to-day operational decisions are inadequate to solve complex challenges, (2) a capacity to think strategically about sustainable competitive advantages, (3) a will to make difficult decisions, and (4) an understanding that, in the words of Ralph H. Kilmann (2004, p. x), "complex problems cannot be solved by simple solutions." Going forward, institutional effectiveness will be defined as ability to clarify strategic priorities, accompanied by the capacity to implement them.

Sustainable institutional educational and business models rely upon the thoughtful integration of strategic and tactical responses. Retired Marine Corps General Tony Zinni and Tony Koltz (2014, p. 12) argue that "politics and policy must be aligned with the strategy, and the strategy must be aligned with the operational design on the ground." They further note the imperative that "decision makers need information, the more solid the better, and the more timely the better" (p. 43). While allowing for the many distinctive characteristics of higher education institutions, we can learn from the knowledge and wisdom acquired by highly effective leaders from other domains. The following descriptors in Table 6.1 differentiate strategic from tactical responses.

Table 6.1   Strategic vs. Tactical Responses

Strategic Responses	*Tactical Responses*
Time horizon: minimum of three years	Actionable within one year
Reenvision mission	Assesses resource implications of mission
Articulates a vision	Embraces accountability
Expresses institutional priorities, purposes, and enduring goals in longer time horizons	Aligns one-year operating objectives with priorities
Examines external challenges, trends, and opportunities	Assesses organizational strengths and weaknesses
Plans are evidence based, ongoing, and include both educational priorities and a sustainable business model	Sets qualitative and quantitative key performance indicators to measure progress and success
Focuses upon sustainable competitive advantages	Thinks about plan execution and use of performance evaluations
Collegiality, creativity, and agility are valued	Results matters
Considers institutional culture	Develops plans to overcome impediments to change
Will to "stop being all things to all people"	Questions "sacred cows"
Develops a broad educational and student support agenda	Allocates financial, human, technological, and facilities resources with annual operating plans and objectives
Ongoing examination of environmental changes	Designs and executes implementation plans
Values the "big picture" and worries about winning the war	Adjusts to unpredictable events and fixates on winning the battle

Institutional Strategic Plans and Tactical Responses

Committed leadership and a balance between long-term strategic initiatives and short-term actions are drivers of institutional transformation in environments too often unaccustomed to change. Efforts to systemically transform higher education should be mindful of detractors and cynicism from within. Some faculty and administrators question the value and applicability of strategic and long-term financial planning.

Others argue that higher education is unique and serves the greater purposes of knowledge acquisition and behavioral growth of its students. Many worry about changes that may impair academic freedom. Some view institutional planning as commercialization and unnecessarily invasive of the academic domain. They posit that the role of college is so distinctive that no good can come from subjecting it to an approach used by other industries. One may, however, reason that while the services rendered by higher education may be unique, lessons can be learned from others who have faced similar challenges over the years and found solutions.

In order to overcome these criticisms, thoughtful attention to processes, scope, and purposes of a strategic plan matters. The time has come for an industry dedicated to data gathering and evaluation of evidence to apply such skills to beneficial internal applications.

Processes and Plans

Strategic planning requires the president and board of trustees agreeing upon processes, scope, and end-game expectations. Their steadfast support for strategic responses to changing market forces is essential. Unaffordable or vague mission statements fail to provide a basis for setting and communicating clear institutional priorities and enduring goals. A clear institutional purpose offers a basis to redesign an institutional academic, student affairs, and business model and for rational allocation of resources. Jim Collins (2001) perceptibly suggests that institutions must "first face brutal facts of reality" and "create a climate where truth is heard" (pp. 70, 74).

Some may wish to consider hiring an external consultant should those in the Office of Institutional Research lack the experience to oversee strategic planning. In either case, leadership must develop a plan-to-plan which provides the board, the president, other senior administrators, and other stakeholders with a mapping of processes, actions, timelines, and responsibilities requisite to develop and execute an institutional strategic plan. Once the board and president agree upon an approach, forums for open communication and collaboration among internal stakeholders should be put in place.

Strategic Plans, Process Management, and the Role of Leaders

Many believe that the president must own the institutional mission, vision, and statement of purpose. Ultimate accountability does reside with the CEO. But the president need not originate all ideas and innovation separate and apart from other internal stakeholders. On the contrary, depersonalization of systemic reform offers a higher potential for strategy to be embraced by a broader constituency and a greater likelihood for priorities to become institutionalized. It is one thing for a president to commit to a plan for change. It is altogether different for the president to be the singular author or driving force behind that change.

Either way, institutional transformation must integrate plans for a new, more vibrant, and sustainable business model into its model for systemic reform. Certain guiding principles, such as improving the quality of education and directly related student support services, offer important guides to planning.

Multiple models for developing an institutional strategic plan are available. John P. Kotter (1996) makes the case for appointing a guiding coalition. In higher education, we are more accustomed to think of a steering committee (SC). Assisted by either the head of institutional research or an external consultant, the president and board should think about the composition of those invited to participate on the SC, its size, and its functions. The SC would report to the CEO and agree upon a timetable to communicate and discuss their findings.

The size, composition, and credentials of an SC merit attention, along with articulation of guiding principles by the president. This calls for the CEO to comment upon the objectives of the SC and to note their responsibilities and which consequences are desirable and others that are unacceptable. Among the latter, one would expect that actions that may adversely impact quality of education and student service support are unacceptable.

The president may nominate the institution's chief academic officer, the head of student affairs, the CFO, and/or the chief information officer to represent administration. Faculty should be invited to participate, with special attention to their expertise, experience in collaborative problem solving, creativity, and whose integrity and credibility are accepted system-wide (Kotter 2001). Representation from student government, the alumni association, and external stakeholders are worthy of consideration. Total participation on the SC of between 12 to 20 members should help assure quality of discourse.

The SC may be used one of two ways. It may oversee the work of other standing committees tasked with distinctive responsibilities, or it may serve as the sole planning committee, while being assigned subcommittee tasks. There are advantages and disadvantages of each approach. Organizational size and

Table 6.2   Planning Committee Schematic

Standing Committee	Tasks	Estimated Timeline
Mission, Vision, and Values	Propose mission, vision, and values	3–6 months
Environmental Scan	Identify and evaluate external opportunities and threats	months 1–3
SWOT Analysis	Examine institutional strengths and weaknesses relative to opportunities and threats	months 4–6
Educational Quality Assurance	Recommend enduring and general education goals and academic priorities	months 1–12
Student Affairs Planning	Propose service improvements and use of technology to improve student retention	months 1–12
Revenue Generation Plans	Recommend creative ways to improve revenue generation from traditional and nontraditional sources	months 1–12
Expense Containment Plans	Study organizational structure and processes and recommend ways to improve institutional effectiveness and efficiency	months 1–12
Informational, Instructional, and Operational Technology Plans	Propose uses of technology to improve learning outcomes and operational efficiencies	months 1–12
Implementation Plans*	Develop action plans and assign responsibilities and timing	Ongoing
Resource Allocation Plans*	CEO, CFO, and board agree upon resource allocation consistent with institutional priorities	Ongoing

*Implementation and resource allocations should be integrated into annual operating plans, featured objectives for the school year, operating and capital budgets, and performance objective setting and evaluation processes.

complexity will help guide appropriate planning processes. Either way, the shared objective is to deliver to the president and board of trustees an evidence-based strategic or prioritized plan within the time frame agreed upon. Some example tasks assigned to members of the SC are shown in Table 6.2.

Continuous Improvement

The magnitude and scope of our changing environment suggests that ongoing leadership commitment to change, strategic, and tactical responses will be the

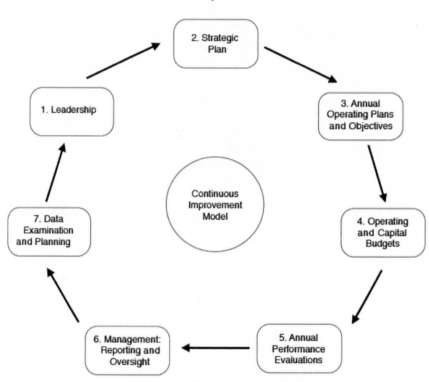

Figure 6.1   Higher Education Continuous Improvement Model.

new normal. Figure 6.1 depicts operationalizing systemic reforms in a higher education setting.

Year-to-year operating plans, management reporting, and oversight assure alignment with strategic priorities while adapting tactically to unpredicted events. All are intended to assure the quality of education and student support services, the informed applications of technology, and the vitality of a business model supportive of sustainable academic quality and an affordable and accessible education. Such ambitious objectives raise questions about the types of skills required of leaders of traditional higher education needed to transform their institutional business models.

INCREASING FINANCIAL SELF-RELIANCE

Until recent years, much of traditional higher education relied upon a revenue-generated business model in which tuition, fees, room and board, subsidies from state and local governments, allocations from endowments, and ancillary enterprises such as bookstores were intended to cover annual operating expenses. Universities with a research mission reflected substantial grant funding on their financial statements, notwithstanding whether true costs of research exceeded funding. To the extent that expenses exceeded revenues, prices for tuition, fees, and room and board increased.

This model became vulnerable at those institutions where enrollments declined and/or reduced funding from public sources was reduced for community colleges, four-year public, and public research universities. Chapter 8 relates lessons learned from exemplars of change who successfully pioneered more self-reliant business models, which will offer insights into revenue-generating success stories. Chapters 8 and 9 offer revenue enhancement and cost containment choices available to institutions.

Redesign of institutional mission, clarifying and communicating institutional priorities, and applying strategic and tactical responses toward the enhanced well-being of students and other internal and external constituents is achievable when built upon what works and either discarding or substantially changing that which no longer serves a purpose. Perhaps most important is the need to understand that educational, student affairs, and business models cannot be allowed to evolve within silos, but as integrated means toward achieving shared goals. Operating and capital budgets and accumulative human resource decisions in the absence of shared commitment to institutional long-term priorities are a formula for failure. Just as society values lifelong learning for individuals, so too must colleges and universities adjust to changing times as going concerns or risk marginalization or a worse fate.

Cost Containment and Operating Efficiencies

Regardless of perspective, political leaders often justify reduced budgetary allocations to higher education based upon a pronounced view that higher education is resistant to reform and does not manage its resources effectively. The Spellings Commission Report noted "with concern the seemingly inexorable increase in college costs, which have outpaced inflation for the past two decades and have made affordability an ever-growing worry for students, families, and policymakers" (U.S. Department of Education 2006, p. 2). Apart from cost savings, hopefully passed along in part to students in the form of reductions in tuition and fees, a leaner, more streamlined, lower labor content processes in a highly efficient operating environment permit administration to allocate more resources toward the quality of instruction and student support.

Improving institutional financial effectiveness relies upon multiple initiatives. For example, process reengineering offers substantial potential to reduce costs while improving quality of educational and support services for students. Investment in operational technologies and delegation of decision-making authority is done to assure migration away from relatively high-labor and paper-intensive content to processes that are more responsive and less costly.

In other industries, the evolution of home banking offers convenient customer services at a far lower operating cost for the bank. In the airlines industry, passenger printing out of boarding passes provides a valuable customer service, with resultant cost benefit reductions to the carriers. The more recent migration to student self-enrollment in courses offers a similar convenience and lowers institutional costs associated with manual paper-intensive processes. Increasing use of predictive analytics and career pathway software offer valuable tools for students to design a coherent approach to degree or certificate completion. Collaborative project teams should examine each and every institutional service and process for the purpose of identifying ways to assure greater efficiency, lower costs, and enhanced services for the end users.

Cost Containment, Educational and Student Service Priorities

A Delta Cost Project study of employment trends and cost structures in higher education observed that in 1990 the ratio of full-time faculty to noninstructional staff was an estimated 2:1 at public non-research universities, and two decades later it was about 1:1. Most growth occurred in professional positions such as business analysts, human resources management, computer support, counselors, and athletics. These positions now average about 20–25 percent of on-campus jobs (Desrochers and Kirshstein 2014, pp. 3–4, 8, 13).

The authors acknowledge that some of this growth was proportional to increasing enrollments. Perhaps, the question is less one of whether tasks and responsibilities assigned to each professional are justifiable than whether a more critical examination of the environment in which they function and the processes governing their activities can transition to more cost-efficient models.

Work to reduce instructional costs has already taken place at many institutions, as evidenced by the shrinking percent of higher education operating budgets allocated to this function. Adjuncts constitute a significant and growing component of the instructional workforce. Class sections are growing in size. Online education is growing rapidly, albeit not in consistently cost-effective ways or with the best quality. Academic departments or disciplines with lower enrollments are either being closed, or fewer faculty are retained.

One way or another, traditional higher education is coming to terms with cost-effective instructional productivity. Some initiatives may not impair the quality of education, while others might. The eventual impact of massive open online courses (MOOCs) on the cost containment side of education remains to be determined. We do know that it is very labor intensive and costly to design and prepare courses taught for the first time online or via blended learning. So, building online education to scale in quality-controlled environments will take time.

More subtle instructional cost factors are worthy of attention. Containment of instructional costs should be considered in a broader institutional context, starting with the institutional mission. So-called mission creep, or gradual expansion of the core institutional statement of purpose, comes at a price. For example, how many four-year public and private colleges and universities have embraced expensive research missions, accompanied by reduced instructional loads for tenure and tenure stream faculty? What is the correlation between the quality of undergraduate instruction and an institutional research mission? Is student retention and graduation more likely when their faculty are full-time and dedicated primarily to instruction?

The time has come to reconsider the core institutional mission from a cost and benefit perspective rather than as an assumed constant. At a national level, it is likely that a market-driven student quest for affordable tuition and accompanying institutional need for enrollment growth will cause many institutions to either exit the expensive playing field of research or more narrowly focus their ambitions on fewer programs where they aspire to national or international recognition.

A second and even less obvious driver of instructional cost derives from a blurring of curriculum, one in which new courses are created, sometimes required, based more upon the passions of faculty than a thoughtful student-centric construct. Institutional agreement upon general education goals is foundational to redesign of curriculum, course offerings, and syllabi. These goals represent a form of contract with students and a commitment to a focused set of deliverables. Conversely, lack of focused curriculum bares incremental costs through a proliferation of courses of indeterminate benefit to students.

Twenty-five years ago, the now-classic *The Lattice and the Ratchet* was released by the Pew Higher Education Research Program (1990). With unrelenting 20-20 vision, the authors diagnosed the causality of a growing and expensive administrative lattice, accompanied by an academic ratchet. The authors urged higher education "to become more competitive—leaner, perhaps meaner, certainly more focused, with simpler organizations and a greater ability to make collective investments in targeted programs and projects" (p. 8).

That so little has changed within the paradigm of traditional higher education since this study was released inspires neither confidence nor optimism. It now appears more likely that unrelenting pressure from such market forces as student enrollment trends, rapid growth of online instruction, and a movement toward either reduced public funding or performance-based funding in certain states may accomplish from without what traditional higher education could not bring about from within.

Organizational Structure

Organizational structure in much of higher education remains complex, relatively static and costly to maintain. Signature approvals for relatively mundane day-to-day transactions are often controlled by relatively few in the hierarchy. Relatively high noninstructional and nonstudent support costs in much of traditional higher education are high. Too little is understood about best practices of enterprise management. Adaptive organizations respond effectively to their evolving environments and are more sustainable by adapting newer and more vibrant behaviors. They are more responsive to their customer needs, less bureaucratic, and more productive.

Attention should be given to organizational structure for the purpose of rendering it more responsive to a changing environment, eliminating or reducing duplicative functions, examining opportunities to cull nonessential administrative staff, and aligning authority with accountability. Integration of financial, educational, student services, technologies, and facilities plans is fundamental to assurance that resources align with institutional priorities. This integrative approach is in marked contrast to functional or unit-based budget creation and may reduce turf conflicts surrounding ineffectual legacy institutional silos.

Substantial expertise about organizational structure, change management, and process innovation resides in business schools at universities. Thomas Davenport and Michael Hammer focus upon process reengineering. Davenport (1993) suggests that one begin with an inventory of major processes and proceed to examine ways to streamline them for efficiency and lower labor content. Hammer (1996) urges us to differentiate between processes before turning attention to individual tasks within those processes. This allows organizations to figure out ways to render structures and processes more effective, eliminate or simplify tasks, and make greater use of operational technology.

Reenvisioning organizational structures and redesigning administrative and professional processes for efficiency offer substantial potential to provide like or better quality of services at reduced cost. Raymond E. Miles and Charles C. Snow (2003) are authorities on organizational structure and behavior. They believe that organizations that retain their vitality and relevance "engage in an ongoing process of evaluating their purposes, questioning verifying and redefining the manner in which they interact with their environments" (p. 3).

Jeffrey K. Liker and James K. Franz (2011), both experts on industrial best practices and The Toyota Way, call for continuous improvement in which top leadership and workers at all levels participate. Notwithstanding

Toyota's recent and repeated errors of quality control and risk management, the processes work when problems are identified, root causes of substandard performance or inefficiencies are understood, detailed plans are completed to remediate the problems, results are carefully monitored, and new and higher performance standards are put in place.

CONCLUDING OBSERVATIONS

We should reflect upon what about higher education needs to change, and what does not. Knowledge creation and delivery and behavioral growth of its students are sacrosanct functions. Institutional legacy, culture, mission, and sense of purpose are valuable. Developments of competencies that will serve graduates well in life and in the workplace are vital functions. If anything, these outcomes are worth enhancing. In this context, sound, evidence-based, and integrative financial planning and management will support these beneficial results while transitioning to a more sustainable business model. This approach encourages strategic resource allocation consistent with institutional priorities and a migration away from day-to-day task management that leaves inefficient operating processes and costly organizational structures intact.

Leaner and more cost-effective organizational structures and operational processes can be achieved while improving the quality of education and student support services. Large multicampus community colleges and universities reflect upon cost savings through consolidation of certain administrative positions and centralizing procurement functions. All operating processes are subject to review and cost and benefit analysis that call for greater use of technology and fewer "touch points" between the party initiating a request and provision of service. Process innovation and structural change are end products of being more responsive to market changes and student and administrative necessities.

From an external stakeholder perspective, the challenges often come down to whether higher education is accountable, transparent, and cost-effective in developing highly talented postsecondary school graduates able to succeed in life and at work. For them, success is attained when higher numbers of students graduate and when they are gainfully employed and less encumbered by student debt. The burden of proof regarding ability to meet these expectations remains with higher education. The greater responsibility, however, is to assure the community college or university graduate traversing the stage at commencement that time and money spent was worthy of the sacrifice.

In the final analysis, our challenge in higher education is to improve upon quality of education and student support services at lower costs. This will require creative and critical thinking, disciplined behaviors, comprehensive evidence-based planning, and a sustained focus on drivers of change that worked for others. Financial analytics and integrative planning are core elements of business model redesign. As such, elevating the financial awareness of board members, administrators, and faculty is requisite to change.

The time has arrived to revamp complex organizational structures so that they are administratively leaner and more responsive to changing market conditions and the needs of their students. Opportunities to eliminate redundant functions should be optimized. Authority to make decisions should align with accountability and responsibilities. Process reengineering offers great potential. There are many ways to become operationally more efficient and effective and less labor intensive and expensive—none of which, by definition, need compromise the core institutional educational mission. Redesign of institutional business models occupies the space whether dedication to a quality education and cost of obtaining it converge.

REFERENCES

Collins, Jim. 2001. *Good to Great: Why Some Companies Make Leap . . . and Others Don't*. New York. Harper Business Press.

Davenport, Thomas H. 1993. *Process Innovation: Reengineering Work through Innovative Technology*. Boston, MA: Harvard Business School Press.

Desrochers, Donna M., and Rita Kirshstein. 2014. *Labor Intensive or Labor Expensive? Changing Staffing and Compensation Patterns in Higher Education*. Delta Cost Project Issue Brief, February 2014. Washington, DC: American Institute for Research.

Gallup. 2015. *The 2015 Inside Higher Ed Survey of College and University Business Officers*. Washington, DC: Gallup and *Inside Higher Ed*.

Hammer, Michael. 1996. *Beyond Reengineering*. New York. Harper Business Press.

Kotter, John P. 1996. *Leading Change*. Boston, MA. Harvard Business School Press.

Kilmann, Ralph H. 2004. Beyond the Quick Fix: Managing Five Tracks to Organizational Success. Washington, DC: Beard Books.

Liker, Jeffrey K., and James K. Franz. 2011. *The Toyota Way to Continuous Improvement: Linking Strategy and Operational Excellence to Achieve Superior Performance*. New York: McGraw Hill.

Miles, Raymond E., and Charles C. Snow. 2003. *Organizational Strategy, Structure, and Process*. Stanford, CA: Stanford University Press.

Pew Higher Education Research Program, The. 1990. "The Lattice and the Ratchet." *Policy Perspectives* 2 (4): 1–8.

U.S. Department of Education. 2006. *A Test of Leadership: Charting the Future of U.S. Higher Education*. Washington, DC: U.S. Department of Education.

Zinni, Tony, and Tony Koltz. 2014. *Before the First Shots Are Fired: How America Can Win Or Lose Off the Battlefield*. New York: Palgrave MacMillan.

Chapter 7

Obstacles and Challenges to Systemic Reforms

Independent State University at Peoria (ISUP) found itself in a difficult situation in the aftermath of the economic trauma of 2008–2009. Statewide unemployment skyrocketed. The state budget, already suffering from under-funded retirement benefits for state employees, evidenced revenue declines as corporate and personal income tax payments contracted. Student enrollment declined as did public budget allocations to public universities.

To compound matters, the university had decided to expand its mission to embrace research 20 years before, and its faculty now included many dedicated research scholars—all of whom belonged to a national labor union. Millions of dollars of loans were borrowed to support an aggressive construction program intended to render ISUP more competitive in its quest for students. The university budget's revenue sources steadily declined between 2009 and 2015, leaving its financial condition unsustainable. The longtime president who oversaw the expansion program decided to retire in 2011. He agreed to remain in office for one additional year in order to allow the board of trustees ample time to find a successor.

A new president, Dr. M. Hartley Baumgarten, assumed the presidency in August 2012. Dr. Baumgarten held a PhD in History from an Ivy League University, had been a department chair, dean of a professional school, and provost of a mid-sized state university in California. Dr. Baumgarten was respected for his collegial style, outgoing persona, and experience working with faculty.

Having been forewarned about ISUP's tenuous financial condition, Dr. Baumgarten and the board of trustees agreed to develop an institutional strategic plan in order to design a more vibrant context for addressing financial and other challenges. Many faculty members supported the new president and welcomed his outreach. The research mission was ratified. Attention would be given to increasing student enrollment in its marquee programs, which included business administration, criminal justice, registered nursing, software engineering, and education.

In addition, ISUP decided to make a major investment to build up its online degree programs. So, the focus would be primarily on revenue generation, although the board and senior administration privately agreed to more effectively contain costs and develop a more agile and inventive institutional culture.

On paper, the five-year strategic plan covering 2013–2018 inspired confidence as a comprehensive instrument that appeared to address all major challenges. State political leaders welcomed the vision articulated by Dr. Baumgarten, and the dawn of a new day for ISUP seemed to be within grasp.

During school year 2014–2015, ISUP's financial condition continued to deteriorate. State funding for ISUP declined still further. Enrollment was down 11 percent compared to its peak in 2007. Faculty and administrators were chafing after three successive years without pay raises. The president and his board of trustees were losing credibility as morale among faculty, administrators and staff declined, and state political leaders expressed concern about their leadership with increasing frequency.

What went wrong? Was the plan itself flawed? Had leaders failed to consider obstacles to change, diagnose the underlying causes, design a multiyear implementation plan to surmount those obstacles, and create a continuous improvement environment? Or, can a plan fail during implementation due to a variety of circumstances that may be unpredictable?

Relatively modest responses by traditional higher education to external challenges have been a source of concern for many years. One may argue that complex and comprehensive higher education institutions are designed to be reflective and evolve slowly. Metered change is one thing. Inconsequential change is altogether something else. This is the fault line separating proponents of the existing business and educational model of higher education and those who feel that the system is too costly and does not deliver results that inspire confidence.

A review of the literature and the President's Commission on Higher Education (1947) make clear that criticism of traditional higher education from senior administrators, faculty, and external stakeholders has been around for a while. The intent of this chapter is to identify potential obstacles to reform and to question certain widely held assumptions along the way.

Critics of higher education point out that tuition price increases over decades reflect institutional incapacity to shed inefficient bureaucratic processes and low occupational demand and low enrollment programs. Some argue that institutions do not add sufficient value to the skills and competencies of graduating seniors relative to their expenses. Some believe that curriculum is too often unfocused and that many institutional mission statements are muddled.

Graduation and employment rates at some community colleges, colleges, and universities are unacceptably low. The mix of faculty and administrators does not reflect the growing ethnic, racial, and national origin minorities of the country as a whole. Many tenured faculty, and some administrators, are allegedly self-serving and weigh personal and professional interests above concerns for their institutions and students.

Institutions determined to redesign their environments are well advised to anticipate the sources of tension and opposition that may render change illusive. Some impediments are obvious, while others are more subtle. Those who fail to chart obstacles to change and develop plans to successfully navigate them, do so at their own peril. Failure to execute institutional strategic plans is not limited to higher education. Mark Morgan, Raymond E. Levitt, and William Malek (2007) note that most private sector companies encounter similar problems. This chapter is by no means a definitive analysis, but denotes factors that render institutional transformation a complicated undertaking.

FRACTURED AND INEFFECTUAL EDUCATIONAL POLICIES

Let's begin by examining the environment in which higher education operates. Certain inefficiencies and inhibitors of change, such as dysfunctional educational policies and practices, are beyond the unilateral control of colleges and universities. Many state and municipality departments of education retain legacy silos in which policies and practices toward P-12 education, community colleges, and universities are treated as separate and apart rather than as parts of a seamless educational continuum.

One cannot assume that sustainable improvement of learning outcomes and prudent use of limited financial resources will occur in higher education in the absence of policy dedicated to improving the effectiveness of instruction at primary and secondary schools and their connectivity with higher education. At present, with a few notable exceptions such as the growing emphasis on early and middle college high schools in New York City, North Carolina, and Texas, there is insufficient evidence of educational policy and practices that foster collaborative intervention strategies among institutions at all levels of public education.

Many community colleges and public universities serving large populations of students in need of remedial education are left to their own devices to solve problems not of their creation, and are criticized for failing to realize graduation for students who are too often woefully underprepared for higher education. Some question whether the proliferation of government regulations and oversight is rendering higher education more risk averse at a time when a need to innovate is needed more than ever (Brewer and Tierney 2011).

There is ample room to question the basic design of P-12 delivery of public education. One may query whether school days are too few, class sessions are too short, teachers are inadequately prepared, and inadequately funded school districts fail to provide instructional software and computers for use by their students. Public policy and funding for education is more geared toward grade-level test results than mastery of broader behavioral and knowledge application competencies that enable their students to perform with proficiency in higher education and the workplace. Education policy too often facilitates student progress through legacy, chronologically driven assembly lines in which at-risk students pass from one grade to the next based more upon their age than mastery of subject matter.

Solutions for complex problems in higher education are more likely when public education policy and practice help mitigate the causes of underperformance along a P-16 continuum. Common core standards, the growing trend toward performance-based funding of higher education, and the recently initiated online accessible federal government college scorecard focus attention on output metrics. They seem less interested in fostering ways to redesign student-centric learning processes or remediating the causes of underperforming schools. As such, it is unclear whether P-16 education policies and practices are part of the solution or the problem.

LEADERS AS CHANGE AGENTS OR TASK MANAGERS

We are ill-advised to assume that leaders in traditional higher education manifest the skills and range of professional experiences needed to replace broken business and learning models with those that add more educational value and are more financially sustainable. Institutional redesign requires behavioral and leadership competencies (see chapter 9) at variance from those needed for maintenance management. Failure of leaders to perform is often traceable to management that lacks the ability to detect and resolve problems (Kilmann 2004).

Robert Birnbaum and Peter D. Eckel (2005) codify the rising performance expectations of college and university presidents, leading us to wonder whether task management renders transformational leadership unrealistic. Yet, many job descriptions and lists of qualifications for college presidents and other senior administrative positions posted on *The Chronicle of Higher Education* and similar outlets for job vacancies remain traditional and do not necessarily reflect awareness of a need for a higher order of skills.

Private discussions with institutional leaders and senior officers of education associations reflect a growing concern about the quality and preparedness of search candidates to lead institutional transformation. Presidents and senior administrators are relied upon to develop and implement strategies that improve the quality of education while rendering it more affordable. Leaders must be respected, purposeful, focused, committed, passionate, effective, inspirational, and collegial agents of change. They must be willing to make difficult decisions. Leaders who do not adeptly perform these functions inhibit institutional reform.

Institutions that attribute greater value to intellect, academic credentials, and a limited range of career experiences over a proven record of performance are vulnerable to disappointing results. Coherent succession planning and leadership development programs are vital. Emergent leaders need exposure to a wider range of career experiences that includes assignments across traditional functional silos such as academic affairs, student services, finance, human resources, operations, public affairs, and facilities management. Institutional progression from at risk to fair, fair to good, or good to great increasingly relies upon transformative leaders with a grasp of broader institutional problems, needs, and capacity to bring about collaborative and integrated solutions. In summation, the assumption that senior administrative incumbents act as leaders or change agents is worthy of closer study.

BOARDS OF TRUSTEES: PART OF THE PROBLEM, PART OF THE SOLUTION, A BIT OF BOTH?

In an ideal world, boards of trustees have the talent, composition, understanding, access to information, and commitment to fulfill their fiduciary responsibilities to the institutions and students they serve. Much is known about "best practices" of boards of trustees. In its most simplistic form, the chief officer (CEO) and board agree upon institutional strategy, and the CEO is charged with its implementation. Boards review and approve strategic plans, human resource and finance policy, and annual operating and capital budgets, hire presidents, and evaluate their performance. Tension rises in proportion to a lack of confidence or trust between board members and the CEO.

More can be learned by considering best practices for boards of trustees. Size, composition, vetting processes, and qualifications matter. Some public and private institutions have boards that are too large to be effective. To the degree that board membership exceeds 15 to 20 trustees, one questions the quality of discourse. Lack of transparency or failure to disclose important information in a full and timely manner to the board erodes confidence in a president. Yet, a president who shares too much information with a board may inadvertently invite micromanaging of day-to-day operations.

The assumption that boards of trustees are highly functional and fully prepared to support institutional redesign may not consistently hold up under closer inspection. Conflicts of interest and governance practices at certain public institutions are cause for concern. When members of boards of trustees or regents are appointed by elected officials, they are susceptible to their political influence.

The case of the Board of Regents in Texas seeking the dismissal of the president of the University of Texas at Austin reflects a drive for power and control by the recently retired governor more than demonstrable failure of its president to perform. Board members of many community colleges are either elected to their positions or are appointed by elected officials. This is problematic to the degree that personal political ambitions or allegiances often trump concerns for institutional priorities. Goldie Blumenstyk (2015, p. 107), longtime reporter for *The Chronicle of Higher Education*, reminds us that of 34 public research universities belonging to the Association of American Universities, 16 presidents resigned or were dismissed in less than three years between 2011 and 2014.

How and when boards act or fail to act can profoundly influence institutions. Some examples come to mind. The rationale behind the original decision of the University of Virginia Board members to oust President Teresa Sullivan is subject to speculation. In the case of Sullivan, it seems that certain board members wanted University of Virginia to move aggressively into online education and the president resisted (Brewer 2014). Sullivan was reinstated after widespread campus demonstrations by students and faculty, which included a vote of no confidence in the board by the faculty senate.

Two more cases come to mind of boards that were seemingly overcome by events. The Pennsylvania State University Board was highly criticized for its handling of the sex abuse scandal relating to the retired defensive football coach Jerry Sandusky and the subsequent decision to fire longtime football coach Joe Paterno. In this case, the university president, Graham Spanier, allegedly withheld vital information from the board about worrisome behaviors by the former assistant coach. Spanier was subsequently discharged by the board, and was criminally indicted. The more recent announcement about the planned closure of Sweet Briar College, temporarily rescinded, raises questions about what the board knew, when they knew it, and what they did about it.

Certain commonalities can be found in the cases of the University of Texas at Austin, University of Virginia, Penn State University, and Sweet Briar College. Board members must receive full, timely, and accurate information from the president in order to make informed decisions. Bad news cannot be withheld pending the next formal meeting of the board. No board member wants to hear or read in the media what should have been communicated in advance by their president. Similarly, presidents need to have full confidence that board members will be supportive, not seek to arbitrarily impose their will on the internal affairs of the institution, and act consistently in the best interests of the institutions they serve. Tumult, surprises, and discord between board members and their presidents inevitably prove disruptive.

Board actions are mission critical toward realizing an enhanced educational and business model for their institutions. Boards must share in the process of institutional redesign and strategic planning and be supportive of measures taken thereafter to realize the benefits of those plans. To the extent that board members are aware of needs for substantive institutional reform, they are obliged to exercise their fiduciary responsibilities diligently in the selection of presidents. Measures intended to assure institutional sustainability may cause opposition from those whose vested interests are adversely affected. This may take the form of votes of "no confidence" in the president, campus demonstrations, protests by alumni, letters or calls to board members, passive-aggressive opposition from disloyal administrators, and/or negative publicity.

In short, the resolve of board members will be tested one way or another. Boards that equivocate amid tensions caused by change will inevitably compromise leadership. High-performance boards are vital to systemic change, but underperforming or dysfunctional boards compromise the abilities of institutional leaders to perform.

SHARED GOVERNANCE: THEORY AND PRACTICE

Many permutations of shared governance exist. In theory, shared governance allows internal stakeholders, mostly faculty, to participate in important academic decisions and opine on broader administrative matters. When functioning as it should in theory, shared governance offers a collaborative forum for leaders and faculty to share information and analysis in setting institutional direction. In this model, college or university faculty are voted to positions in a senate by their peers. Institutions with collective bargaining agreements with faculty often define which functions are subject to shared governance with administration within their contracts.

In the best of all worlds, shared governance need not impede change, provided that reality aligns with theory. Much depends upon goodwill and trust between faculty and administrators. Faculty have the professional experiences to make important substantive contributions to academic matters such as curriculum and review of new programs.

The question is whether, and to what degree, shared governance is subject to imperfection. Leaders who obfuscate, disregard faculty opinion, or fail to inform or simply ignore rules of engagement invite opposition to initiatives without regard to the merit of changes undertaken. One may also find structural flaws brought about by fragmentation of committees and inability to develop effective integrative mechanisms to analyze complex issues at the institutional level (Morrill 2007).

Presidents and boards who cede too much authority to shared governance find that their ability to lead is restricted during crises. One needs to consider whether decision-making authority is ceded to shared governance and over which domains it applies. Or, is shared governance a forum for information sharing and tendering recommendations for senior administrators to take into consideration before making decisions? A discourse model is about collaborative problem solving, whereas shared governance with authority to make decisions may be more about power and control. Governance that limits the ability of administrators to respond effectively to changing times may prove dysfunctional and an obstacle to reform. The assumption, on the other hand, that tenured faculty and faculty unions are consistently intransigent in opposition to change is subject to review on an institution-by-institution basis.

The whole issue about the role of faculty unions, their prevailing practices, and how tenured faculty act is open to a more definitive study. Faculty unions are designed to safeguard the financial and other interests of their members. They serve at the will of their members, as reflected by elections. As such, faculty unions and their labor contracts with higher education institutions may define which actions are subject to shared governance. A widely accepted view is that rights not ceded to shared governance remain with administration to decide upon.

Senior administrators and their boards of trustees are well advised to thoughtfully consider ways to engage faculty and implement plans accordingly. In the words of one leading authority on higher education in the United States, "The rise of academic unions helped to increase salaries during the 1970s, but contributed to an increasingly adversarial relationship between faculty and administration in some universities" (Altbach 2005, p. 289). Whether real or imagined, Altbach (2005) argues that many faculty are given to resisting perceived administrative encroachments into their domains. Edward J. Valeau, a retired community college president, and John Petersen, a retired accreditation commission president, observe that faculty unions and their members often "see themselves as the true management of their colleges" (Valeau and Petersen 2011, p. 37).

Higher education is vulnerable to centrifugal forces that can undermine execution of institutional plans no matter how well intentioned and designed. Some believe, as stated by economist and academic Bob Martin (2013, p. 33), "As it stands now, shared governance is fragmented governance." As it is, faculty have dual roles in many institutions via attending to their professional duties and participating in shared governance. In some cases, this breeds conflicts of interests. William G. Bowen and Eugene M. Tobin (2015) offer a

balanced and substantive examination of the role of faculty in shared governance in their book *Locus of Authority*. And, Derek Bok (2013) offers further
insights in *Higher Education in America*. A true test of presidents relates to
their effectiveness in either sustaining the participation, support, and confidence of faculty while changing institutional design or figuring out ways to
overcome intransigent opposition to reform.

FLAWED STRATEGY

Institutional strategic plans may provide thoughtful redesign and revitaliza-
tion of institutional mission, enduring goals and priorities, or may fall short of
the mark, sometimes due to errors of omission or commission. The intent of a
strategic plan is to "advance the institution to new heights" (Alexander 2015).

When done correctly, a strategic plan articulates clear, concise, realistic,
affordable, and inspirational mission and vision statements. The plan sets
forth institutional enduring goals, values, and priorities. It values institutional
legacy while defining the journey ahead. It is largely built upon a body of
relevant evidence that is thoughtfully considered during environmental scans
and so-called strengths, weaknesses, opportunities, and threats or challenges
(SWOT/SWOC) analyses. Its formulation processes are transparent and inclusive. Key performance indicators allow for objective measurement of progress.

Regrettably, opportunities for error abound, in part due to the complexity
of this undertaking. Some examples come to mind. Mission statements should
be inspirational and offer realistic criteria for decision-making by providing
a statement of institutional purpose. What are the consequences in the eventuality that institutions embrace a research agenda within the mission that
is no longer affordable? Can community colleges afford to offer unfunded
community education, lifelong learning, or customized job training activities
at subsidized prices even if such activities fall within their mission? Reflection upon institutional mission statements offers an opportunity to reconsider
or reset directional signals for academic and student affairs and financial
planning. Vague or unaffordable mission statements compromise subsequent
thinking, planning, and decision-making.

Incomplete, anecdotal, or biased data gathering and analysis undermines
the foundation upon which priorities are defined. Preexisting assumptions
should be questioned. Institutions, professional schools, or academic programs that devalue the importance of evidence are poorly positioned to
identify challenges and opportunities, or allocate resources in support of their
priorities.

Conversely, sound data analysis facilitates support for those programs
most likely to sustain competitive advantages. Institutions attempting to be

all things to all people are more likely to underperform their competitors by disbursing limited resources hither and thither. Institutions with declining enrollments or low retention rates are especially in need of strategic evidence-based solutions. Concerns about enrollment and unacceptably low retention rates have been voiced as early as in the 1950s (Thelin 2004). Inadequate use of data renders an institution less able to understand the sources of strategic challenges and opportunities, and respond appropriately.

Finally, contemporary enrollment and funding challenges at many institutions compel integration of multiyear strategic and financial plans with a like duration. With or without strategic plans, institutions must define their value propositions and make resource allocation decisions supportive of stated priorities. Disaggregation of educational, student services, technology, and facilities plans from financial planning is an exercise in folly.

FAILURE TO "OPERATIONALIZE" THE PLAN

The realization of institutional mission, vision, and enduring goals is attainable in proportion to the effectiveness with which strategic plans are acted upon. Goals are more likely to be realized when implementation or annual operating plans and objectives derive from a master plan. This calls for designing and executing action plans, assigning responsibility and accountability to administrators, monitoring and reporting on progress, sustaining transparency, and allocating financial and other resources in support of priorities.

It also calls for aligning annual performance evaluations with results that will support well-conceived strategies. Stated differently, a purely aspirational strategic plan lacking a data-based foundation is hallucinatory. Similarly, ineffectual execution of a strategic plan raises questions about the credibility of those at the institutional helm. In the ultimate sense, the president owns the plan, and internal constituents soon discover through his or her actions whether a commitment from the top should be taken seriously.

INSTITUTIONAL CULTURE

Institutional behaviors and practices can prove problematic when attempting to implement even thoughtful and inspirational institutional strategic plans. In the broadest sense, an institution's culture is the sum of values, beliefs, assumptions, and behaviors of those who work there. Just as agile and innovative cultures characterize successful high-tech companies, alleged change-resistant behaviors in higher education inhibit realignment of priorities and implementation of plans. A subtler manifestation of culture arises when obsessive concerns about process and collegiality supplant dedication to performance, student needs, academic excellence, and cost-effective operations. Correctly or incorrectly, many within academe are criticized for placing their own interests ahead of the needs of others (Rhodes 2001).

The greater the distance between a prevailing culture and the one needed to sustain systemic change at a college or university, the more likely that old habits will undermine progress and performance. The William H. Bergquist and Kenneth Pawlak (2007) study, *Engaging the Six Cultures of the Academy*, examines the imperative of integrating divergent cultures. Institutional strategic plans that envision material reform and change need to be mindful of prevailing cultural attributes.

A successful transformation, for example, to a market-driven model of program concentration and educational delivery will be difficult to achieve if pervasive behaviors are change resistant, risk averse, and teaching-centric rather than learning-centric. Edgar H. Schein (2004) explores the intricacies of organizational behavior and concludes that many institutions are a composite of many subcultures, which cautions us about misuse of generalizations.

A subtler characteristic of institutional culture that restricts progress stems from an overly controlled environment in which planning and decision-making is concentrated in the office of the president and/or members of the CEO cabinet. Disconnects between authority and accountability at the levels of upper-middle and middle management induce insecurity, higher cost, and operational inefficiencies while repressing innovation. Layered bureaucracies have ways of being unaccountable and creating "make-work" for others.

Many institutions that rely upon government subsidies or on passing along cost increases to students through tuition increases find a need to be increasingly more self-reliant financially. A culture of self-reliance places a premium on behaviors that include entrepreneurship, agility, innovation, a spirit of competition, risk-taking, evidence-based planning, and a will to make difficult decisions. This changing self-awareness should be compared with prevailing behaviors. Some believe that a "cultural audit"—benchmarking of preexisting values and behaviors—merits consideration. The greater the gap between actual values and behaviors relative to those required to sustain systemic change will very likely impede progress. The authors of the Spellings Commission Report observed: "Our yearlong examination of the challenges facing higher education has brought us to the uneasy conclusion that the sector's past attainments have led our nation to unwarranted complacency about its future" (U.S. Department of Education 2006, p. ix).

Nearly 60 years earlier, the so-called *Truman Commission Report* noted: "Educational leaders felt an uneasy sense of shortcoming . . . that somehow colleges had not kept pace with changing societal conditions"

(President's Commission on Higher Education 1947, p. 21). Some reasonable lag between societal change and curriculum adaptation may be expected, yet two government-sponsored reports issued approximately 60 years apart shared similar concerns. Deliberate and metered responses to challenges and opportunities are one thing. Institutional redesign takes time and hard work until the benefits are realized. The frustration of many external stakeholders with higher education reflects a perception that much of postsecondary education remains captive to a change-resistant culture.

STRUCTURAL AND HUMAN RESOURCE IMPEDIMENTS TO CHANGE

College and university administrators and faculty function within silos that may limit their broader understanding of institutional priorities and student needs. The larger the university, the more one is apt to find a rich array of professional or career-oriented schools, academic departments, and disciplines. Institutions of any size will have specialized activities that focus attention upon instruction, student affairs, enrollment, finance, facilities management, human resources, information technology, external relations, and fundraising. Community colleges often include workforce development, remedial education, and community education in the mix.

The norm is that professionals are hired and promoted within these silos, sometimes cynically called fiefdoms. Administrators understand the challenges facing functions for which they are directly responsible and attempt to find solutions for problems arising within their silos. Sometimes professionals evolve and develop a broader vision, skills, and an awareness of the institution as a whole. Others sustain a limited vision, awareness, or even caring about the greater whole. Expressed differently, silos in higher education are detrimental to systemic change, and are apt to remain in place in the absence of succession planning and leadership development from within.

The role of the head of human resources in the design and nurturing of future leaders should not be underestimated, and relies upon unrestrained commitment from the president. From a human resource perspective, hiring, developing, and promoting from within silos is the norm in higher education. Can professionals within traditional silos function effectively in an environment that places a premium on teamwork and codevelop solutions with administrators and faculty in other silos? Do recognition and reward systems apply to those who share performance objectives? From a cost and efficiency standpoint, traditional silos are expensive to maintain, may contain redundant activities, or fail to share resources across functional areas of responsibility.

Systemic reforms place a premium on the will and capacity of senior administrators and faculty to support institutional priorities at what may be perceived as a sacrifice to one's vested interests and career opportunities. In fairness, many talented leaders emerge from within this environment, perhaps due more to personal ability than to their institutional structure and career path. Raymond E. Miles and Chuck Snow (2003, p. 6) observe, "The ability to enact a new or different [organizational] environment is significantly constrained by what is known about allocating, structuring and developing resources." In short, one must think about how organizational structure can significantly limit plan execution.

UNWIELDY MANAGEMENT REPORTING AND PROCESSES

Design and approval of an institutional strategic plan, and accompanying implementation plans, may also fail in the absence of management reporting and processes that track progress on an ongoing basis. If management reports fail to inform senior administrators with timely, accurate, and actionable quantitative and qualitative data, they are dependent upon hearsay, impressions, and anecdotal input. Imperfect sources of information are woefully inaccurate as a basis for plan adjustments, decision-making, and sustaining forward progress.

Senior administrators disconnected from periodic oversight of progress relative to strategic and annual priorities may find that drift occurs as their direct reports engage in day-to-day task management and fail to devote time, energy, and other resources to plan execution. Voluminous reports with data that cannot be acted upon and poorly run meetings are counterproductive. Lack of attention to highly focused progress reports undermines a sense of ownership and accountability.

In this context, senior administrators who fail to ask probing questions when progress reports are made lose opportunities to detect slippage in a timely manner and take action accordingly. Worse yet, their subordinates may deduce that reporting on progress is perfunctory. Ineffective reporting and review of progress compromise accountability. Legacy accounting systems were designed to assure accurate reporting for financial statements, but are often insufficient to meet management needs.

Labor-intensive activities and elongated approval processes, namely an ineffective bureaucracy, sap the time and energy critical to systemic reform. Manual preparation or customization of management reports are apt to prove less accurate and expensive to produce. Irrational organizational behavior sustains a cadre of middle and upper-middle management without empowering them to make decisions essential to their areas of responsibility.

The more signatures needed to approve a new program, expense, or authorize a job offer, the lesser is the accountability for decisions made. Worse yet, time needed to effect change and implement necessary reform is siphoned off to high-cost and low-yield activities.

FAILURE TO ADAPT HUMAN RESOURCES PRACTICES TO SYSTEMIC CHANGE

Ambitious and inspirational plans may prove unrealizable if performance evaluation processes are disconnected from strategic priorities and annual operating objectives. Institutions relying upon evaluation processes for administrators and faculty primarily based upon job descriptions are poorly positioned to drive a change agenda for lack of accountability for results.

Imagine an institution where administrators, faculty, and staff are accustomed to favorable performance reviews, yet enrollment declines, retention rates of students are low, morale is awful, there are no consequences for negative or ineffectual behaviors, facilities are in disrepair, accreditors voice concern about institutional effectiveness, and the financial condition is unsustainable. Failure of the president to hold himself or herself and others accountable for results will serve to enable institutional resistance to change.

BUDGET DECISIONS AND RESOURCE ALLOCATION

Fundamental outcomes of institutional strategic plans include institutional mission, purposes, priorities, and initiatives. The same holds true for schools, colleges, academic departments, and administrative functions within the institution. Casting new and concise directions assume the will and ability to allocate financial, technological, facilities, and people resources in support of articulated goals and objectives. On the other hand, budget approvals based upon legacy ways of spending are counterproductive.

What are the consequences of antiquated resource allocation practices? Important initiatives and priorities are likely to be underfunded, hence suffer from lack of financial and other essential resources needed to succeed. On the other hand, less consequential programs and routine functions have little incentive to change their ways. Worse yet, across-the-board decisions to direct all academic, service, and administrative functions to reduce operating expenses by a fixed percentage from one year to the next is leadership by default.

Imposition of across-the-board fixed budget reductions of expenses for all units offers the attractiveness of being easy to apply, requiring little thinking, and less apt to be controversial. On the surface, it is equitable. Yet, failure to fund institutional priorities places them on a starvation diet. A one-size-fits-all approach to budget reduction of certain expenses will undermine the best of plans.

ACCREDITORS AND ACCREDITATION PROCESSES

Peer review of community colleges, universities, and professional programs by regional and professional accreditation associations is subject to increasing reflection and scrutiny by internal and external stakeholders alike. Many questions have arisen. Do accreditation associations offer critical third-party review and assurance of quality? Are they champions or obstacles to change? Does their cost outweigh their benefit? A more definitive study of these questions awaits.

Six regional accreditation associations in the United States perform institutional reviews. Scores of professional associations accredit career programs ranging from health care to business administration. Suffice it to say that generalizations about their effectiveness, or lack of same, are misguided. One may find illustrations of accreditation processes that stifle innovation. We are also apt to come across cases of accredited institutions forced to close for lack of financial resources, or instances of alleged unprofessional conduct by one or more associations. On the other hand, peer review offers the advantages of content experts examining their member institutions according to known standards and performance criteria.

The first author can share insights gained from two accreditation experiences. Having served as president of a community college undergoing reaccreditation from the Middle States Commission on Higher Education, it was clear that on this occasion the residual benefits outweighed the costs. He had a similar experience while serving as vice chairman of the board of trustees of a college in Florida that was visited by the Southern Association of Colleges and Schools. The preparatory self-study and residual benefits of accreditation offered valid third-party observation of areas in need of attention. The associations were student centric and asked the right questions about how we assured their learning outcomes and addressed institutional and financial effectiveness.

Some officials in federal and state government question the role and effectiveness of accreditors as an industry overseer. Accusations of their being too institutionally friendly abound. In fairness, similar complaints about allegedly friendly behaviors by certain state and federal agencies in the transportation, highway safety, banking, environment, and other sectors of the economy can be found as well. Generalizations of this sort tend to embed elements of truth and fiction. Many in higher education worry about the prospect of government oversight replacing peer review. Given the highly partisan state of national and state politics, there is reason for many in higher education to be concerned about government oversight that may intrude upon institutional autonomy and academic freedom. The point of this discussion is that institutions driving a redesign agenda are well advised to collaborate with their accreditors to provide evidence that a voluntary system works.

CONCLUDING OBSERVATIONS

Systemic flaws and impediments to change are many and are formidable. Some obstacles are readily detectable, while others are subtler and more nuanced. Comprehensive research universities and community colleges, along with smaller four-year institutions, face a plethora of challenges ranging from rising tuition to a perception of declining quality of education. Institutional performance expectations are rising, along with demands upon their presidents. Meanwhile, resources are increasingly constrained.

By considering the many barriers to change, leaders, their boards, and faculty are better positioned to plan and respond effectively. The national socioeconomic consequences of the financial health and performance of traditional higher education are direct. The implications of institutional incapacity to adapt to changing times are seen in enrollment numbers, as students and their families are increasingly becoming value conscious. In the final analysis, policy makers, educational leaders, their boards, administrators, and faculties have difficult choices to make. Their ability to act judiciously and effectively will be borne out by the sustainability of their institutions.

REFERENCES

Alexander, Livingston. 2015. Correspondence with the first author, 14 December 2015.

Altbach, Philip G. 2005. "Harsh Realities: The Professoriate Faces a New Century." In *American Higher Education in the Twenty-First Century*, edited by Philip G. Altbach, Patricia J. Gumport, and Robert O. Berdahl. 2nd Ed. Baltimore, MD: The Johns Hopkins University Press.

Bergquist, William H., and Kenneth Pawlak. 2007. *Engaging the Six Cultures of the Academy: Revised and Expanded Editing of the Four Cultures of the Academy*. San Francisco, CA: John Wiley & Sons.

Birnbaum, Robert, and Peter D. Eckel. 2005. "The Dilemma of Presidential Leadership." In *American Higher Education in the Twenty-First Century*, edited by Philip

G. Altbach, Patricia J. Gumport, and Robert O. Berdahl. 2nd Ed. Baltimore, MD: The Johns Hopkins University Press.

Blumenstyk, Goldie. 2015. *American Higher Education in Crisis? What Everyone Needs to Know.* New York: Oxford University Press.

Bok, Derek. 2013. *Higher Education in America.* Princeton, NJ: Princeton University Press.

Bowen, William G., and Eugene M. Tobin. 2015. *Locus of Authority: The Evolution of Faculty Roles in the Governance of Higher Education.* Princeton, NJ: Princeton University Press.

Brewer, Dominic J., and William G. Tierney. 2011. "Barriers to Innovation in U.S. Higher Education." In *Reinventing Higher Education: The Promise of Innovation.* Cambridge, MA: Harvard Education Press.

Brewer, Talbot. "The Coup that Failed: How the Near-Sacking of a University President Exposed the Fault Lines of American Higher Education." *The Hedgehog Review* 16 (2). Available online at: www.iasc-culture.org/THR.

Kilmann, Ralph H. 2004. *Beyond the Quick Fix: Managing Five Tracks to Organizational Success.* Washington, DC: Beard Books.

Martin, Robert E. 2013. "Incentives, Information and the Public Interest: Higher Education Governance as a Barrier to Cost Containment." In *Stretching the Higher Education Dollar: How Innovation Can Improve Access, Equity, and Affordability,* edited by Andrew P. Kelly and Kevin Carey. Cambridge, MA: Harvard Education Press.

Morgan, Mark, Raymond E. Levitt, and William Malek. 2007. *Executing Your Strategy: How to Break It Down and Get It Done.* Cambridge, MA: Harvard Business School Press.

Morrill, Richard L. 2007. *Strategic Leadership: Integrating Strategy and Leadership in Colleges and Universities.* Lanham, MD: Rowman & Littlefield.

President's Commission on Higher Education. 1947. *Higher Education for Democracy.* Six Volumes edited by George F. Zook et al. Washington, DC: Government Printing Office.

Rhodes, Frank H. T. 2001. *The Role of the American University: The Creation of the Future.* 2001. Ithaca, NY: Cornell University Press.

Selingo, Jeffrey J. 2013. *College (Un)Bound: The Future of Higher Education and What It Means for Students.* New York: Houghton Mifflin Harcourt.

Schein, Edgar H. 2004. *Organizational Culture and Leadership.* 3rd Ed. San Francisco, CA: Jossey-Bass.

Thelin, John R. 2004. *A History of American Higher Education.* Baltimore, MD: The Johns Hopkins University Press.

U.S. Department of Education. 2006. *A Test of Leadership: Charting the Future of U.S. Higher Education.* A Report of the Commission Appointed by Secretary of Education Margaret Spellings. Washington, DC: U.S. Department of Education.

Valeau, Edward J., and John C. Petersen. 2011. "Systemic Change, Approval Processes and Governance: The Role of the Board of Trustees." In *Increasing Effectiveness of the Community College Financial Model: A Global Perspective for the Global Economy,* edited by Stewart E. Sutin, Daniel Derrico, Rosalind Latiner Raby, and Edward J. Valeau. New York: Palgrave Macmillan.

Chapter 8

Reflecting Upon Lessons Learned from Exemplars

In June 2015, Flexible State University at Daytona (FSUD) named a new president, Dr. Jane Piedmont, with the intent of improving upon the university's academic performance and developing a sustainable financial model. The 11-member board was impressed by Piedmont's accomplishments while leading Maine State and Technical University at Bar Harbor. She had previously served as provost of Cooperstown Community College in upstate New York.

FSUD served a student population of an estimated 8,000 full-time undergraduate students and 3,500 graduate students, most of whom lived along the east coast of Florida between St. Augustine and Vero Beach. Tuition had increased by 46 percent during the past 10 years, yet balancing the annual budget remained troublesome. The FSUD board of trustees made clear during the selection process that improvement upon a six-year graduation rate of 48 percent was imperative in order to support regional economic growth and that both a sustainable financial model and low tuition increases were important outcomes.

Piedmont understood that unique institutional characteristics merited consideration. As a former history professor, Piedmont also valued learning from the experiences of others. While feeling the pressure to make immediate decisions, Piedmont managed to convince the board to support a six-month period of inquiry and planning, with the objective of rendering substantive recommendations thereafter.

President Piedmont nominated three planning committees, each comprising faculty, administrators, and student leaders. An Educational and Student Services Innovation Committee was asked to study models that served similar institutions well; FSUD's qualitative and quantitative data would be subject to inquiry as well. A Technological Innovation Committee would compare FSUD's delivery system relative to "best practices" in higher education.

Finally, a Financial Resources Innovation Committee was named to study opportunities to generate incremental revenues from nontraditional initiatives and reduce operating expenses. In each case, the committees were tasked with studying exemplars of change and identifying lessons learned.

Educational quality, student learning outcomes, and affordable tuition constitute the nexus at which academic, student, and business affairs converge. Although financial planning and budgets fall under the purview of the chief financial officer (CFO), all leaders bear responsibility for institutional sustainability, affordable tuition, quality of learning, and student support services. Much can be gained by nurturing symmetry between these functions and by examining exemplars of change. What did they accomplish? How? And, what lessons can be learned from their initiatives?

Two early leaders in educational reform come to mind. For example, during the presidency of Charles William Elliot at Harvard University, their graduate department became a Graduate School of Arts and Sciences, the medical school curriculum expanded to four years, with a bachelor's degree required beforehand, the curriculum for undergraduates encouraged more electives, and the School of Business Administration was launched. In many ways, Elliot envisioned the modern American university and transformed Harvard in the process.

In 1910, Abraham Flexner, an educator from Louisville, was invited by the Carnegie Foundation to examine medical school education in the United States. The so-called Flexner Report contributed to reshaping medical school curriculum, changing the role and credentials of faculty and creating competitive admissions standards. Flexner (2010) envisioned redesign of contemporary medical education in the United States. Both Elliot and Flexner envisioned education that offered more value, ways to narrow the gap between educational needs, and ways to achieve desirable outcomes. Elliot and Flexner were visionaries and clear thinkers who made a difference.

This chapter explores institutional and individual exemplars of reform whose accomplishments may inspire others. Some improved the quality of education and/or their respective delivery models. Others developed revenues through nontraditional activities or by containing costs. Some applied instructional, student service, and operational software for the benefit of their students, faculty, and staff. All displayed creative energies and the ability to translate vision to plans and design to action. Reform of higher education's education and business models are attainable.

Our study does not comment upon massive open online courses (MOOCs). While MOOCs offer intriguing potential, they remain in an incubation mode in which the quality of education, support services, retention rates, the migration from noncredit to credit, and the business model continue to evolve. Georgia Tech recently launched a master's degree in computer science as a form of a MOOC. The success and potential portability of their model to other programs and institutions will prove informative.

EDUCATIONAL DELIVERY MODELS

Higher education has been profoundly influenced by emerging technologies that improve institutional capacity to inquire about, communicate with, learn about, and service our students. Online education offers an example of a profoundly different delivery model that came of age during the latter part of the twentieth century. For-profit colleges and universities were among the early adopters of online education, and aggressively grew their enrollments through offering courses, certificates, and degrees primarily to adult learners.

Over time, concerns arose about behaviors of certain for-profit colleges in terms of quality of education, sales practices, relatively low graduation rates, and comparatively high defaults on repayment of student loans. As awareness of these problems became known, their aggregate enrollment declined. Yet, for-profits proved that adult learners represent a growing market segment for student enrollment and tuition revenues and that economies can be found through standardization of curriculum and courses. As aggregate enrollment at for-profits declined during recent years, several nonprofit public and private institutions began to occupy that space.

Four nonprofit institutions in particular devoted substantial resources to online education, thereby partially filling the enrollment space vacated by for-profits. The Royal Melbourne Institute of Technology (RMIT), Webster University, Southern New Hampshire University (SNHU), Arizona State University (ASU)/EdPlus, Penn State University's World Campus, and Western Governors University (WGU) are worthy of special attention. In these cases, substantial planning occurs, technology and student support resources assist students and faculty, high potential target markets receive attention, and enrollment and revenue generation have grown. Each appears to offer sound education and business models.

RMIT University

The RMIT University has emerged as a global leader in higher education outreach. Specializing in offering competency-based education (CBE) around a few targeted disciplines, RMIT has in recent years taken a proactive global expansionary stand. With overseas locations in Indonesia, Spain, and Vietnam, RMIT lives up to its slogan as a "global university of technology, design, and enterprise."[1] RMIT uses a twin-hub model where students at any of the campuses have an opportunity to take some of their coursework in an additional foreign location (RMIT 2015b). Many students and faculty members take advantage of this twin-hub experience by conducting research and coursework in two or more countries.

RMIT Europe opened in 2013 and is headquartered at its branch campus in Barcelona, which serves as a hub for the rest of Europe. From this location, RMIT partners with more than 115 universities throughout Europe. The hub model is one that leverages partnerships to provide students and faculty members with exchange, internships, and research opportunities.

The value-added experience RMIT offers to Vietnamese students since it first opened in 2001 is an opportunity to enroll in a top-rated Australian university on Vietnamese soil. RMIT Vietnam offers degrees from campuses in Hanoi and Ho Chi Minh City. All courses are offered in English. RMIT boasts the only fully foreign-owned university in Vietnam. Enrollments exceeded 3,000 students in 2015, a trend that will undoubtedly continue to rise.

The competencies graduates learn at RMIT are focused on skills needed in the workforce, and the value is recognized by current and prospective students. Denise Cuthbert (2013), dean of the School of Graduate Research, mentioned how important it is that RMIT maintains a close relationship with government leaders in local and international contexts. These relationships are what helped the government of Vietnam entrust land to RMIT in Ho Chi Minh City, an offer the government has not extended to any other foreign university.

Whether it's in Melbourne or at one of its several overseas locations, RMIT also focuses on developing strong relationships with local and international industry partners, which offers students internship opportunities and graduates excellent options for potential employment. We highlight RMIT as an exemplar in establishing local and international partnerships that have helped RMIT rise to world-class status in recent years.

Webster University

Webster University is an example of an institution that has transformed over time into one that is primarily focused on meeting the needs of a twenty-first-century student body. Established in 1915 in a suburb of St. Louis as a Catholic women's college, Webster later expanded its enrollments to include students of both genders in the early 1960s and to a lay governance model in 1967. It operates under a nonprofit, private higher education model.

Webster's rapid expansion across the United States and overseas is because university administrators follow a university-wide strategic plan titled *Global Impact for the Next Century*. "The world is changing, and Webster University is changing with it," states Elizabeth J. Stroble (Webster University 2015b). Webster's current strategic direction is rooted on four core values:

student-centered focus, learning that joins theory and practice, diversity and inclusion, and global citizenship. This values-focused approach is attractive to stakeholders at all levels and has helped Webster gain higher recognition. It is also grounded in a university-wide approach that aligns well with the Higher Education Leadership Wheel we introduced in chapter 1.

Webster graduates enter the workforce having been exposed to local, national, and international experiences and global citizenship opportunities that center on the role they will play in industry and community well into the future. With 60 campuses in the United States, Webster also has international branch campuses in Africa (Ghana), Asia (China and Thailand[2]), and Europe (Austria, Greece, the Netherlands, and Switzerland) (Webster University 2016). This international footprint highlights a unique strength of the Webster University model that is ideal in establishing networking, study abroad, internship, and job placement opportunities well beyond what normal higher education institutions are able to accomplish on their own.

Penn State World Campus (PSWC)

Based upon selection criteria that include faculty credentials and training, graduation rates, student debt, academic, student and career services, technology, and student engagement, *U.S. News & World Report* in 2015 ranked PSWC among the top three best online bachelor degree universities. Educational and student service quality controls are valued.

PSWC was launched during the 2000–2001 school year. Graduates receive a normal Pennsylvania State University diploma, and faculty come from their residence programs. Full-time students pay a flat rate of US$6,500 per semester full-time enrollment for a minimum of 12 credit hours (there is no upper limit). Assuming eight semesters of full-time study at 16 credit hours per semester and no increase in tuition, a degree from PSWC cost US$52,000 in 2015–2016 dollars.

Liberal arts majors are offered in addition to career-oriented degrees in business, education, energy, engineering, health and family services, nursing, and computer sciences. Courses are offered asynchronously. Approximately 14,000 full-time, part-time, undergraduate, and graduate students enrolled for the school year 2015–2016.

A telephone interview with Rick Shearer (2015), director, PSWC Learning Design, offers additional perspective. Courses and instruction are designed to be equal to or better than residence-based learning. A continuous improvement environment is sustained, with new or different readings constituting 5 to 10 percent of all reading assignments. Course designers, support staff and faculty retain contact throughout the student learning experience. Their model allows for a certain percentage of revenue retention to reinvest in PSWC.

Perceived challenges going forward include an increasingly crowded field of online competition, building to scale, cost containment, and a need to continuously add value for their students. Lessons learned by PSWC may serve the institution well in terms of adding to a more complete understanding of the contemporary student life experience. Attention to academic rigor, the learning experience and integration with the broader Penn State education and student support infrastructure characterizes this initiative.

The activities, achievements, and challenges facing PSWC are documented in the Pennsylvania State University Faculty Senate Report (Smutz et al. 2015). The report notes the presence of quality controls that include requiring successful completion of a five-course certification by new faculty and that all faculty are reviewed and appointed by academic colleges and departments.

The financial results are impressive. School year 2013–2014 reflected US$106.5 million in tuition revenues, of which US$62 million were distributed among other colleges and campuses of Penn State. An increase to US$115.8 million in tuition revenues are projected for 2014–2015, of which US$62.5 million will be distributed (Smutz et al. 2015). Undergraduate retention was 62 percent in 2013–2014, and 82 percent for graduate students (Smutz et al. 2015).

The report observes that challenges include the rapid pace of changing technologies, the need to further build to scale for purposes of improving their operating efficiencies, and the increasing competition. Notwithstanding these challenges, PSWC's goal is to increase student enrollment to 45,000 by 2025 (Smutz et al. 2015). The business model aligns with the educational mission for both PSWC and the Penn State System.

EdPlus at Arizona State University

ASU is a large, public research university that has adopted an employer- and student-centric approach to delivery of its online education to a national audience. Unlike SNHU, which created separate subsidiaries for online education and CBE, ASU's EdPlus functions within the traditional institutional structure. By way of context, ASU has an estimated 83,000 students enrolled. Tuition and fee schedules are subject to review and approval by the Arizona legislature, and their financial statements are reviewed by the state auditor. After years of defunding by the state government, Arizona's public research and four-year and community colleges had to figure out ways to become more self-reliant financially.

Under the leadership of EdPlus Executive Vice President and Dean Phil Regier, supported by its president, Michael M. Crow, ASU has shown a will to experiment. It partners with Starbucks to offer online degree-based education to qualified Starbuck employees regardless of their location. As of 2015, an estimated 13,000 students were enrolled in EdPlus (Lewin 2015).

According to Howard Schultz, chief executive officer (CEO) of Starbucks, "If any Starbucks barista could finish a bachelor's degree with full tuition reimbursement through Arizona State University . . . wouldn't that represent an important step forward in enabling the kinds of life-changing opportunities their parents and grandparents had? We sure think so" (Shultz and Crow 2014). According to ASU Crow, "We're trying to demonstrate a model in which corporations and universities work together to help kids finish college" (Crow 2015b).

Starbuck employees who work at company-owned stores and average at least 20 hours a week of work are eligible for reimbursement. From its side, ASU reduces standard tuition by 42 percent for Starbuck employees. Many employees are expected to qualify for federal grants, such as Pell, and will be reimbursed the differential in tuition by Starbucks (Crow 2015a).

Phil Regier (2015a; 2015b) was interviewed on two occasions for this book, and he shared many insights on EdPlus progress. Although all faculty for EdPlus come from ASU academic departments, and are either full-time or adjunct, all must successfully complete a two-week boot camp training program.

Faculty play a key role in supplying feedback to students. There is no upper limit on enrollment per course section. EdPlus does not retain operating income, but returns it to ASU's central coffers. The president of ASU chairs their EdPlus Steering Committee, and EdPlus operates on two-year budget cycles. Educational planning is student centric. Students pay the same tuition regardless of whether they are from Arizona, another state, or another country.

EdPlus envisions international opportunities and domestic partnerships as a vehicle for growth. Within a span of a few years, ASU grew from an initial student enrollment of 400 to more than 13,000 and included 70 degree programs by 2014. Pursuant with their home page, EdPlus (2015) "is committed to being a leader in online learning and global education. EdPlus will be a focal point for blending technology with teaching and learning ecosystems, in order to achieve greater scale, more efficient delivery and better learning outcomes in traditional and non-traditional settings."

Much thought was given to tuition pricing. It differs between ASU students who study in residence and those who enroll online. Depending upon the program, students enrolled online pay between US\$490 and US\$533 per credit hour, regardless of residency. Assuming for now 120 credits required to graduate and no increase in annual increases, a degree from ASU's EdPlus will cost between US\$58,800 and US\$63,960. Nonresident tuition and fees for EdPlus is discounted by 30 percent compared with on-campus instruction for nonresidents.

The audited annual financial statements of ASU do not comment upon the gross tuition revenues derived from EdPlus nor their net financial contributions to the university, which is consistent with the way that other integrated units of the university are treated. ASU's EdPlus has aggressive plans to grow its enrollment in the years ahead and thereby help offset the reductions of state funding.

Southern New Hampshire University, College of Online and Continuing Education, and College for America (CfA)

According to its home page, SNHU was founded in 1932 as a nonprofit private New Hampshire School for Accounting and Secretarial Science. After other name changes over the years, its current name was adopted in 2001. Accredited by New England Association of Schools and Colleges, SNHU named Paul LeBlanc as its president in 2003. Although SNHU is still organized around its schools of liberal arts, business, and education, it has achieved remarkable growth through its College of Online and Continuing Education subsidiary, which offers more than 80 undergraduate majors in various career tracks and liberal arts. Many of the insights for this section were derived through a phone interview with Paul LeBlanc (2015).

SNHU's online subsidiary student enrollment totals are among the five largest in the United States. By 2014–2015, an estimated 55,000 students were enrolled, and it has been called "the Amazon.com of higher education" (Kahn 2014). It produces a significant surplus for the University, 11 percent in FY2015, has a coterie of full-time faculty in addition to using adjuncts. SNHU's online enterprise contributes financial resources to its physical campus and projected gross annual revenues of an estimated US$375 million for FY2015. More recently, SNHU launched still another subsidiary, College for America (CfA), which delivers its programs through an online CBE model.

As of now, CfA offers associate degrees in business and nonclinical health care, and bachelor degrees in communications and health care management. Programs are based upon the skill needs of their corporate partners that include Anthem Blue Cross and Blue Shield, Sodexho, Goodwill Industries, ConAgra Foods, Panera's, FedEx, City of Memphis, and McDonalds. Unlike WGU, SNHU online and CfA do not use faculty in conventional ways. Skill sets are determined in collaboration with employer advisors and using data analytics. Attainment of 20 learning goals and 120 competencies are required for graduation with an associate's degree and 240 competencies for the bachelors.

In a manner similar to WGU, CfA terms are 26-week long. Evidence of competency attainment includes submission of papers and project assignments. Successful completion of project assignments is foundational to student progress. CfA uses academic coaches and reviewers rather than instructors, and what has been called a direct assessment model to track student progress. CfA is approved on an experimental basis by the U.S. Department of Education, and its students are eligible for federal aid and Pell Grants. Advancement is based upon proven mastery of designated learning outcomes. CfA was the first such program approved by the U.S. Department of Education.

CfA sustains quality standards, and is determined to provide substantive feedback to their students within 48 hours of project completion and submission. In addition, CfA's stated value proposition to those employers who send their workers is based upon enhancement of occupational skills, employee retention, and setting higher career goals. As with WGU, and SNHU's online subsidiary, curricula is standardized. All offer proactive 24/7 interaction with faculty and/or other student support services intended to foster student persistence and graduation. Their operating philosophy and quality controls are geared to adult learners. Using a subscription model of US$1,250 in FY2015 every six months, CfA is priced to reach students of very modest means.

A phone interview with Paul LeBlanc (2015) offered additional insights into SNHU's success. He acknowledges the importance of advice from Clayton Christiansen, who served on the SNHU Board of Trustees for many years, and of their strategic approach to change. A culture of "robust data analytics" characterizes their planning and decision-making processes, as well as forming the basis for interactions with students. Software tracks student progress, and students who are perceived to be slipping are contacted by staff.

Anticipating the difficult road ahead among for-profits and their perceived outlook for declining student enrollment and market share, SNHU carefully selected regions more likely to be receptive to online degree programs offered by a nonprofit university. Their video messages were thoughtfully crafted.

LeBlanc supports an entrepreneurial model in which CfA and the College for Online and Continuing Education are treated as separate subsidiaries. This approach expedites planning and decision-making processes through operational autonomy from the residential campus. SNHU has defined performance standards for a host of core functions that resemble the way that well-run corporate enterprises function.

Response times are monitored to assure expeditious answers to student inquiry, movement from inquiry to enrollment, and affording transfer credit for those who come from other institutions. Two-day turnaround standards are set for responding to financial aid applications. Student inquiries to a service center were compressed from 1 week to 8.5 minutes. LeBlanc refers to reengineered processes as "speed to lead." Students are constantly monitored to detect real or potential performance problems, and student support staff proactively initiate contact as needed.

Just as SNHU offers degree programs in three formats, namely, residence, online, and CBE, so too does it charge differentiated tuition. As of 2015, per annum tuition for the residence-based programs was US$29,274 plus fees of between US$1,703 and US$2,146. Online education tuition is US$320 per credit hour for nonactive duty military. Assuming 30 credit hours for a full-time student, tuition pricing per annum is US$9,600 or 32.8 percent the cost of a residence program to attain the same SNHU degree.

Further assuming 120 credit hours or four years to graduation, and no increase in tuition, a four-year degree will cost US$38,400. CfA charges an annual tuition of US$2,500, much or all paid by employers. Referring to tuition pricing for CfA, LeBlanc was quoted as saying, "This is the most remarkably priced college degree in the country, and the truth is that the price is the least remarkable thing about it. . . . What draws students and employers is the promise of mastering competencies they can immediately apply in their workplace" (Fain 2014a). The comparatively lower cost of SNHU's online and CfA tuition reflect sustainable business models that support a focused curriculum. Media-based and employer-centric marketing supplant more expensive visitation teams.

Competency-Based Education and Distance Education

Among many innovations in curriculum design and program delivery in higher education that have emerged during recent years, CBE seems to offer the most price-competitive venue for career education in the United States. Its evolution, approaches to planning, critical success factors, positions of accreditation associations, and lessons learned are worthy of attention. Special attention is given to two early adopters, namely WGU and CfA, a subsidiary of SNHU. Many community colleges, public and private non-profit universities such as the Kentucky Community and Technical College System, the University of Wisconsin, Austin Community College, Sinclair Community College, and Bellevue College (WA) appear to be moving in this direction.

The U.S. Department of Education and accreditors are taking CBE seriously (Bounds, Jr. 2015). According to Paul Fain (2014b), who tracks CBE for *Inside Higher Ed*, by 2014 many colleges or universities either already offer CBE at some level or are planning to do so. According to the same article, the U.S. Department of Education appears ready to approve so-called direct assessment programs on an experimental basis, which is important due to federal aid and grant implications. The Lumina Foundation, which has a long-term interest in fostering system change in traditional higher education, has formed the Competency-Based Attainment Network, as a cohort support group for institutions moving toward adoption of CBE.

Unlike synchronous or most asynchronous courses offered through conventional online channels, CBE is self-paced, so students progress as they demonstrate evidence of skill acquisition. The most able and dedicated students can graduate ahead of their peers, while others do not advance as quickly and may find their education is more expensive. In the case of both WGU and CfA, employers play an important role in defining the skills and competencies requisite to curriculum design and outcome measurement. It is then up to academic leaders, faculty members, and support staff to develop and deliver curriculum and help keep students on track.

Western Governors University

A distinctive nonprofit private CBE-based institution, WGU was founded in 1997 with the support of 19 governors in the Western United States. Early financial assistance was provided by educational foundations, with the involvement of many corporate leaders. In 2015, WGU student enrollment stood at 58,000, charges between US$2,890 per six-month term in business, administration, teaching, and information technology programs, and US$4,250 in pre-licensure nursing.

On average, WGU supports a delivery system that enables students to complete a bachelor's degree within three years at a total tuition price of between US$18,000 and US$25,512, inclusive of all learning materials. WGU is accredited by the Northwest Commission on Colleges and Universities (Thomas 2015). Their relatively affordable tuition structure reflects a highly focused, no-frills curriculum, notwithstanding their reliance upon full-time faculty as opposed to the growing industry trend toward the use of adjunct faculty.

According to their home page, WGU's (2016) mission is "to improve quality and expand access to post-secondary education by providing a means for individuals to learn independent of time and place to earn competency-based degrees and other credentials that are credible to both academic institutions and employers." Flexibility, affordable tuition, and career success are integral to WGU's statement of purpose. WGU offers degrees in well-defined career occupations including teaching, business administration, information technology, and certain health professions. Employer satisfaction surveys of WGU alumni workplace performance conducted in 2013 by Harris Interactive reflect exceptionally high ratings.

WGU has worked diligently over the years on a continuous improvement model. According to Sally Johnstone, vice president for academic advancement, WGU uses a standardized curriculum, all of which is subject to ongoing review by academics and employers. All faculty are full-time. New faculty are required to attend on-site training programs, offered at several locations, and are then mentored by current faculty prior to assuming their responsibilities.

Student progress is based upon demonstrated mastery of learning outcomes associated with courses. All faculty are focused on students' success in their academic program of study. WGU assessments are designed and evaluated by professionals who do not directly support their students. Each student support faculty member normally works with 80–90 students and proactively coaches and mentors these students to help them master the learning outcomes.

Students can enroll at any time. Each term is six months in duration. Courses map to learning outcomes, and students' progress is based upon demonstrated mastery of specific competencies. Programs are aligned with workforce needs as defined by employers. WGU takes advantage of the latest technologies and learning science developments to help students succeed (Johnstone 2015).

Accreditors and Preapproval Criteria for Experimental CBE Sites

Interest in CBE has risen among a number of community colleges, four-year colleges, and universities. A recent article in *Insider Higher Ed* observes that an estimated 200 institutions either already have begun offering CBE or are on track to do so in a so-called direct assessment model (Fain 2014c). This has caused the U.S. Department of Education (USDOE) and regional accreditation associations, through its Council of Regional Accrediting Commissions (C-RAC), to work on common standards by which to evaluate learning outcomes and institutional effectiveness.

The role of faculty in the learning and student interaction process is among the variables receiving close attention by USDOE and the accreditors. Both USDOE and C-RAC are developing guidance for direct assessment CBE programs. C-RAC's approach appears to offer a foundation and pathway for accreditation of CBE by member institutions.

A press release from C-RAC on 2 June 2015 offers insight into their current thinking. C-RAC distinguishes between credit-based CBE and a so-called direct assessment program. In credit-based CBE, such as the WGU model, student competencies are expected to aggregate at the program or degree level, and "each student is required to demonstrate mastery of every competency." This approach is akin to awarding credit for course or competency completion, and instructors are expected to validate student mastery of skill attainment.

C-RAC notes that a direct assessment model for programs or degrees that do not track back to a credit-based course must receive prior approval from their accreditation association. Adequacy and qualifications of instructional staff are subject to review. In addition, accreditors will "evaluate and approve the institution's methodology for determining the credit hour equivalence of the direct assessment measures" (C-RAC 2015). This is a prima facie indication that accreditors will require proof statements from their member institutions that learning outcomes and other accreditation standards will be applied fairly, fully, and equally to all member institutions, regardless of whether they sustain residence programs, online education, or either form of CBE.

In a letter dated 9 June 2015, and directed to executive directors of the six regional accreditation associations, USDOE observes that it has the authority to grant waivers for CBE student access to federal aid for pre-approved "experimental sites" to institutions able to ensure quality in their application of CBE to the satisfaction of their accreditation associations. The cover letter makes clear that this authority will be applied to a limited number of institutions and sets forth certain rules of engagement or criteria governing accreditation commissions' actions.

The broad language applies to assessing the qualifications and role of faculty members, program design, and documentation requirements for course and credit-based CBE and direct assessment. In doing so, USDOE left no room for interpretation of unacceptable institutional behavior, namely, "It is incumbent on the institution to demonstrate that students are not left 'to educate themselves', a chief characteristic of correspondence programs" (USDOE 2015). In view of prior criticisms by USDOE of regional accreditors for a variety of perceived shortcomings, assignment of responsibility and the effort to define criteria for the approval process merit further attention.

ENTREPRENEURSHIP, REVENUE GENERATION, AND THE EDUCATIONAL MISSION

Our thesis is that sustainable business models align with and support basic educational priorities, serve the needs of students, and either grow revenues through ancillary activities or improve operational efficiencies in ways that benefit students. The University of Pittsburgh Medical Center (UPMC) and the early growth years at Tuskegee exemplify ways that financial and resources were generated through educational entrepreneurship. UPMC and Tuskegee directly supported their core academic mission through generating resources from ancillary enterprises, and deployed hands-on management techniques worthy of private sector companies.

UPMC and the University of Pittsburgh Health Sciences

Nowadays UPMC is a separate nonprofit legal entity providing health care, insurance, and clinical research services. It primarily serves the needs of residents in Western Pennsylvania. It owns hospitals, medical practices, laboratories, research, rehabilitation, and assisted living facilities. In 2014, UPMC generated US$11.4 billion of total operating revenues (UPMC 2014). It also partners with the University of Pittsburgh Health Sciences in many ways that render both institutions more effective.

The externally audited financial statements also reflect that UPMC made payments to the University of Pittsburgh in the amount of US$152.3 million in 2014 for the clinical services provided by certain faculty members and medical students. An additional payment of US$107.4 million was made to the University of Pittsburgh for research and academic support. The Financial Report of the University of Pittsburgh for Fiscal Year 2014 reflects still more payments from UPMC due to affiliation agreements reached over time. In short, UMPC and University of Pittsburgh Health Sciences sustain a symbiotic relationship in which each enterprise is integral to the success of the other.

UPMC embraces medical entrepreneurship and supports core educational priorities of health sciences at the University of Pittsburgh. How did this happen? Is their model portable? What lessons can we learn?

One cannot separate the successes of UPMC from the leader who launched this enterprise, namely Thomas P. Detre. The story of his achievements, the team he brought together to lead UPMC, and the evolution of UPMC and the University of Pittsburgh Health Sciences are captured in articles that appeared in the *Pittsburgh Quarterly* (Dietrich II 2009), *Academic Medicine* (Levine 2008), and *A History of UPMC: Beyond the Bounds* (Brignano 2009). This is supplemented by insights gained through many conversations during the years of our friendship.

Although Detre passed away several years ago, his legacy and the model he developed endures. In 1973, the university recruited Detre, then psychiatrist-in-chief at Yale-New Haven Hospital, a tenured professor of psychiatric medicine at Yale, to head the Western Psychiatric Hospital (WPH). Little did the University of Pittsburgh understand the full range of Detre's attributes. As it happened, Detre was a highly effective fund-raiser, an extraordinary recruiter of top faculty and administrative talent, and an impressive generator of research grants. Detre was also a tough negotiator, sustaining certain operational autonomy for UPMC and authoring a revenue-retention scheme that allowed for reinvestment of internally generated revenues (Hart 2010, pp. 16–17).

In 1984, Detre was named senior vice president for health sciences. During the years after his appointment, energy, vision, and centralized planning characterized the transformation from a confederation of hospitals, then collectively known as the University Health Center of Pittsburgh, to what is now known as UPMC. Detre and his team centralized controls, developed operational efficiencies, and a coherent organizational structure.

Systemic transformation in this model did not permit institutional autonomy. Detre held the joint positions of CEO of UPMC and eventually rose to the senior vice chancellor for health sciences at the University of Pittsburgh.[3]

The vision nurtured by Detre was that UMPC and Pitt's medical school and health sciences were inseparable, and that a multiplier effect in value creation should exceed the sum of the parts. This was articulated as follows:

> In an academic health center, research and clinical success are synergistic and interdependent. In-depth, committed, strategic collaboration between the clinical and the academic enterprises will enhance the success of both beyond that which would occur with an investment in either alone. (Levine et al. 2008, p. 8)

A measure of one's legacy as an educational leader is the sustainability of the educational and business model beyond the tenure of the pioneer.

Tom Detre's contribution to the University of Pittsburgh, UPMC, and the broad communities they serve are testimony to his lasting contributions. Detre had vision, drive, intelligence, and determination to excel. He was intuitive, respected, and known to rely upon evidence-based decisions. Detre was a medical entrepreneur who was committed to performance excellence at UPMC, while being dedicated to the academic and research mission of health sciences.

UPMC-Pitt Medical School offers a proof statement that a high-functioning business model in higher education can be compatible with quality of education. This model also reflects the benefits derived from a highly centralized administrative structure that minimized redundant functions. Resources generated by UPMC help to sustain highly rated health care and medical school education.

Tuskegee University

The formative years of Tuskegee University reflect the ingenuity and dedication of its founder, Booker T. Washington.[4] On 4 July 1881, the Tuskegee Normal and Industrial Institute (now Tuskegee University) opened its doors to 30 male and female African American students (Washington 2004). Booker T. Washington, a young graduate of Hampton Institute, was its founder. Washington's autobiography affords insights into his leadership style.

Financial necessity, combined with a focus on trade skills education, led to an evolving work-study program in which students cleared land, helped design and construct buildings, and manufactured bricks for use of Tuskegee. Bricks were also sold locally to raise revenues. According to Washington (2004, p. 61), "Most of our students came to us in poverty, from the cabins of cotton, sugar and rice plantations. I felt that building the school themselves would give them valuable self-reliance and skills, from brick making and masonry to blacksmithing, carpentry and architecture."

Washington was dedicated to institutional and individual self-reliance, thus insisting upon learning skills and a trade as fundamental education for Tuskegee graduates. Academic subjects were taught as well. While students were charged for room and board, they could receive credit from work performed at the school to apply toward their fees. Washington was a prolific fund-raiser and was able to cover the annual per student tuition of US$50 through donations.

Three years after Tuskegee opened its doors, a night school was established. By 1901, Tuskegee's enrollment had grown to 1,400 day students and 457 night students, and it had 66 buildings, 62 of which were built by students, a 2,300-acre campus, and offered majors in 30 "industrial departments" (pp. 60–61, 73, 100–103). Some might argue that Tuskegee was the prototype of modern-day career-oriented technical and community colleges in the United States.

While Tuskegee received a relatively modest annual appropriation from the state government of Alabama, institutional growth of physical facilities and student enrollment created resource needs that benefited from fund-raising, reliance upon student workers, and generating ancillary revenues through the sale of bricks and agricultural produce yielded from their land. Luis Harlan (1972, p. 158), a biographer of Washington, observes a "pragmatic bargain" in which the leader of Tuskegee sacrificed accommodation with a dominant and hostile segregationist environment in order attain "educational and economic gain" for his institution. Notwithstanding criticisms of Washington, the achievements of Tuskegee as a trade-focused college and as a financially self-reliant institution are above reproach.

COST CONTAINMENT, OPERATING EFFICIENCIES, AND AFFORDABLE TUITION

It may be said that generating incremental revenues through new or ancillary activities may be aspirational; institutions literally own their expenses. To some reasonable degree, certain expenses are discretionary and may be compressed. This section presents exemplars of cost containment where operating expenses are controlled, and quality of education and student services are sustained.

Grove City College (GCC)

During a guest lecture in a University of Pittsburgh doctoral-level course in 2014, Dick Jewell (who had recently retired as president of GCC) advised our graduate students, "When our students cross the stage at graduation to receive their diploma, I want to know that I'm shaking the hand of an educated person." GCC effectively controls expenses, and supports laudatory student attainment without sacrifice to learning outcomes, educational, and spiritual priorities. As stated on its home page, GCC (2016) is dedicated to "a well-rounded curriculum that helps students see the broad intellectual ideas, people and events that have shaped, and continue to shape, our world."

What do we know about GCC? Its website is informative. It is a faith-based private liberal arts college located about 50 miles north of Pittsburgh. During 2014–2015, just over 2,400 students were enrolled in either liberal arts majors or in career programs that included accounting, business, computer science, primary and secondary education, and electrical or mechanical engineering. GCC's four-year graduation rate was 78 percent.

All education is delivered in a conventional residence mode. GCC was rated by *Consumers Digest* in 2014 as the number one value private liberal arts college in the United States. Other top ten colleges include Williams, Amherst, Claremont McKenna, and Middlebury. *Consumer Digest* selection criteria include student academic performance indicators; four- and six-year graduation rates; and cost of tuition, room, and board. During the school year 2015–2016, the fully loaded price of tuition, room, and board was US$24,956, of which US$16,154 was for tuition.

A closer study of GCC's distinctive business model is revealing. The following notes are largely based upon a coauthored position paper by Jewell and Sutin (2012). Unlike most of its peer group, GCC does not discount tuition—so the sticker tuition price applies to all students. Students are expected to live on campus, with limited exceptions. Last year 97 percent of all students were in residency halls. Faculty are hired and retained based upon their perceived content expertise and a passion for instruction.

A normal teaching load is four courses per semester. This more closely resembles the instructional load at a community college. Staff, faculty, and administrators, including the president, are on one-year renewable contracts. GCC does not offer tenure and does not have labor unions. Instructors come to GCC because they want to, and most remain. GCC relies primarily upon enrollment and tuition revenues to cover operating expenses.

Allocations from endowments and capital campaigns primarily fund new construction, student scholarships, and other forms of financial aid. GCC rejects funding from either the state or the federal government. Retirement pensions were shifted from a defined benefits program to defined contribution. GCC abhors debt, although it did borrow to help finance two new buildings and does use a revolving bank line of credit to cover temporary cash needs. Finally, GCC carefully monitors operating, professional, and staff productivity. GCC's value proposition for its students is discernible.

Community College of Allegheny County (CCAC): Reflections from 2003–2007

CCAC is a large, urban community college serving the educational needs of thousands of students in Allegheny and Washington counties in Pennsylvania through a system of four large campuses and several lower enrollment centers. Toward the end of August 2003, barely two weeks into the first author's presidency at CCAC, our externally audited consolidated financial statements arrived. They reflected a US$2.4 million reduction of net assets for the fiscal year 2002–2003, which is how fund accounting terminology classifies an operating loss. That fall the state government reduced appropriations to the operating budget of community colleges by 10 percent relative to the prior year, marking a departure from its statutory requirement of providing one-third of operating revenues.

CCAC's financial situation worsened in the weeks that ensued. Health care insurance premiums increased by 39 percent for 2004. Contractually mandated salary increases for members of our two labor unions (American Federation of Teachers [AFT] and Service Employees International Union [SEIU]) were scheduled to increase costs by US$1.5 million for the next school year. The CFO's pro forma financial projection indicated that CCAC's net annual operating loss would rise to US$15 million in three years in the absence of significant intervention. This sum exceeded the financial reserves of the college (Sutin 2011).

After notifying the board of trustees that the financial model of CCAC was broken, our team developed a comprehensive financial intervention plan for review and approval by the board. Idea generation eventually came from many sources in ongoing college-wide collaboration. Short-term emergency measures called for increasing tuition pricing of most programs by 8 percent. An additional 20 percent premium was charged to students in more costly nursing and other health career programs (Sutin 2011). The emergency plan also called for reduction of nonfaculty staff by 10 percent over a one-year period of time—beginning with a retirement incentive plan.

Further initiatives were agreed upon. Analysis of data indicated that many course sections had been offered at attendance levels below our calculated breakeven point of nine students. That was unsustainable. Enrollment guidelines were given to deans of instruction for the purpose of increasing the size of course sections, with the understanding that certain disciplines such as English required more faculty input and should enroll comparatively fewer students. Others were based more upon test grading and could handle larger enrollment without sacrificing quality. Travel, dues, and memberships in professional associations were reduced by 30 percent. The president's travel budget was lowered by 40 percent (CCAC 2004b). We decided to insource more campus security at a significant savings.

These measures, and others, set the basis for stabilization of CCAC's financial condition. By fiscal year 2007–2008, CCAC's audited financial reports stated an increase of US$6.6 million in net assets or what may be termed a net operating surplus. The average annual increase in tuition during the 2003–2007 time period reflected the prevailing rate of inflation inclusive of the one-time 8 percent increase. Importantly, open lines of communication with faculty and staff members were retained for purposes of exploring options beyond the emergency plan.

The initial environment of shared concern led to collaboration with the leadership of our unit of the AFT and SEIU. The AFT assumed a leadership role in helping CCAC gain acceptance to a consortium of K-12 school districts in Allegheny County, which brought about a substantial reduction of administrative costs while maintaining like or superior health care benefits. SEIU leaders invited senior CCAC administrators to attend many of their executive committee meetings at which several proposals were presented for our consideration. Collaboration with labor unions may appear by some as counterintuitive, but it did take place as we had shared concerns for institutional sustainability.

Reorganization of our administrative structure and reduction of nonfaculty positions was more complicated and faced tougher opposition. CCAC had evolved as a somewhat loose confederation of campuses, each with their own standards and different job descriptions for like positions. Campus loyalties trumped institutional priorities. Redundancy of many functions was noticeable.

With support from CCAC's board of trustees, a plan was adopted to develop a more integrated institution. An outside consultant was hired, namely David Peirce, the former head of the Virginia Community College System, and retired president of the American Association of Community Colleges. We agreed with his recommendations that each campus executive, now called a campus president, would also hold system-wide functional responsibilities.

Under the new scheme, the head of one campus was named institutional chief academic officer. Another was named vice president of student affairs for the system. The third was CFO, and the fourth was named to head up workforce training. This eliminated four senior positions. Henceforth, the job of each was leadership and delegation more than task management.

Deans of instruction, student affairs, and chief business officers on each campus were held accountable to manage day-to-day operations. CCAC also migrated from a job description as a basis for annual performance evaluations to management by objectives. These changes caused a shock to a campus-centric change-resistant institutional culture and did not occur smoothly. Many changes endured beyond 2007; some did not.

Facilities Management at University of Pittsburgh: A Story of Student-Centric Change

Colleges and universities have ample opportunities to improve service quality for students and reduce expenses. Redesign and transition from labor-intensive processes to highly productive operations can be achieved by engaging workers and utilizing technology to facilitate communications and provide essential management reports. This work is unglamorous and rarely captures media attention.

The facilities management situation facing Jim Earle when he was named assistant vice chancellor for business at the University of Pittsburgh, the choices he made, and the beneficial outcomes allow us to better understand how creative solutions can be found that improve operational and student support services while lowering expenses. The sources for the following comments came from a graduate school course Earle co-instructed with the first author on Higher Education Budget Management, supplemented by his email on 13 July 2015.

Prior leadership had sustained an arms-length relationship with employees responsible for repair and custodial services, all of whom belonged to the SEIU. Morale was low. The unit lacked a mission statement and the requisite core values. Communication channels were often dysfunctional. Productivity was unsatisfactory, as were perceptions of service quality by students living in dormitories. In short, customer satisfaction was low and cost of services was higher than it needed to be. Earle was named head of this function with a mandate from executive leadership to fix the problems.

Earle devoted substantial time and energy to gathering information to better understand the problems, analyzing the findings, and developing an implementation plan. Earle knew that complex problems required comprehensive solutions. By nature a highly open, sensitive, and motivational leader, Earle approached the workforce with respectful and nonhierarchical communications and invited team members to develop collaborative solutions.

In time, all committed to a regimen of continuous student services without regard to the day of the week or the hour of the day. They agreed upon a mission statement and values. Decisions were made to adopt a computerized maintenance management system (CMMS). Employees were named to a task force to evaluate and select an appropriate CMMS. As a result, there was improved awareness among employees of the beneficial results of the system acquired, combined with a sense of ownership. The unit culture had begun to shift from hierarchical "we-they" relations to one of common ownership of the performance results. Communications were open and honest.

The process of CMMS selection and the resulting applications proved highly beneficial. Student requests for services now went directly to portable units help by repair and custodial employees rather than through a centralized and inefficient log-in center. Accountability for service provided could now be tracked to the individual employees on call. All students who requested services automatically receive online survey requests to evaluate the quality of the service they were provided.

Labor productivity could be tracked. Work schedules for routine preventative maintenance were in place, which is far less costly than corrective maintenance. Measurable performance standards were agreed upon as a basis of pride rather than contract negotiation. Union leaders now suggest a 24-hour service turn-around for nonemergency repairs instead of the previous 48-hour time frame.

Other key performance indicators, such as inventory, are also tracked by CMMS. Inventory levels were reduced from a running average of US$1 million to an estimated US$400,000. Perhaps more important, employees are committed to high service quality standards and are excited about finding still further ways to improve efficiency and lower costs. The cost savings generated by CMMS offset the purchase price in less than one year.

Collaborative Intervention: An Emerging Success Story in New York City

This section is devoted to an emergent effort in New York City to develop systemic and seamless solutions to facilitate advancement by students in high school to community colleges and universities. It is not the only such initiative in the United States, but is worthy of attention due to its rapid growth and the partnership between City University of New York (CUNY), the New York City Board of Education, and local employers.

High dropout rates from many public high schools, and the numbers of graduates in need of developmental or remedial education courses calls for more innovative solutions. Vertical integration of high school and college education offers an alternative approach that inspires confidence.

The early or middle college school has long been a vehicle by which a limited number of public school districts in the United States and postsecondary institutions collaborate to educate at-risk students from low-income families. Those who enroll pursue a high school diploma and often go on to obtain professional certification, an associate's or bachelor's degree. LaGuardia Community College was an early adopter of this model. In the case of CUNY, early college or middle college is a subset of a more comprehensive collaborative initiative.

Similar early college initiatives exist in Texas, North Carolina, and other states, so focusing attention on New York is illustrative of achievements by others as well. Further insight into their progress came about through phone interviews with Ann Freibel, associate dean of academic affairs at LaGuardia; Brian Donnelly, deputy director, Early College Initiative at CUNY; and John Capman, research analyst at CUNY. This was supplemented by information materials sent by Donnelly and data culled from CUNY Collaborative Programs and the Early College Initiative on their homepages.

The planning and operational components of the New York City Early College Initiative involve participation by representatives from CUNY, the Board of Education, and private sector employers. They share efforts to select new principals, define curriculum guidelines, and agree upon the technical and soft skills desired of students. Faculty members develop curricula within prescribed guidelines.

Pathways in Technology Early College High Schools (P-TECHs) are a smaller version of the early college and serve approximately 100 students per high school grade. These schools are dedicated to a STEM curriculum for students with special interests in these majors. Both the P-TECH and the conventional early or middle college afford seamless pathways to a CUNY participating institution. As of 2014–2015, early college enrollment was 6,807 in 17 early colleges. Summer enrichment, college success, and college transition programs are made available to early college students. This is indicative of 360 degree planning and collaborative work that characterizes the Early College Initiative in New York City (CUNY 2016).

The results are impressive. Eighty-seven percent of the 2013 high school cohort in early college graduated from high school and averaged successful completion of 28 college credits. Seventy-seven percent of the 2011 cohort went on to college. CUNY and public school partners sustain a continuous improvement model for the purpose of improving upon these results. Higher retention rates and successful progression at community colleges and universities reduce deployment of financial and other resources needed to support students in remedial or developmental education courses.

EMERGENT TECHNOLOGIES

Creative application of software and data mining offers a wide range of opportunities to enhance academic and student services planning, evaluate performance metrics, and share tools with faculty members and students to self-direct their activities. Mining data and integrating resultant analytics into planning are increasingly understood as essential rather than optional building blocks. For example, Nuventive and like companies provide suites of software products to facilitate performance measurement of student learning outcomes. Civitas Learning (CL) offers *predictive analytics* that better enable students to chart their plans of study more effectively, while facilitating support from faculty members, their advisors, student support services, and administrators.

According to Angela Baldasare (2015), assistant provost for institutional research, University of Arizona, this supports more efficient and timely interventions for at-risk students in particular. Kurt Ewen, presidential fellow at Valencia College, Florida, observes that predictive analytics data from CL's web-based applications offer actionable insights and help the college determine when and how to better allocate resources to support students based upon evidence rather than assumptions. Software from Viridis Learning triangulates data between students, college, and employers in ways that better position students to make informed decisions on their educational concentration, while positioning college faculty to adapt curriculum in a continuous change environment.

Unlike private industry, where mammoth multibillion dollar enterprises can internally generate software solutions, higher education institutions lack the scale or critical mass to do so. Yet, institutional effectiveness increasingly relies upon instructional, operational, and data reporting software that are enablers of performance improvement. The opportunities to further improve institutional efficiencies and effectiveness through selective application of software are bountiful.

CONCLUDING OBSERVATIONS AND LESSONS LEARNED

Higher education offers far more stories of innovation and conspicuous achievement than limitations of time and space allow coverage of within the confines of this chapter. In the aggregate, they suggest that more change is occurring within community colleges, colleges, and universities than is conceded by its many critiques. Success stories don't sell newspapers or magazines and rarely appear in broadcast media. But institutional achievements in higher education go well beyond those noted in this chapter and offer lessons that others can learn from.

Other mature industries, such as banking, transportation, and consumer shopping have made great strides in developing customer-centric technologically driven solutions that materially improve service quality while yielding significant productivity gains to customer and service provider alike. Home banking services such as bill payer dramatically lower operating expenses while offering a suite of value-added services for customers. The airlines industry achieved similar results by shifting from hard copy to e-tickets and customer printing of boarding passes. Both industries reenvisioned core processes, invested in operating and data reporting software, and effectively transferred ownership of discrete processes to their customers. They figured out how to make a knowledge economy work to their competitive advantage.

The exemplars cited in this chapter are indicative of an increasing awareness within higher education that challenges to improve upon the quality of learning, educational outcomes, quality of service, affordable education, career and liberal arts education, and sustainable business models can no longer be treated as separate and distinct. An overarching lesson learned from exemplars is that we can learn from others and that collaborative solutions are attainable. The following commonalities from success stories provide important markers to chart progress in the years ahead:

1. CBE offers exceptional potential to deliver verifiable skills-based career education identified by employers at more affordable prices, with instructional costs contained by offering a highly focused prescriptive no-frills free curriculum.
2. Nonprofit community colleges, colleges, and universities can meet the educational needs of nontraditional adult learners and generate substantial revenues in the process, provided that they dedicate requisite resources to sustain quality of education, offer competitive tuition, and sustain proactive and comprehensive student support services.
3. Selective and thoughtful risk taking can generate supplemental revenues through ancillary activities in support of the academic mission.
4. Quality education at a more affordable tuition is attainable provided that student attainment is central to planning, more attention is given to instruction, and operating efficiencies improve.
5. Early or middle colleges offer more seamless solutions toward successfully guiding at-risk students from one level of education to another, offering the potential for improving high school and postsecondary degree attainment while reducing the cost of subject matter repetition.
6. Collaborative solutions are attainable to the extent that an environment of trust exists between administrators, faculty, students, public officials, and business leaders.
7. Instructional and operational technology facilitates both learning and cost-effective administration and instruction.
8. Solutions to a more affordable and higher quality of education require a strategic and integrative approach that is entrepreneurial in style and planning that is collaborative and evidence based, demanding in execution, and student centric at the core.
9. Accountability, transparency and results matter.

Public confidence has to be earned through delivering a consistently high-quality and affordable education and graduating a high percentage of students who enroll. Graduates of community colleges, four-year colleges, and universities better able to "think" and "do" are the ultimate gauge by which educators and their institutions will be judged. Does higher education as a whole need to change? You bet. Are some within higher education resistant to change? Probably. But are there success stories to learn from? Absolutely.

NOTES

1. RMIT partners with the University of Pelita Harapan in Jakarta, Indonesia, to offer English-speaking programs and joint business degrees. Other overseas locations where RMIT currently partners with local higher education institutions to offer degrees include China, Singapore, and Sri Lanka (RMIT 2015a).

2. Like many higher education institutions that own and operate branch campuses overseas, we recognize the challenges Webster University has had in its expansion overseas. Perhaps most notable among these difficulties in recent years has been at the Webster University–Thailand (WUT) campus in Bangkok, where several shortcomings were highlighted in internal and external critiques (Redden 2015; Webster University 2015a). Senior administrators remain committed to help WUT continually improve and overcome its shortcomings and meet the international standard it espouses for all of its campuses (Webster University 2015a).

3. From 2004 to the time of his death in 2010, Detre held the titles of Emeritus Distinguished Senior Vice Chancellor for Health Sciences and Emeritus Distinguished Service Professor of Psychiatry (Hart 2010, p. 16).

4. We recognize the various perspectives (both for and against) which past and current scholars express regarding Washington's sometimes controversial views regarding education, including the importance of technical education (see, for instance, Du Bois 1903; Norrell 2003).

REFERENCES

Arizona State University/EdPlus homepage: available at: https://edplus.asu.edu

Associated Press, April 8, 2015. available online at: www.yahoofinance.com

Baldasare, Angela. 2015. Phone interview with the author, Pittsburgh, PA to Tucson, AZ, 15 May 2015.

Bounds, Jr., Herman. 2015. Letter from Herman Bounds, Director, Accreditation Group to Accrediting Agency Executive Directors. Washington, DC: Office of Postsecondary Education, U.S. Department of Education, 9 June 2015.

Brignano, Mary. *A History of UPMC: Beyond the Bounds. D*orrance Publishing, Pittsburgh, 2009.

Chandler, Dana. 2015. *Guide to the Papers of Booker T. Washington: The Tuskegee Collection.*

City University of New York (CUNY). 2016. Early College Initiative at CUNY. New York: CUNY. Available online at: http://www.earlycollege.cuny.edu/results; accessed on 1 February 2016.

Consumer Digest. Top Values for Colleges and Universities, 2014 edition.

Council of Regional Accrediting Associations. 2015. *Regional Accreditors Announce Common Framework for Defining and Approving Competency-Based Education Programs.* Press Release, 2 June 2015, Washington, DC.

Crow, Michael M. 2015a. *Designing the New American University*. Baltimore, MD: John Hopkins University Press.

Crow, Michael M. 2015b. "Talking Head: The State of the Public University." *New York Times*, Education Life, April 12, 2015, 8.

Cuthbert, Denise. 2013. Discussions with W. James Jacob at the Asia-Pacific Higher Education Research Partnership Meeting, RMIT University Vietnam, Ho Chi Minh City, 3 June 2013.

Dietrich II, William S. 2009. "Against the Odds." *Pittsburgh Quarterly* Summer.

Donnelly, Brian. 2015. Phone interviews, Pittsburgh, PA to Brooklyn, NY, 13 April, 15 May, and 23 July 2015.

Du Bois, W. E. B. 1903. *The Souls of Black Folk: Essays and Sketches*. Chicago: A. C. McClurg & Co.

Earle, Jim. 2015. Email correspondence to the first author, 13 July 2015.

Ewen, Kurt. 2015. Phone interview, Pittsburgh, PA to Orland, FL, 8 May 2015.

Fain, Paul. 2014a. "Competency and Affordability." *InsideHigherEd*, May 6, 2014. Available online at: https://www.insidehighered.com/news/2014/05/06/college-america-hits-10000-mark-new-competency-based-bachelors-degrees; accessed on 1 February 2016.

Fain, Paul. 2014b. "Defining Competency." *InsideHigherEd*, June 17, 2015. Available online at: https://www.insidehighered.com/news/2015/06/17/new-letters-us-and-accreditors-provide-framework-approval-competency-based-degrees; accessed on 1 February 2016.

Fain, Paul. 2014c. "Experimenting With Aid." *InsideHigherEd*, July 23, 2014. Available online at: https://www.insidehighered.com/news/2014/07/23/competency-based-education-gets-boost-education-department; accessed on 1 February 2016.

Flexner, Abraham. 1910. *Medical Education in the United States and Canada*. Bulletin Number Four (The Flexner Report). New York: The Carnegie Foundation for the Advancement of Teaching. Available online at: http://archive.carnegiefoundation.org/pdfs/elibrary/Carnegie_Flexner_Report.pdf; accessed on 1 February 2016.

Freibel, Anne. 2015. Phone interview with the author, Pittsburgh, PA to Queens, NY, 29 January 2015.

Grove City College (GCC). 2016. *Who We Are*. Grove City, PA: GCC. Available online at: http://www.gcc.edu/about/whoweare; accessed on 1 February 2016.

Hechinger, John. 2013. "Southern New Hampshire, a Little College That's a Giant Online." *Bloomberg Businessweek*, May 9, 2013. Available online at: http://www.bloomberg.com/bw/articles/2013–05-09/southern-new-hampshire-a-little-college-thats-a-giant-online; accessed on 1 February 2016.

Harlan, Louis R. 1972. *Booker T. Washington: The Making of a Black Leader, 1856–1901*. New York: Oxford University Press.

Hart, Peter. 2010. "Obituary: Thomas P. Detre." *University Times*, Vol. 43, No. 4, October 14, pp. 16–17.

Jewell, Richard, and Stewart E. Sutin. 2012. "Value-Based education: A Vision for a Higher Education Business Model," Presentation, American Enterprise Institute Conference, Washington, DC, 2 August 2012.

Johnstone, Sally. 2015. Phone interview with the author, Pittsburgh, PA to Salt Lake City, UT, 1 July 2015.

Kahn, Gabriel. January 2, 2014. "The Amazon of Higher Education: How tiny, struggling Southern New Hampshire University has become a behemoth." *Slate*.

Available online at: http://www.slate.com/articles/life/education/2014/01/southern_new_hampshire_university_how_paul_leblanc_s_tiny_school_has_become. html; accessed on 1 February 2016.

LeBlanc, Paul. 2015. Phone interview with the author, Pittsburgh, PA to Manchester, NH, 17 February 2015.

Levine, Arthur et al. 2008. "The Relationship Between the University of Pittsburgh School of Medicine and the University of Pittsburgh Medical Center: A Profile in Synergy." *Academic Medicine* 83 (9): 816–826.

Lewin, Tamar. 2015. "Promising Full College Credit, Arizona State Offers Online Freshman Program." *New York Times*, April 23, 2015, A14.

"National University Rankings." 2015. *U.S. News & World Report.*

Norrell, Robert J. 2003. "Booker T. Washington: Understanding the Wizard of Tuskegee." *The Journal of Blacks in Higher Education* 42: 96–109.

Penn State World Campus. 2016. *Homepage.* University Park, PA: Pennsylvania State University. Available at: http://www.worldcampus.psu.edu; accessed on 1 February 2016.

Redden, Elizabeth. 2015. "Revealing Review of a Thai Campus." *Inside Higher Ed*, 14 April 2015.

Regier, Phil. 2015a. Phone interview with the author, Pittsburgh, PA to Phoenix, AZ, 3 March 2015.

Regier, Phil. 2015b. Phone interview with the author, Pittsburgh, PA to Phoenix, AZ, 1 April 2015.

RMIT. 2015a. *International Partners.* Melbourne: RMIT. Available online at: https://www.rmit.edu.au; accessed on 27 October 2015.

RMIT. 2015b. *RMIT Vietnam Background.* Melbourne: RMIT. Available online at: https://www.rmit.edu.au; accessed on 27 October 2015.

Smutz, Wayne, Jane Keary-Thomas, Janet May Dillon, Rachel Heverly, and Tinamarie Illar. 2013. *Penn State World Campus: Today and Tomorrow.* Faculty Senate Report. University Park, PA: Pennsylvania State University.

Shultz, Howard, and Crow, Michael. 2014. "America Can't Afford College That's Unaffordable." *HuffPost Business*, November 6, 2014. Available online at: http://huffingtonpost.com/howard-schultz/american-cant-wait-colle_b_5427559.html; accessed on 1 February 2016.

Shearer, Phil. 2015. Phone interview with the author, Pittsburgh, PA to University Park, PA, 23 February 2015.

Southern New Hampshire University (SNHU). 2016. *Homepage.* Manchester, NH: SNHU. Available online at: http://www.snhu.edu/about; accessed on 1 February 2016.

Sutin, Stewart E. 2011. "Response to a Financial Crisis: Case Study of CCAC 2003–2008." In *Increasing the Effectiveness of the Community College Financial Model: A Global Perspective for the Global Economy*, edited by Stewart E. Sutin, Daniel Derrico, Rosalind Latiner Raby, and Edward J. Valeau (pp. 241–250). New York: Palgrave Macmillan.

Thomas, Pat. 2015. "Governor Sandoval Announces New Online, Competency-Based University." Press Release, 16 June 2015. Reno, NV: WKOLO. Available online at: http://www.kolotv.com/home/headlines/Governor-Sandoval-Announces-

New-Online-Competency-Based-University-for-Nevada-307640431.html; accessed on 1 February 2016.

University of Pittsburgh. 2014. *Financial Report, Fiscal Year 2014*. Pittsburgh, PA: University of Pittsburgh.

University of Pittsburgh Medical Center (UPMC). 2014. *Audited Consolidated Financial Statements, Year Ended June 30, 2014*. Pittsburgh, PA: UPMC.

Western Governor's University (WGU). 2016. *About WGU*. Salt Lake City, UT: WGU. Available online at: www.wgu.edu/about; accessed on 1 February 2016.

Washington, Booker T. 1901. *Up from Slavery: An Autobiography*. New York: Doubleday.

Webster University. 2015a. *International Site Review Report on: Thailand, Bangkok and Cha-am Campuses*. St. Louis, MO: Webster University.

Webster University. 2015b. *Webster University Strategic Plan: Global Impact for the Next Century*. St. Louis, MO: Webster University.

Webster University. 2016. *Worldwide Locations*. St. Louis, MO: Webster University. Available online at: http://www.webster.edu/worldwide/; accessed on 18 March 2016.

Chapter 9

Strategic and Transformative Leaders

Custer College in Kennebunk, Maine, was founded in 1872 as a nonsectarian coeducational four-year liberal arts institution. During subsequent decades, Custer grew and prospered. By 1998, Custer's enrollment had grown to 1,800 students on an attractive 104-acre campus. It was looked upon as a desirable alternative for applicants from affluent families in Middle Atlantic States and New England based upon the rigor of its curriculum, quality of faculty, and intimate learning environment. Students also looked favorably upon Custer due to its proximity to Boston and the Maine coast. Tuition pricing placed Custer among the top 25 percent in its peer group on a national scale.

Custer sustained a diversified liberal arts curriculum and was especially proud of its English, history, philosophy, foreign languages, theater arts, and music departments. In the aggregate, 24 percent of its students were enrolled in these majors as of 1998. It supported nonacademic activities that included 16 varsity sports for men and women athletes and a wide range of intramural sports and clubs. The educational and financial outlook was positive. In this context, faculty lobbied the president, board of trustees, and alumni for expanded participation in university decisions through shared governance.

In the interest of maintaining a harmonious relationship with faculty, it was agreed that administrative and academic issues alike would be subject to review and recommendations of the faculty senate. Yet, the board of trustees' resolution authorizing an expanded role for shared governance in college decision-making was ambiguous as to whether the faculty senate was empowered to make decisions. So long as Custer prospered, their environment was collegial and shared governance was neither a pressing concern for college leaders nor for their board of trustees.

The president, who had presided over 16 years of unprecedented growth, announced her retirement in June 1997. One year later, the board of trustees

151

announced that Dr. Jordan LeFontaine would assume the presidency. LeFontaine, a distinguished graduate of Custer, held a PhD in English Literature from a prestigious Ivy League University. An author of many best-selling historical fiction books, one of which won the Etinboro Book Club Award, Dr. Lefontaine also taught for many years at a highly regarded university in California. His attributes included public speaking, national recognition as a scholar and author, and roots as a distinguished Custer Alumni. This endeared Dr. LeFontaine to faculty, students, and the alumni association. His appointment was heralded as a significant opportunity for Custer to achieve national recognition.

After assuming the presidency, Dr. LeFontaine and the board of trustees agreed to develop an aggressive three-part plan designed to elevate Custer from a respected regional college to one worthy of national recognition. The plan called for an enrollment increase of 600 students between 2000 and 2005 to a total of 2,400. Master's degrees and research faculty would be added to the six departments noted above. Custer would apply to its regional accreditation association for university designation.

A facility master plan called for construction of two new dormitories, modernizing and expanding the student union, refurbishing the main liberal arts center for learning, and building an 800-seat capacity theater for the performing arts and a new gymnasium to include a physical fitness center. The financial plan called for a US$95 million bond issue, with Dr. LeFontaine raising an additional US$30 million from well-heeled alumni. Although Custer's endowment was a modest US$28 million, its financial statements reflected a balanced budget during the past 20 years, and informal conversations with wealthy alumni were promising. Everyone agreed that Custer's aspirations for a national identity required an aggressive construction and building refurbishment plan. The faculty senate overwhelmingly endorsed the plans.

Custer's ambitions were predicated upon an optimistic outlook for the national economy and continued capital gains in the stock market that would better position alumni to make donations. The chief business officer, whose concerns about adding so much debt to the balance sheet were not heeded, had elected to accept a position at another college. So, when the US equities markets lost almost 50 percent of their value between 2000 and 2002 as when the so-called tech bubble burst, no one at Custer was prepared to deal with the ensuing fallout from the financial crisis. Many alumni, who had pledged a total of US$22 million to the building fund, suffered investment losses and withdrew their pledges.

An already-complicated situation was made worse since Custer had already launched its growth plan. New faculty had been hired in anticipation of enrollment growth, and most of the new construction was nearing completion. Some of the families who had planned to fund their children's education *at Custer could no longer afford to do so. Enrollment declined from a peak of 1,800 to 1,627 during school year 2002–2003. Worse yet, freshman enrollment dropped from a target of 700 to 528.*

What choices were available to president LeFontaine, the board of trustees, and others at Custer? Was the president equipped to deal with the financial crisis at hand? What is the role of leaders in responding to crises? How would shared governance function during trying times? What sorts of behaviors, values, skills, and competencies characterize those best able to perform amid formidable challenges? What strategic options should Custer consider?

Leaders are increasingly defined by the way they enable their institutions to either adapt to a transitioning regional, national, and global context or fail to do so. Many challenges facing President LeFontaine at Custer can be found elsewhere. They include volatile financial markets, spontaneity of communications among students using social media, unpredictable public funding, the changing demography of student enrollment, technological innovations, the rapid growth of online learning, and demands for improved graduation rates, affordable tuition, and increasing government oversight. This places a premium on leadership capacity to develop strategic responses, set long-term direction, and form a team to effectively plan for the longer term while effectively managing day-to-day operations.

Our chapter on exemplars informs us about leaders committed to quality education and student support services while exhibiting business proficiency. Arizona State University (ASU), Southern New Hampshire University (SNHU), and Pennsylvania State University (PSU) grew substantial national online learning enterprises to occupy space vacated by retrenching for-profit institutions. ASU and PSU did so within their prevailing university structures. SNHU launched a separate operating subsidiary.

Tom Detre developed a synergistic relationship between the University of Pittsburgh School of Medicine and University of Pittsburgh Medical Center. Booker T. Washington was dedicated to affordable education and acquisition of trade skills by students at Tuskegee. Jim Earle overhauled facilities management at the University of Pittsburgh, thereby providing improved services for students while increasing operational productivity and better controlling costs. Grove City College has a history of lean administration and providing high-quality education at a very competitive tuition rate. All defined success differently, without compromising the quality of learning at their campuses.

Redesigning of institutional business and educational models requires transformative leaders who think and act strategically, make difficult decisions, undertake evidence-based planning, manage constrained human and financial resources effectively, seize opportunities, solve problems, inspire others, and are innovative, entrepreneurial, and passionate. Such leaders are pragmatic, blessed with vision, understand how to acquire and apply requisite resources to toward priorities. This chapter comments upon certain behaviors, values, skills, and competencies of effective leaders, their roles and responsibilities, and processes supportive of sustainable systemic reforms.

TRAITS OF EFFECTIVE LEADERS: THE ART AND SCIENCE OF LEADERSHIP

The report commissioned by U.S. Secretary of Education Margaret Spellings in 2006 called upon higher education to change its ways. The report did not mince words while stating "our yearlong examination of the challenges facing higher education has brought us to the uneasy conclusion that the sector's past attainments have led our nation to unwarranted complacency about its future" (U.S. Department of Education 2006, p. vi). The report's contributors further observed:

> History is littered with examples of industries that, at their peril, failed to respond to—or even to notice—changes in the world around them, from railroads to steel manufacturers. Without serious self-examination and reform, institutions of higher education risk falling into the same trap, seeing their market share substantially reduced and their services increasingly characterized by obsolescence. (p. ix)

The socioeconomic trauma caused by the meltdown of financial markets in 2000–2002 and again in 2008–2009, subsequent reductions of funding for public sector institutions, intensified competition for enrollment, increasing concerns about the relevance of a liberal arts education, and technological advancements have created an increasingly complicated environment. This is expressed somewhat differently by Edgar H. Schein (2004, p. 401), "As the world becomes more complex and interdependent, the ability to think systematically, to analyze fields of forces and understand their joint causal effects on each other, and to abandon simple linear causal logic in favor of complex models become more critical to learning."

 Leadership styles reflect an individual's character, personality, and capacity to motivate others. Some highly effective leaders are reflective and inspire others by their deeds and by sharing wisdom. Mahatma Gandhi and Nelson Mandela come to mind. Others are highly inspirational communicators who galvanize public opinion. Martin Luther King, Franklin Delano Roosevelt, and Winston Churchill are among those who shared this exceptional gift. Edward R. Morrow, a heralded US news commentator during World War II, once reportedly said of Winston Churchill that he mobilized the English language and sent it to war.

A commonality among extraordinary leaders is their passion, deep personal commitment, courage, and ability to inspire others to perform at levels that might otherwise prove illusive. Leadership styles vary considerably, are unique to the individual, and are less subject to a "makeover" through training and development. Good leaders care for the well-being of those who work for them, are decisive, and find ways to win. John E. Roueche, George A. Baker, and Richard R. Rose (1989, p. 11) define transformational leaders as those able to "influence the values, attitudes, beliefs and behaviors of others by working with and through them in order to accomplish the college's mission and purpose." They observe that "followers understand and appreciate the need for change" (p. 11). The sum of these attributes may be thought of as the art of leadership.

A compelling question emerges. Are effective leaders "born or made?" In truth, there is no simple answer. Notwithstanding one's innate talent,

Table 9.1   Characteristics of Transformative Leaders in Higher Education

Behaviors and Values	Skills and Competencies
An exemplar of honesty, integrity, humility, and worthy of trust	Says and does the right things; a role model
Is a reflective and strategic thinker	Asks probing questions, challenges traditional assumptions, listens, processes, analyzes, has an open mind, and explains reasoning; aware of context, challenges, and opportunities
Is a visionary	Champions mission, vision and enduring goals driven—builds toward the future
Holds self and others accountable for student and institutional achievements	Hires the right people: is devoted to plan development and execution, oversight processes, and measurable objectives—manages the present
Is a communicator; inspires and motivates others	Institutionalizes reforms through consensus and team building and shared commitment to priorities
Is supportive and cares for others	Accepts responsibility for actions of others, respects their concerns; a mentor and coach to future leaders
Is transparent	Defines metrics of success and provides access to information
Is adaptable to change, innovative and resilient	Sustains ongoing awareness of changing environment supported by data gathering, analysis, planning, and problem solving; is pragmatic
Is fair minded and exhibits balanced judgment	Bases decisions on evidence; makes difficult personnel and financial decisions—resolves conflicts
Is committed to learning and growing	A lifelong learner: develops financial and technological literacy; asks the right questions
A "Capacity Builder"	An advocate for resource needs to support strategic goals
Is passionate about beneficial outcomes for students	Identifies obstacles; develops and implements plans to overcome

most of us benefit from a combination of learning experiences, mentoring, and a career progression that exposes us to challenges and opportunities for professional growth. Career development and graduate school programs are unlikely to modify the behaviors of those lacking a moral compass or manifesting dysfunctional social skills.

This places a premium upon the ability of boards of trustees and chief executive officers (CEOs) to understand the behaviors, values, skills, and competencies needed by senior administrators to function effectively. A leader's ability to activate processes and actions that drive change may be called the science of leadership, which benefit from formal training and professional experiences. Higher education needs more leaders able to inspire and guide systemic reform (see Table 9.1).

STRATEGIC THINKING AND TRANSFORMATIVE LEADERS

Higher education occupies a space in which challenges, threats, and opportunities converge. It behooves leaders to be cognizant of external stimuli and their implications and act thoughtfully and decisively. John P. Kotter (1996), an authority on leadership at the Harvard Business School, counsels that "visible crises can be enormously helpful in catching people's attention and pushing up urgency levels" (p. 45). He further believes that two foundational elements of sustainable change are a shared sense of urgency and a low level of complacency.

In 2013, Witt Kieffer, a higher education executive search and consulting firm, interviewed 14 presidents. A consensus view emerged that "pressure from boards has intensified as challenges have multiplied . . . and this new era calls for a visionary, inspirational new leader, able to lead the cabinet, trustees and the entire campus community in new directions" (Goldstein et al. 2013, p. 7). Strategic thinking and their modus operandi differentiate transformative leaders in higher education from others. Strategic thinkers understand complex environments and circumstances, welcome contested views, accept ambiguity, consider implications of a transitioning context, and conceptualize responses. Further, they understand the "calculated relationship between the ends, ways and means" (Harrison 2013, p. 4). Fallen and Scott (2009, p. 51) reference Francis Bacon, who reportedly said "we rise to great heights by a winding staircase."

A study by Bain & Company in 2012 noted that the increasingly precarious financial condition of many institutions is that have more debt and liabilities to service and insufficient cash reserves to do so (Dinneen and Dretler 2012). The authors call upon institutions to "(1) develop a clear strategy, focused on the core (2) reduce support and administrative costs (3) free up capital in non-core assets and (4) strategically invest in innovative models" (pp. 3–4). The authors define core as roughly those functions and programs that are mission critical and where the most resources are invested for the greatest returns. Postsecondary education values knowledge creation, learning, reflective thinking, character and skill development, and transmitting knowledge. This places a premium on leaders with a higher order of intellect and an ability to nurture inquiry. They draw upon existing institutional strengths, address weaknesses, and welcome collaboration. Transformative leaders have a clear vision of the future, exercise sound judgment, thoughtfully articulate priorities, and find solutions.

According to Richard Rumelt (2011, pp. 66–67), "Leadership inspires and motivates self-sacrifice . . . with careful attention to obstacles and action." Gardner (1990, p. i) describes leadership as "the process of persuasion or example by which an individual induces a group to pursue desired objectives." Leaders understand and care about the needs of persons for whom they are responsible (Rath and Conchie 2008). Phrased differently, the CEO should have a vision of the endgame, cultivate processes that inspire confidence, and implement recommendations consistent with institutional mission, student needs, enduring goals, and financial realities.

Institutional Strategizing

Institutional strategic plans offer institutions an opportunity to revisit mission and vision and collaboratively develop a clear sense of direction and priorities. Evidence-based planning is foundational to prudent decision-making. Determinants of success include transparent processes in which administrators, faculty, staff, and students identify and discuss problems and find solutions. Leaders encourage discourse among senior administrators, the board of trustees, staff, students, and alumni.

A plan-to-plan defines the deliberative process, designates research and analysis tasks, assigns responsibilities to committees, and sets timelines for task completion. Toward the end of the process, an implementation plan positions the institution to operationalize transition from broad long-term goals to short-term action plans and objectives. As such, if a strategy identifies what needs to be done, then tactics set forth an implementation blueprint to assure effective plan execution. Responsibilities for follow-up are assigned and progress is monitored.

The CEO and members of his or her cabinet should carefully determine whom to invite to participate in strategic planning committees, their selection criteria and responsibilities. The intent is to recruit a team able to think reflectively, adopt innovative solutions to complex problems, examine relevant data whenever and wherever applicable, question prevailing assumptions, and provide a thoughtful and transformative institutional design. This requires a team that is representative of various constituencies, diverse, highly credible, trustworthy, and receptive to so-called outside-the-box thinking.

Those selected should be capable of respectful discourse. Superior analytical, problem solving, and communications skills are desirable. Some may be highly innovative, while others are more pragmatic. All should be passionate about concerns for students and the institution. In consideration of these observations, leaders should not hesitate to exclude from deliberations those persons incapable of respectful discourse or collaborative problem solving.

Preliminary decisions need to be made regarding the proposed scope of a strategic plan, how it will be used, and for what purposes. One approach is to remain at a strategic level in which mission and vision statements and enduring goals to guide future actions and tactical plans appear. Another approach can be more ambitious and call for task forces or committees to address a broader mix of functionally specific needs. Institutions are more likely to benefit from plans that are substantive while avoiding temptation to microplan everything and anything.

Committee structure, composition, and functioning may vary with no one approach being necessarily superior. Kotter argues for a guiding coalition to drive reform. Higher education leaders might call this a steering committee. Some may prefer one larger central planning committee. Larger and more complex institutions may find it preferable to constitute a steering committee, with separate subcommittees charged with one or more responsibilities. For example, one subcommittee may undertake an environmental scan and an analysis of institutional strengths, weakness, opportunities, and threats (SWOT). This committee would devote special attention to gathering data and analyzing its implications.

Another team might work on a multiyear business plan that considers revenue -generating and cost-saving initiatives and ways to develop a more sustainable business model. Other committees might examine instructional and student services and operational technologies for the purposes of improving their effectiveness and productivity. Done correctly, this effort should be foundational for subsequent academic, technology, facilities, human resources, and student affairs master plans.

Guiding Principles and Strategic Planning

Presidential articulation of guiding principles helps frame issues to be explored by committees. In doing so, care should be expended to avoid conflicting with the mandate of various planning committees. Illustrations of guiding principles may include the following:

- A president's vision for the future
- Enduring goals must be student-centric, consistent with the institutional mission, and not compromise the quality of education and student support services
- Developing integrative educational, student services, and business plans that render tuition and fees competitive and assure institutional sustainability
- Encouraging creative thinking and innovation
- Questioning prevailing assumptions
- Sustaining institutional agility and avoiding overcommitment of resources to permit adjustments to unpredicted challenges and opportunities
- Goals and objectives will be accompanied by measurable qualitative and quantitative performance indicators

Mission Statements

Mission statements define an institution's reason for being, while vision statements define aspirations for the future. They are student-centric and realistic relative to resources and offer criteria to help guide future plans and day-to-day decisions. Conversely, mission creep generates cost and dilutes resources from other more critical functions. Statements crafted for public relations purposes are more apt to be understood as fluff and send negative signals to internal and external stakeholders alike.

Strategic Planning and Institutional Transformation

Strategic planning affords institutions an opportunity to redesign their educational, business, and student services environment by building upon what works well and calling for adaptive change as may be needed. Given the time and resources needed to develop a comprehensive strategic plan, one is ill-advised to raise expectations of change and transformation in the absence of a top-down commitment from leadership and the board of trustees to act on it.

What are some attributes of good planning, and pitfalls to avoid? Tony Zinni and Tony Koltz (2014, p. 42) advise that "the first step of good decision making is to clearly define the problem, followed by sound analysis, assessment and decision-making." Rumelt (2011) reminds us of the importance of drawing upon existing strengths, while selecting objectives that address critical issues, avoiding fluff, public relations jargon, or aspiring to the impossible. Kotter (1996) stresses the power of vision, the need to surmount obstacles, the importance of developing and communicating proof statements based upon short-term accomplishments, and the imperative of anchoring change in the institutional culture.

John Davis (2013) encourages a rational planning model, leaders who understand the prevailing institutional culture and have an ability to identify requisite changes. Schein (2004) advises leaders to manage through cultural evolution as institutions adapt to a changing context. Michael Fullan and Geoff Scott (2009, p. 27) observe, "We are not against good critique, but against abstract discussion that leads nowhere." Zemsky (2010) cautions against using excessive rhetoric, vilifying others who hold opposing views, or attempting to reform tenure or accreditation. Raymond E. Miles and Charles C. Snow (2003, p. 3) observe that "ineffectual organizations struggle with structure, process and mechanisms." Schein (2004) warns leaders to avoid anecdotal information or "feel." Clayton M. Christensen and Henry J. Eyring (2011, p. xxiii) inform us that "the typical university must change more quickly and more fundamentally than it has been doing." Richard Alfred (2006) believes that thinking and acting strategically is a crucial component of leadership, be it in the private sector or academe.

Evidence-Based Planning

Strategic planning, institutional transformation, and year-to-year operations benefit from a confluence of effective leadership, dedicated administrators and faculty, and the prudential use of relevant quantitative and qualitative data to identify problems, challenges, trends, opportunities, and threats and develop thoughtful solutions. At the front end, data gathering and analysis clarify choices and priorities for leaders. Management reporting allows leaders, administrators, and faculty to chart progress relative to agreed-upon objectives, plans of action, and key performance indicators. Ongoing examination of data offers a basis for mid-course corrections should certain initiatives encounter difficulties, while positioning the institution to build upon success.

Data mining offers an extraordinary basis for setting institutional, school, department, and program priorities and making informed decisions. Reliance upon data does not guarantee achievement of desired results, given the complexities of plan execution. But it does offer an objective basis for determining priorities, solving problems, decision-making, and continuous improvement of institutional performance across a wide range of core activities.

Analytical Tools: Environmental Scans, SWOT, and Competitor Analyses

Contemporary drivers of change include demography, technology, public policy, funding, increasing sensitivity to student debt, a pronounced orientation of students toward career programs in high-demand occupations, a shift toward increasingly value-conscious parents and students, and an altering competitive landscape. Bodies of evidence afford institutions an opportunity to identify emergent trends, study relevant data, and assess their implications.

Uses of instructional, student support, and operational software render some institutions more effective than others. Eroding medium household income, coupled with rising financial awareness of accumulative student debt, adversely weigh upon enrollment trends at many relatively expensive non-flagship public universities and costly nonelite private colleges. Adult learners who work full-time and study online or through night school at local community colleges represent an opportunity for some and a challenge for others. ASU, Penn State, SNHU, and WGU are among those who tapped into this growth market in the United States through a mix of distance education and, in the case of WGU and SNHU, competency-based education (CBE).

Additional variables merit consideration. The shift toward more career-directed students calls upon the liberal arts to define their value propositions, focus their curriculum, and offer proof statements of their achievements. The emergence of social media as the prevalent communications tool of younger adults offers extraordinary opportunities to those who leverage ways of tapping these platforms to facilitate student performance and better assure retention.

Continued technological and services innovation by highly creative private sector companies in the higher education space offers extraordinary opportunities to outsource technology or services too expensive to develop from within. Demands for institutional transparency, accountability, improved outcomes for students, and affordable tuition, combined with lower funding from public sources, hold profound implications for institutional redesign and development of more vibrant education and business models.

ACADEMIC LEADERSHIP, CURRICULUM, PRODUCTIVITY, AND PROGRAM REVIEW

Within higher education, provosts, deans, and faculty are accountable for knowledge creation, quality of the learning experience, relevant curriculum, effective pedagogy, and market-driven delivery systems. Within the academy, tapping "human agency," as noted by Richard L. Morrill (2007, p. 108), is especially important when defining institutional mission, purposes, and core functions. By progressively doing so, reform of curriculum and programs is more attainable.

Faculty productivity has become something of a bellwether for leaders seeking to better control expenses. Traditional ways of doing so have included increasing enrollment in course sections, hiring more adjunct faculty, offering more courses and programs online, and passing along more administrative duties to faculty as secretarial ranks are culled. We are informed by the Delta Cost Project studies that instructional expenses have declined as a percentage of operating budgets in many sectors of higher education, between 2000 and 2010 (Desrochers and Kirshstdein 2012).

But has increased faculty productivity adversely influenced the quality of education and the learning experience? What other options may lower academic expenses further without harmful consequences? We now turn attention to other planning tools available to the provost or chief academic officer that offer more potential to contain costs and improve the quality of education than solely focusing linear attention on the productivity of faculty.

Program Review and Academic Leaders

Periodic program, academic discipline, and department reviews (henceforth referred to simply as program reviews) should be conducted along three dimensions. The first reflects upon a student-centric curriculum, continuous improvement of educational quality, delivery models, resource needs, and financial and instructional considerations on a case-by-case basis. The second level examines the full portfolio of programs from a broader institutional and strategic perspective. The third considers programs within a broader competitive marketplace. The provost and academic deans have resource allocation decisions to make, and one-dimensional program reviews may no longer suffice.

Outcomes of system-wide program reviews can be consequential. Programs with robust enrollment may require additional resources in order to sustain competitive advantages. In other cases, data may suggest maintaining current levels of support. Programs with low enrollment and declining market demand suggest that program consolidations, downsizing, or elimination may require consideration.

Processes deployed should include faculty engagement, and encompass student-centric curriculum analysis and broader financial considerations. Enrollment and student achievement metrics to include graduation trends and job placements should be examined. Zemsky (2013, p. 20) describes curriculum and program offerings as "a supermarket where students are shoppers and professors are merchants." Provosts are called upon to differentiate between programs in high demand relative to others with low enrollment and make resource allocation decisions accordingly.

Available literature offers important perspective. For example, Robert Dickerson (2010) comments on metrics that include program evolution and expectations, five-year trend analysis of external enrollment trends, competitive positioning, internal and external challenges and opportunities, and resource needs. In addition to standard retrospective analysis, the evaluative process should be forward thinking as well. What may occur within the next three to five years that may cause concern or create opportunities? What unilateral actions from within may positively or negatively alter the education and business models?

Dickerson (2010, p. 45) believes that thinking skills "depend not only on what the mind knows but on how it evaluates any new fact or argument." Conversely, those who hold steadfast to routine ways of acting and thinking inevitably become part of the problem more often than the solution. Seen through this lens, provosts and deans focus on not only the quality of education but also the cost-effective solutions. This requires a high order of financial literacy and enterprise management skills.

Changes in a competitive academic marketplace inevitably weigh upon program attractiveness and financial sustainability. Christensen and Eyring (2011) call upon leaders in higher education to devote special attention to innovation and expense reduction. Program reviews offer an opportunity to align resources in support of affordable and sustainable academic priorities. In this context, the dramatic enrollment shift to online learning, the emergence of CBE as an alternative design for career programs, and the evolution of massive open online courses are changing the rules of engagement.

As an example, we regularly see television advertising in Pittsburgh of online education from SNHU and ASU. Emergent technologies, a growing body of adult learners, and significantly improved instructional software and student support software and online delivery platforms represent threats to tradition-bound institutions and growth opportunities for those more able and willing to adapt to changing times (see Figure 9.1).

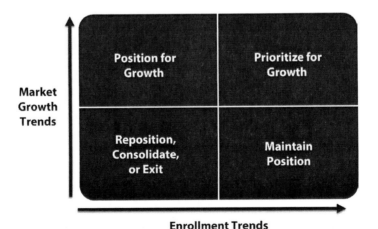

Figure 9.1   Program Review and Resource Allocation Guide.

TRANSITIONING FROM PLAN TO ACTION AND ACTION TO RESULTS: THE CEO IN ACTION

On 11 October 2014, the highly regarded author Walter Isaacson, referring to the late Steve Jobs of Apple fame, said, "Vision without execution is hallucination" (della Cava 2014). Execution of plan and vision differentiates those who act thoughtfully from others who traverse the contemplative and analytical processes to an operational cycle. Data-based analyses inform choices. It is up to leaders to select wisely, make timely decisions, communicate priorities, assign responsibilities, monitor progress, report on results and make mid-course adjustments as necessary, and hold themselves and others accountable for progress relative to predetermined key performance indicators.

According to Miles and Snow (2003, p. 6), "Top management has both the opportunity and the requirement to view the organization as a total system—a collection of people, structures and processes that must be aligned with the organization's chosen environment." In the complex and evolving world of the academy, words may impress, actions command attention, but results differentiate those who guide their institutions forward from others who muddle by. Transformative leaders may or may not be likable, but they must be persons of integrity who command respect from their constituents.

We can learn from the experiences and insights of others. Larry Bossidy (2002), a former executive from General Electric, became a successful CEO at Honeywell and led their corporate turnaround. The insights he culled from those experiences speak to critical success factors required to transition from plan to execution. Bossidy comments on the importance of CEO people skills, behaviors, and tactics. Implementation plans are indispensable. They embrace strategic goals, call for specific actions, and require commitment and discipline.

According to Bossidy, commitment cannot be delegated. He further cautions leaders to hire the right people to do the right things and not to confuse daily tasks with plan execution. Jim Collins (2001) advises replacing hierarchy and bureaucracy with a culture of discipline as we transition to a knowledge age economy. He further observes, "People are not your most important asset . . . the right people are" (p. 51).

Role of the Chief Financial (Business) Officer

In view of increasing concerns about institutional financial sustainability and affordable tuition, the CFO must function at a high level in two primary domains. First, the basic functions of a CFO include delivery of financial reports that are timely, accurate, carefully analyzed, and clearly communicative. The CFO assures the integrity of accounting, procurement, and payment systems against abuses from fraud or embezzlement.

As important, the CFO is a change agent who worries as much about student costs as the institutional condition. CFO's engage other senior administrators, including the presidents' cabinet, to work collaboratively toward continuous improvement of educational, student support, technology, facilities, and human resource services. The CFO assures allocation of financial and other resources consistent with institutional priorities. The latter requires long- and short-term financial planning consistent with the duration of the institutional strategic plan and annual operating plans and budgets. This requires a high order of integrity, honesty, unselfish collaboration, and resilience.

CEOs count upon their CFOs to safeguard the institutional financial condition by assuring adequate liquidity to pay bills in a timely manner and avoiding unsustainable levels of debt. The increasing tension over affordable tuition, student enrollment, and academic performance calls upon CFOs to evidence a high level of financial acumen and to be deliberative and creative change agents. CFOs may worry at night about actual and potential financial problems and propose solutions by day. Our evermore challenging context places a premium on CFOs who take a lead role in changing the institutional business model, while helping develop resources to support student-centric outcomes. Their institutional loyalty, integrity, and honesty must be beyond reproach.

An effective CFO manifests not only superior financial skills, but exemplary personal behavior and communication skills. A CFO must command the respect, if not necessarily the affection, of other members of the CEO's cabinet. CFOs ask tough, yet fair, questions. They are well positioned to take a supportive role in integrating operational technology for purpose of rendering operations more efficient, less labor intensive, and cheaper.

CFOs should advocate migration to low labor content, technologically driven operational processes. Outsourcing of certain functions should be explored by the CFO and internal partners to pursue equal or superior quality at a lower cost. As the provost is the architect of institutional education performance, then CFOs must hold like responsibilities for overhauling the business model. Reaching across silos as partners in planning, sharing common cause, and generating ideas are fundamental to simultaneous improvement of educational quality and the business model.

Integrative Leadership Model

The Integrative Leadership Model draws upon institutional processes that offer a comparatively higher likelihood of transformation toward the future in a continuous improvement environment. As suggested by Bossidy (2002) and Collins (2001), process is an enabler, but not a substitute for the right people to generate ideas and evidence the passion, commitment, and capacity to manage change. The right people, in turn, rely upon thoughtful processes that guide continuous improvement and innovation cycles (see Figure 9.2).

Transformation of traditional higher education is more likely accomplished when institutions build upon such prevailing values as respect for inquiry, deliberation, analysis, and collaboration in an environment committed to plan execution. Integrative leadership models offer one tactical approach to plan execution. There are other models.

In 2012, the American Association of Community Colleges completed a substantial review of prevailing situational realities and the challenges ahead for its member institutions and issued a report, "Reclaiming the American Dream: Community Colleges and the Nation's Future." Their study called for broad institutional redesign and reflected the following understanding:

> The work of effective institutional change requires a strengthened infrastructure of support, including strategically focused professional development programs, technologies for learning and learning analytics, and institutional capacity for collecting, analyzing, and using data to inform a student success agenda. (AACC, p. 19)

Their report also found "student success rates that are unacceptably low, employment preparation that is inadequately connected to job market needs,

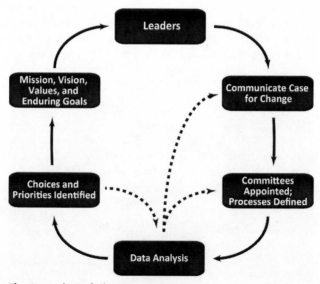

Figure 9.2 The Strategic Redesign Process.

and disconnects in transitions between high schools, community colleges and baccalaureate institutions" (p. viii).

Integrative models call for leaders to sustain commitment at all key process junctures. They select the right people for committees and assure the integrity of inquiry. Planning is based upon a body of relevant evidence. A reflective and questioning posture assures that operating assumptions, prevailing mission, preexisting academic programs, and student services are subject to full and rigorous analysis and discussion. Operations are reviewed for the purpose of making them more efficient and less costly.

Enduring goals should be integrated at the institutional level and should set priorities to help guide decisions for the duration of the plan. Implementation plans and annual operating objectives align with core elements of the strategic plan. At both the strategic and annual planning levels, it is imperative to integrate education and business considerations and planning. This requires setting forth specific plans of action, allocating resources in support of stated priorities and action plans, making leadership commitment to measurable performance objectives, an oversight process that examines progress and reviews data, and making tactical adjustments to action plans as may be required (see Figure 9.3).

A culture of accountability, effective two-way communications, and commitment to transparency are important enablers of institutional transformation. So too are such values as honesty and ethical standards characterized by behavior in which bad news is reported immediately, those who deliver the messages are not chastised, and leaders recognize outstanding performance by others rather than assuming the credit themselves. In short, good behaviors make for good processes, while dysfunctional behaviors undermine the best of plans and intentions.

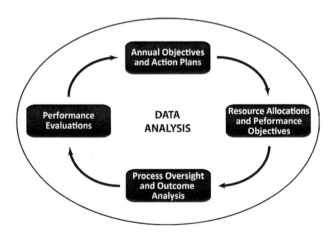

Figure 9.3   Operationalizing the Redesign Process.

Making Choices

Institutional business models change in some proportion to initiatives that offer more robust revenue-generating opportunities and expense savings. We know that tuition pricing by early entrants to CBE is dramatically lower. Curriculum is highly concentrated, prescriptive, and defined by employers.

Expressed differently, each element of instruction and student support services in CBE offers a perceptible cost and benefit for the student. Those who provide online education to a broad national base achieve scale that allows for more competitive tuition pricing than that which is available to students who study on campus. Our earlier chapter on exemplars of change noted the profound beneficial consequences from raising revenues from ancillary activities. Online education, however, has not traditionally rewarded dabblers who enter this competitive domain underresourced, underfunded, and lacking commitment.

Other high-impact initiatives are worthy of consideration. The significant potential to improve educational performance, possibly at lower cost through reducing the need for redundant remedial coursework, for students in New York's Early College Initiative through collaborative intervention should be closely examined. For example, sequencing programs at residence campuses to facilitate 36-month degrees can dramatically alter revenue generation by using facilities otherwise unoccupied during the summer. Incremental revenue gains can be forecasted. Students may be offered predefined tuition reimbursements payable upon graduation.

Let us consider the cost implications of tenure stream faculty members versus instruction-focused faculty. Undergraduate students largely value the quality of instruction and access to faculty. The quality of instruction at Grove City College, also mentioned previously, is highly regarded. Instruction load for their faculty is 24 credit hours per annum, and tuition pricing is competitive. Community colleges are also instruction oriented and normally require similar loads. On the other hand, universities devoted to a research mission may require somewhere between 9 and 12 credit hours per annum from research scholars, not to mention paying for periodic sabbaticals. The cost differential between research and instructional faculty is consequential.

Many universities that value their research mission now find a need to reflect upon options. Some non-flagship public universities may rethink how many research faculty are affordable. Flagship public universities and top-tier private universities that hold a research mission as core may consider dedicating instruction-oriented faculty to undergraduates, while reserving more costly research faculty to work with their graduate students. Finally, organizational structure and processes should be subject to periodic review to assure their continuing vitality and cost-effectiveness, with a preparedness to consolidate and free up critical resources for instruction and direct student support services by reducing administrative overhead.

Successful adaptation of such initiatives requires transformative leadership, careful planning, a will to shift the paradigm of traditional delivery models, and the courage to do so. None of the above changes assumes that either tenure or faculty unions, per se, intrinsically cause the erosion of education or business models. Transitioning from current realities to tomorrow's vision will more likely come about through evolution than revolutionary change.

Donor Giving and Institutional Business Models

The legacy business model of traditional higher education is revenue driven, with attention primarily focusing on enrollment-driven tuition and fee revenues, public subsidies, and allocations from endowments. Accordingly, presidents have often been selected based upon a perceived capacity to represent the institutional interests effectively as a public speaker, an advocate for budget allocations from state and federal sources and as a fund-raiser through donor giving. All of these functions remain important, but changing market conditions set the bar for performance at a higher level and require more inclusive competencies.

We present a hypothetical simulation as a way of testing these assumptions. At the risk of oversimplification, we assume the following:

1. A hypothetical university sustains a US$1 billion annual operating budget that remains about the same over a three-year time frame.
2. The president targets a US$1 billion donor giving program to be achieved within three years.
3. The endowment campaign is successful and US$1 billion of new monies have been raised.
4. Eighty percent of the increased endowment is "restricted" and cannot be applied to cover annual operating expenses, while some smaller proportion of these funds will effectively go toward operating funds by endowing chairs for faculty and student scholarships.
5. Twenty percent, or US$200 million, is set aside as unrestricted funds.
6. State statutes and institutional prudence limit annual allocations of up to 5 percent from the unrestricted funds, hence permitting up to US$10 million of a US$1 billion increase in the endowment to be applied to the annual operating budget. This equates to 1 percent of the annual operating budget.
7. Had the university set a target of reducing its operating expenses by 2 percent per annum, net of increases to salaries and benefits and other mandated expenses such as health insurance premiums, compliance, property maintenance and repairs, and so forth on a sustainable basis for each

of the next five years the potential annual savings would be approximately US$20 million each year.

8. The university is able to launch revenue-generating initiatives to grow monies from nontraditional sources, with a net increase in new funds of US$30 million over the same period.

9. The accumulative financial consequence of expense reduction during the next five years would be approximately US$100 million, US$30 million in new revenues, and US$50 million from endowment disbursements.

What is our point? Donor giving, while very important, will not unilaterally remedy an otherwise unsustainable business model, nor will it render tuition and fee pricing more attractive. Systemic reforms must occur through multiple sources, inclusive of growing revenues from nontraditional sources, disbursements from endowments, and expense reduction. Institutional leaders are well advised to consider (1) what levels of tuition and fees are likely to appeal to future students "x" years into the future, (2) which programs will be the most attractive, and (3) how to strategically plan or redesign business models from there backward. This realization speaks to the skills requisite of leaders in higher education to improve educational quality and become substantially more efficient.

GOVERNANCE, LEADERSHIP, AND INSTITUTIONAL TRANSFORMATION

Boards of trustees, and boards of regents in some states, bear fiduciary responsibility for institutional performance and actions. The selection criteria and process for board appointments are subject to variance from one institution to another and from one state to another. Under ideal circumstances, board members act in accordance with their responsibilities. They care, are independent thinkers, and ask questions intended to make informed decisions. They are entrusted with selecting, evaluating, rewarding, and, when necessary, disciplining institutional CEOs.

Their functions include review and approval of strategic plans, annual operating plans, operating and capital budgets, policy, and key administrative appointments. They review reports presented by senior administrators and ask questions as necessary to fulfill their responsibilities. As such, boards verify organizational mission and purposes, ensure resource adequacy, and are expected to act within the law, while sustaining a rigorous code of ethical conduct (Ingram 2003). A study by McKinsey & Co. suggests that boards and senior administrators bear responsibilities to "assess the will and skill of leadership, managers, and staff to pursue change" (Auguste et al. 2010, p. 16).

A need for institutional transformation places a premium on criteria to select a CEO. When the board feels a sense of urgency for reform, it is imperative to look beyond credentials, appearances, and formal job responsibilities. Boards need to identify the behavioral characteristics deemed critical, accomplishments to date and to examine the candidate's track record as a change agent. What was accomplished? How? With what results? Most institutions nowadays need CEOs who walk the walk, not those who only talk the talk.

Weighed against the challenges of a rapidly changing environment, the bar by which to judge CEO performance has risen. Eloquence and a perceived ability to raise monies from donors no longer suffices. Once finalists have been decided upon, due diligence helps mitigate against potential embarrassment.

Beyond CEO selection, boards and CEOs share a high level of mutual dependency. Boards rely upon CEOs as their primary source of information. Reports that are complete, timely, objective, and honest serve as the basis upon which board decisions and resolutions are passed.

At the same time, CEOs depend upon full and unrelenting board support when driving institutional transformation. Difficult decisions that cause change may cause public pushback in the form of faculty votes of no confidence or passive-aggressive behaviors by administrators opposed to a reform agenda. Back-channel communications to board members or attempts to embarrass CEOs through stirring up negative publicity are among the tools in the arsenal of proponents of the status quo. It is incumbent upon board members to avoid micromanagement of the CEO. At the same time, the CEO must share good and bad news alike in the interest of mutual trust.

CONCLUDING OBSERVATIONS

Expectations of institutional leaders are formidable. The problems and challenges facing higher education were years in the making. Most challenges are complex and not given to simple solutions. This places a premium on revisioning the attributes of leaders in general and in particular the president, provost, and CFO. Boards are well advised to work with their search firms to not only agree upon selection criteria, but to figure out ways of ascertaining their potential for institutional transformation in particular.

We can, however, take heart from the achievements of others. Exemplars cited in this book are but a few among many. We know what attributes are required of transformative leaders, which processes function and which do not. We need not reinvent the proverbial wheel to succeed, but we must have the heart, mind, and soul to do so. To paraphrase words reportedly spoken by Mahatma Gandhi, if we can close the gap between what we do and what we can do, most of the world's problems can be solved.

REFERENCES

Alfred, Richard L. 2006. *Managing the Big Picture in Colleges and Universities.* Westport, CT: Praeger.

American Association of Community Colleges (AACC). 2012. *Reclaiming the American Dream: A Report from the 21st-Century Commission on the Future of Community Colleges.* Washington, DC: AACC.

Auguste, Byron G., Adam Cota, Kartik Jayaram, and Martha C. A. Laboissière. 2010. *Winning by Degrees: The Strategies of Highly Productive Higher Education Institutions.* Seattle, WA: McKinsey & Co.

Bossidy, Larry, and Charan Ram. 2003. *Execution: The Discipline of Getting Things Done.* New York: Crown Business.

Christensen, Clayton M., and Henry J. Eyring. 2011. *The Innovative University.* San Francisco: Jossey-Bass.

Collins, Jim. 2001. *Good to Great.* New York: Harper Collins.

Davis, John. 2003. *Learning to Lead: A Handbook for Postsecondary Administrators.* Landham, MD: Rowman & Littlefield.

della Cava, Marco. 2014. "'Jobs' author Isaacson tackles tech history." *USA Today,* October 6.

Denneen, Jeff, and Tom Dretler. 2012. *The Financially Sustainable University.* Boston, MA: Bain & Company.

Desrochers, Donna M., and Rita J. Kirschstein. 2012. *College Spending in a Turbulent Decade: Findings from the Delta Cost Project.* Washington, DC: American Institute for Research.

Dickerson, Robert. 2010. *Prioritizing Academic Programs and Services: Reallocating Resources to Achieve Strategic Balance.* San Francisco: Jossey-Bass.

Fullan, Michael, and Geoff Scott. 2009. *Turn Around Leadership for Higher Education.* San Francisco: Jossey-Bass.

Gardner, John W. 1990. *On Leadership.* New York: The Free Press.

Goldstein, Karen L, Alice Miller, and Jane Courson. 2014. *Reinventing Leadership in Higher Education: A Confidential Survey of College Presidents.* Oak Brook, IL: Witt/Kiefer.

Harrison, Ross. 2013. *Strategic Thinking in 3D.* Washington, DC: Potomac Books.

Ingram, Richard T. 2003. *Ten Basic Responsibilities of Non Profit Boards.* Board Source. Washington, DC: Board Source.

Kotter, John P. 2008. *A Sense of Urgency.* Boston, MA: Harvard Business Press.

Miles, Raymond E., and Charles C. Snow. 2003. *Organizational Strategy, Structure and Process.* Palo Alto, CA: Stanford University Press.

Morrill, Richard L. 2007. *Strategic Leadership: Integrating Strategy and Leadership in Colleges and Universities.* Lanham, MD: Roman & Littlefield.

Rath, Tom, and Barry Conchie. 2008. *Strengths Based Leadership: Great Leaders, Teams, and Why People Follow.* New York: Gallup Press.

Roueche, John E., George A. Baker III, and Robert R. Rose. 1989. *Shared Vision: Transformational Leadership in American Community Colleges.* Washington, DC: The Community College Press.

Rumelt, Richard. 2011. *Good Strategy, Bad Strategy: The Difference and Why It Matters*. New York: Crown Business Press.

Schein, Edgar H. 2004. *Organizational Culture and Leadership*. 3rd Ed. San Francisco: Jossey-Bass.

U.S. Department of Education. 2006. *A Test of Leadership: Charting the Future of U.S. Higher Education*. A Report of the Commission Appointed by Secretary of Education Margaret Spellings. Washington, DC: U.S. Department of Education.

Zemsky, Robert. 2013. *Checklist for Change: Making American Higher Education a Sustainable Enterprise*. New Brunswick, NJ: Rutgers University Press.

Zemsky, Robert. 2010. *Making Reform Work*. New Brunswick, NJ: Rutgers University Press.

Zinni, Tony, and Tony Koltz. 2014. *Before the First Shots Are Fired: How America Can Win Or Lose Off the Battlefield*. New York: Palgrave MacMillan.

Chapter 10

Connecting the Dots

The Education Imperative

Institutional transformation in almost any sector of an economy is an arduous and complex undertaking, with outcomes often being less predictable than one might imagine. If most organizations evolve slowly in response to external and internal stimuli, much of higher education may be characterized as occupying the lower quadrant of adaptability. The reasons are many.

Not without cause, legacies are valued. Mission statements often endure beyond the duration of presidents. Reflective thinking is a virtue. Ambiguity and contesting ideas are often accepted as inherent to knowledge creation and deliberative collegial processes. Autonomy is sacrosanct, yet may breed insularity. Depending upon the institution, tenured faculty, under-committed leadership, shared governance, institutional culture, alumni, government officials, and behaviors of board members may constitute centrifugal forces that undermine efforts toward institutional redesign.

Organizational structures comprising silo-oriented functional units, schools, professions, and academic departments often do not lend themselves to collaboration across internal boundaries. Meritorious ambitions to change are one thing. Goal attainment may be something altogether different in an environment in which change is not the norm. So, why bother?

Macro socioeconomic realities compel consideration of institutional reform. External stakeholders such as government officials, employers, and leaders of trade and professional associations understand the risks associated with underperforming educational systems. Increasing global competition in a knowledge-age economy places a premium on a highly skilled and productive workforce. Nations rely upon a highly functioning educational system at all levels to deliver a qualitatively accomplished and quantitatively ample workforce.

Consumption-driven economies need a critical mass of reasonably compensated workers and professionals with sufficient disposable income to be acquisitive. An implied social contract between national leaders and those they govern calls for opportunity creation for economically disenfranchised citizens. When seen through this lens, a highly functioning educational system at all levels plays a critical role in shrinking a skills gap and sustaining economic growth. A College Board Research Brief asserted:

> Globalization has dramatically changed the way we live and work in our now knowledge-based society and, with this change, an urgent need for an increasingly skilled workforce demands that the United States re-imagine its approach to education. To be competitive in a global economy, students in the United States need to become flexible, lifelong learners who adapt to the new challenges that will emerge in college and career. (Di Giacomo et al. 2013, p. 1)

The authors of the *Spellings Commission Report* framed this discussion of the US national interest as follows:

> We may still have more than our share of the world's best universities. But a lot of other countries have followed our lead, and they are now educating more of their citizens to more advanced levels than we are. Worse, they are passing us at a time when education is more important to our collective prosperity than ever. (U.S. Department of Education 2014, p. x)

A recent Organisation for Economic and Co-operative Development (OECD) (2014, p. 14) *Education at a Glance* study offers a more global socioeconomic assessment:

> Across OECD countries, 73% of people without an upper secondary education find themselves at or below the median level of earnings, while only 27% of university graduates do. Educational attainment is the measure by which people are being sorted into poverty or relative wealth; and the skills distribution in a society—its inclusiveness, or lack thereof—is manifested in the degree of income inequality in the society. Countries with large proportions of low-skilled adults are also those with high levels of income inequality.

Germany recognizes the connectivity between national socioeconomic interests and education. A recent article in *University World News* informs us that 40 percent of first-year university students are majoring in math, informatics, natural sciences, or technology/engineering (MINT) compared to the OECD average of 27 percent. This is also reflected in the commitment of the German federal government, in agreement with the states, to increase funding to improve upon the quality of teaching and research during the next five years

(Gardner 2015). One may hypothesize that pre-university education in Germany both is high quality and affords special attention to a MINT-oriented curriculum.

The case for reform from within higher education is equally compelling. Many institutional leaders have concluded that their revenue-driven business models are unsustainable over the medium- to long term (see chapter 3 for details). Their view is confirmed by downgrades of an increasing number of colleges and universities by credit rating agencies. Enrollment declines have occurred at many non-flagship public universities, community colleges, and four-year liberal arts colleges.

Many public sector institutions receive less support from state and local governments than in the past, expressed in both absolute dollars and on a full-time (student) equivalent basis. The outlook for better times ahead is not promising in view of the rising costs of promised retirement benefits for government employees and mandated increases in the state share of Medicaid benefits. Some question the value and relevance, not to mention the cost, of a liberal arts degree at many private colleges.

Meanwhile, increases of many nondiscretionary costs such as facilities repairs and maintenance, technology acquisition and servicing, cyber and campus security, compliance with government regulations, and increasing demands for student and academic support services are daunting. Those who invest in new construction and renovation through bond and other forms of long-term debt may find that payments of principal plus interest are onerous consumers of operating budgets.

REFLECTIONS ON CHALLENGES AND OPPORTUNITIES

Technology

Technology is one of the most singularly significant game changers in higher education. It has multiple applications. For example, technology offers a platform for highly engaging and interactive online education in a synchronous, asynchronous, or self-directed mode (competency-based education). Instructors can be inventive in student engagement through including podcasts, integrating use of blogs, wikis or discussion boards, creating problem-solving teams, developing simulations, and posing problems for open forum debate.

Other examples come to mind. Creative applications of instructional software are designed to assist a generation acclimated to visual learning. The Kahn Academy, for instance, provides user-friendly, free online visual learning modules in subjects like math for younger learners. At Kahn, problem solving is a visual and fun experience. Other interactive software for postsecondary school students provide feedback as work is performed in writing, reading comprehension, math, and other subjects.

A plethora of exciting, student-centric technology applications have been developed that support an efficient and effective learning progression. Some enable faculty and/or student support services to identify performance concerns prior to course completion for those enrolled in online learning. Predictive analytics and career pathway applications enable institutions and students alike to more effectively map their course sequences in support of degree and career goals.

Institutions such as Southern New Hampshire University, Arizona State's EdPlus, Penn State World Campus, RMIT, and Western Governors University (WGU) understand that technology acquisition is part of a greater whole required to assure student achievement. They invest substantial resources in staff and student support services. Faculty are carefully trained and receive ongoing staff support. Comprehensive curriculum planning occurs as programs and course content are standardized. Planning considerations include faculty selection, training, support, and sometimes reenvisioning the role of faculty in the learning process. Each supports large and rapidly growing undergraduate online education.

Students enrolled at WGU select a career track and are expected to evidence mastery of skill acquisition through competency-based education. Likewise, Southern New Hampshire University has launched College for America in this domain. Many other universities are moving in this direction. Arizona State and Penn State are major players in the online learning space. They remain part of the existing university structure and draw upon faculty selected from their academic programs. All align institutional and student interests and understand the importance of integrating educational and business models. These institutions are responding to demands from working adults for a quality learning experience and degree completion. In so doing, they are generating substantial incremental revenues while offering relatively attractive tuition pricing.

Many noninstructional forms of operational and management reporting technology can be found. Operating software can materially reduce labor content and enhance staff productivity. Student learning assessment, institutional effectiveness, and management reporting applications position academic and business administrators to collect and analyze data and plan more effectively. Some institutions have tapped into social media to market themselves, even to transform the ways they communicate with their students. Private enterprise long ago understood that operational efficiencies driven by simpler processes and supported by technology are mission critical for survival. As such, technology is considered an investment, rather than an expense.

Institutions that undervalue technology do so at their own peril, while others that embrace its capacity to improve quality and affordability of education are better positioned for the future. Technology offers opportunities to innovate, and success is a function of adopting a broad and enduring institutional commitment. Innovation and careful planning appear in many ways.

According to *U.S. News and World Report*, the number 1 ranked online MBA degree is offered by Temple University, whose instructional and support services construct is impressive. More recently, Georgia Tech launched a master's degree program in computer science in a massive open online course (MOOC) environment. Drexel's School of Education is an international leader as an online learning enterprise. More recently, L. Rafael Reif, president of Massachusetts Institute of Technology, invited faculty to participate in a Task Force on The Future of MIT Education. Reif's (2014) letter acknowledging receipt of their report stated:

> The past few years have brought mounting evidence that higher education stands at a crossroads. As with any disruptive technology, MOOCs have been viewed with enthusism in many quarters and skepticism in some. However, the underlying facts are inarguable: that the rising cost of education, combined with the transformative potential of online teaching and learning technologies, presents a long-term challenge that no university can afford to ignore.

As a globally conscious society, we are increasingly inquisitive and communicative and have become lifelong learners through keyword searches on the Internet, use of apps, and social media. We regularly tap into these resources to satisfy knowledge acquisition needs, ranging from keeping in touch with world and national news, weather reports, stock market performance, or sports.

If we wish to learn more about historical events, global geography, medicine, or improve foreign-language skills, we can do so at will. As such, we form our own learning communities. Some participate on blogs or develop Facebook, Twitter, Pinterest, Instagram, or LinkedIn relationships with persons who share like interests. In short, independent or group learning experiences have increasingly become part of societal everyday behaviors and experiences. Higher education's task is to figure out the implications of these pronounced trends and align its products and services accordingly.

A look into the future of higher education suggests a learning environment of increasing technologically literate faculty, administrators, and staff—one that is less operationally and administratively labor intensive, more student-centric, reflective of high-quality interactive learning and skill acquisition experiences, and offering more affordable tuition. Leaders, faculty, business, and student support staff will develop a technology vision and map plans of action backward from that point.

Some institutions will opt for strategic alliances or joint ventures with technology companies or outsource certain services to render software acquisition and support services more affordable. They will sustain fidelity to their core academic mission, while managing their enterprise as a high-performance service industry manifesting a sustainable business model. Investments in technology by leaders in this space may well exceed new construction costs. Professional development and training of faculty, administrators, and support staff will be the norm rather than the exception. Visionary leaders will be technologically attuned and attract smart people as central to this paradigm shift. Student enrollment will be less geographically driven, with increasing access to a world of global learners.

Accountability, Skills Gap, and Priority Setting

Higher education is learning the hard way that public officials will not hesitate to frame the debate and provide their own performance metrics in the absence of institutional transparency through Internet access to a homepage scorecard or dashboard. At one extreme, direct and indirect intrusions into institutional autonomy, such as the earlier illustrations of Florida and Texas, pose a real and present danger to traditional instructional and operational institutional independence.

Some criticism of higher education may reflect latent anti-intellectual sentiments amid those who value "doers" more than "thinkers." A more balanced view poses legitimate concerns about change-resistant institutional cultures and gloomy growth prospects for regional and national economies in the absence of systemic reform. Notwithstanding a perceptible decline of public funding for higher education in many states, especially relative to full-time equivalent student enrollments, many government officials set higher performance expectations such as improving graduation rates and more affordable tuition. Fairly or unfairly, those who disburse monies infuse themselves into the accountability debate.

Accountability and priority setting are two-edged swords. At the national level, some public officials vent about the need for a high-performance education, yet exhibit reckless fiscal behaviors when appropriations decisions are made. Although operating funds for public education come from state and local budgets, nothing restrains federal government appropriations to improve teacher education programs, fund more research, or improve access of high-risk students from lower-income families to supplemental education.

There is no constitutional restraint upon budgeting monies to improve access to learning technologies in underfunded schools or to support the further growth of competency-based learning and middle and early college partnerships. State education policies and practices, with some notable exceptions, are themselves behind the times by arguably focusing too much attention on governance, power, and control and too little on quality improvement of learning environments. The horrific situation of public schools in Detroit, as one of many severely underfunded urban and rural school districts, offers an example of a bankrupt municipality whose students are adrift.

The fractured ways in which municipalities, states, and the federal government go about their business in the United States leaves much to be desired. Debates over national security are usually framed in narrow military terms rather than reflecting the imperative of sustaining a competitive economy. Societies that decay from within are at risk as residents are undereducated and face lifetime socioeconomic disenfranchisement. Jaime P. Merisotis (2013, p. 1), president of Lumina Foundation, made his concerns known as follows:

> At its core, the strength of this nation—or any nation—is its people, the sum total of talents, skills and abilities inherent in its citizenry. Only with sufficient talent, and the right kinds of talent, can a nation truly succeed. Talent development, then, must be America's prime objective, and it's not a task we can tackle by conducting business as usual. We can't expect our citizens to meet the demands of the 21st century economy and society without a 21st century education. Americans need an education that imparts rigorous, relevant learning—an education that provides the tools that are necessary to thrive in the face of rapid, inevitable change. In short, our citizens need high-quality, credentialed, college-level learning—and they need it in greater numbers than ever before.

Preoccupation with output metrics such as common core testing and graduation rates is folly in the absence of redesigning a P-16 educational system. Systemic underperformance calls for far more effective alignment of public education policies, practices, and funding priorities to remediate the causes. Degree attainment is important. Graduating an educated person is more consequential yet.

Within the walls of higher education, accountability is more accurately measured by achievement on all matters resting within the control of leaders, faculty, and staff. Educators who act as victims, or are characterized by attitude deficits, are more likely to set low expectations for themselves and their students and underperform relative to their potential. On the other hand, those who take ownership for making a difference will find ways to persist with continuous improvement initiatives and will engage students more effectively in learning. Accordingly, faculty at all levels are well positioned to review curriculum and pedagogy and adapt to changes intended to motivate as well as instruct, but rely upon educational leaders to afford them the opportunities to engage in change.

Educational leaders are called upon to create collaborative processes that energize faculty and inspire them to propose changes that can ultimately be reflected in qualitative and quantitative measurement. All have an opportunity to draw upon data to examine what works and what does not and formulate plans accordingly. At the end of the day, education serves multiple purposes. At the grass roots, students benefit from skills development and degree attainment. Employers gain by hiring more productive and effective employees. Municipal, state, and federal government coffers recover their investments in education through a more robust economy and increasing tax revenues.

Education investment dollars ultimately recycle in ways unattainable when students drop out and are unable to earn livable incomes. Societies evolve in curious and often unpredictable ways. Is an educated society in the national self-interest, and does it merit strategic funding priority? Accountability, when seen through this lens, is subject to shared ownership between public officials and educators.

STRATEGIC AND TRANSFORMATIVE LEADERSHIP

In many ways, we are influenced by our life experiences. One such moment comes to mind. Some years ago, the first author attended a senior executive offsite retreat hosted by the chairman and CEO of Mellon Bank. Our guest speaker was retired army lieutenant general Hal Moore, the central character in the book and movie *We Were Soldiers*. When asked to define the attributes of a leader, General Moore cited concern for one's troops, judgment, and finding a way to win.

In higher education, we may think of our students, faculty, administrators, and staff as our troops. Leaders bear the ultimate and inescapable burden of assuring that students benefit from a first-class education and that their sacrifices of money and time are rewarded with talents they could not otherwise attain on their own. These are times when expectations rise from without, tensions mount from within, criticism is more persistent, and financial resources are more constrained. Leaders are called upon to find a way to win!

We know much about what does not transform institutional performance. An institution's educational and business model are unlikely to undergo material change as a consequence of case-by-case decision-making, year-to-year tactical adjustments to budgets, teaching loads, or recruitment plans. One-off periodic program reviews done out of context from institutional offerings and from market realities may yield attractive binders. They may inform, but are unlikely to bring about consequential change.

Task management may be necessary, but is akin to maintenance management. Tenured faculty and their unions may win justifiable rights and benefits through negotiations, but how does this support requisite reforms or their students? On the other hand, students may find attractive an upscale cuisine and infamous climbing walls, but how will they react to servicing their debt obligations? Leaders may enjoy the trappings of their offices, but what will be their legacies? Inquiry and collaborative processes matter, but too often do not translate into action.

Fundamental redesign occurs when leaders think and act strategically and encourage others to do so. Much is known about other manifestations of change. Lead indicators of institutional transformation are identifiable. Institutional missions are inspirational, realizable, and affordable and represent a broad collective view. Priorities and enduring goals are agreed upon, communicated, and serve as a basis for resource allocation. Planning is system-wide, student-centric, and based upon analysis of evidence. Data is actionable and acted upon. Stakeholders understand the importance of sustainable competitive advantages that serve the interests of students and draw students more on the basis of demonstrable academic and behavioral value propositions than slick marketing campaigns.

Institutional transformation comes as much from doing things the right way as from adherence to a grand design. This is highlighted by leaders who are guided by core values and who have developed essential characteristics outlined in the Higher Education Leadership Wheel. Annual operating plans derive from strategy. Professional performance objectives are qualitatively or quantitatively measurable, and evaluations relate to functional, unit, and institutional goals. Staff at all levels are held accountable relative to pre-agreed-upon performance objectives. Oversight processes and management reporting are activated to assure plan execution.

Organizational structures are simpler and more adaptable to change. Technologies contribute to improvement of student learning and a transition from high-to-low labor content processes. Learning outcomes are consistent with curriculum characteristics. More students graduate. They are better prepared for work, further study, and assumption of broader postgraduation responsibilities.

At the end of the day, the kind of business models needed nowadays in higher education combine several core elements. Entrepreneurial initiatives yield revenue growth otherwise unattainable. Expense reduction initiatives improve upon effectiveness and efficiencies without detracting from the quality of learning. Business-, academic-, and student support plans are inseparable and mutually dependent. Transformative leaders institutionalize such behaviors, and the institutional cultures reflect greater agility and responsiveness to changing times.

Institutions devote time to succession planning so that forward momentum is assured by those nurtured within leadership incubators. Transformative leaders are unselfish and unrelenting capacity builders, who are uncompromisingly devoted to the students they serve. They are guided by core values and have developed over a lifetime essential leadership characteristics. They find a way to win!

REFERENCES

Di Giacomo, F. Tony, Bethany G. Fishbein, Wanda Monthey, and Catherine Pack. 2013. *Global Competency Education*. Research Brief 2013-1. Washington, DC: College Board. Available online at: http://www.research.collegeboard.org; accessed on 2 February 2016.

Gardner, Michael. 2015. "More money for higher education and research." *University World News*, Issue No. 392. Available online at: www.universityworldnews.com; accessed on 2 February 2016.

Lumina Foundation. 2014. *A Stronger Nation Through Higher Education: Annual Progress Report*. Indianapolis, IN: Lumina Foundation. Available online at: http://www.luminafoundation.org; accessed on 2 February 2016.

Organisation for Economic and Co-operative Development (OECD). 2014. *Education at a Glance 2014: OECD Indicators*. Paris: OECD Publishing. Available online at: http://www.oecd.org/edu/Education-at-a-Glance-2014.pdf; accessed on 2 February 2016.

Reif, L. Rafael. 2014. *Letter Regarding the Final Report of the Institute-wide Task Force on the Future of MIT Education*. Press Release, 4 August 2014. Cambridge, MA: MIT News Office. Available online at: http://news.mit.edu/2014/letter-final-report-institute-wide-task-force-future-mit-education; accessed on 2 February 2016.

U.S. Department of Education. 2006. *A Test of Leadership: Charting the Future of U.S. Higher Education*. Washington, DC: U.S. Department of Education. Available online at: https://www2.ed.gov/about/bdscomm/list/hiedfuture/reports/final-report.pdf; accessed on 2 February 2016.

Index

185

About the Authors

Stewart E. Sutin is professor of higher education in the School of Education at the University of Pittsburgh. Dr. Sutin entered public higher education ten years ago after a 29-year career in the banking industry that included serving as head of international banking operations at Mellon and as president of Bank of Boston International. He led efforts to develop and implement global business strategies and worked on projects with consulting teams from McKinsey, Boston Consulting Group, and Booz Allen Hamilton. Dr. Sutin codeveloped and launched two global business institutes and was named president and chairman, board of directors, Banker's Association for Finance and Trade (a subsidiary of the American Banker's Association). He developed expertise in strategic planning, product and service innovation, risk management, operating efficiencies, financial and human resource planning and management, and "turn-around" leadership for individual business units.

In 2003, Dr. Sutin became the seventh president and chief executive officer of Community College of Allegheny County, an enterprise that provided credit and community education to more than 60,000 students year over year through a complex multicampus, multicenter delivery network. During his tenure in office, Dr. Sutin led development and implementation of multiyear strategic, educational, student affair, financial, and technology plans. Annual operating plans, budgets, and performance metrics were aligned with enduring goals. Special attention was afforded leadership development, equitable recruitment, and promotion practices, evidence-based decision-making, teamwork, and a focus on system-wide academic and student affair standards. Dr. Sutin served on the boards of trustees of two universities and on graduate school advisory boards at Carnegie Mellon, University of Pittsburgh, Brandeis, Duquesne, and the University of Miami. He also chaired the Pittsburgh Council on Higher Education.

Dr. Sutin serves as a member of the faculty of administrative and policy studies in the School of Education at the University of Pittsburgh as clinical professor in higher education management. He instructs courses in leadership, strategic planning, budget and financial management, and human resource management. His research, publication, and public presentation focus attention on improvement of the business model of higher education. Recent books and studies he has coedited and coauthored include *Value-Based Education: Vision for a Higher Education Business Model, Increasing Effectiveness of the Community College Financial Model,* and *Community Engagement in Higher Education: Policy Reforms and Practice.* He has conducted leadership workshops at the President's Academy of the American Association of Community Colleges and for individual institutions.

Dr. Sutin holds a PhD from the University of Texas at Austin, an MA from Georgetown, and a BA from Penn State. He attended executive education programs at the University of Michigan Graduate School of Business and at the Harvard University Graduate School of Education. He served in the US Army Reserves and was honorably discharged with rank of Captain in 1978.

W. James Jacob is Associate Professor of International Higher Education in the School of Education at the University of Pittsburgh. His research and leadership interests include higher education strategic planning, academic affairs, quality assurance, organizational development, organizational effectiveness, and indigenous education issues of culture, language, and identity as they relate to postsecondary education.

He is the coeditor of two-book series related to the development of comparative, international, and development education scholarship: *International and Development Education* and *Pittsburgh Studies in Comparative and International Education.* His most recent books include *Community Engagement in Higher Education: Policy Reforms and Practice; Indigenous Education: Language, Culture, and Identity; Policy Debates in Comparative, International, and Development Education; Beyond the Comparative:*

Advancing Theory and Its Application to Practice; and *Inequality in Education: Comparative and International Perspectives.*

Since 2007, Dr. Jacob has served as the director of the Institute for International Studies in Education at the University of Pittsburgh. He is currently a Fulbright Senior Specialist (2015–2020), where he offers capacity building expertise to governments on higher education. Dr. Jacob holds a PhD in education from the University of California, Los Angeles, a master's in organizational behavior from Brigham Young University's Marriott School of Management, and an MA in international development from BYU's Kennedy Center for International Studies.